Contents

Acknowledgements

The publisher wishes to thank the following for their help with the reading and production of the book: Maz Loton, Jon Moore and Cathy Turner. Thanks are also due to Debbie Board for her technical editorial work and to Laura Ingham for her designs for this series.

The publisher is indebted to the Association of Accounting Technicians for its help and advice to our authors and editors during the preparation of this text.

Authors

David Cox has more than twenty years' experience teaching accountancy students over a wide range of levels. Formerly with the Management and Professional Studies Department at Worcester College of Technology, he now lectures on a freelance basis and carries out educational consultancy work in accountancy studies. He is author and joint author of a number of textbooks in the areas of accounting, finance and banking.

Michael Fardon has extensive teaching experience of a wide range of banking, business and accountancy courses at Worcester College of Technology. He now specialises in writing business and financial texts and is General Editor at Osborne Books. He is also an educational consultant and has worked extensively in the areas of vocational business curriculum development.

Introduction

what this book covers

This book has been written specifically to cover the 'Processing bookkeeping transactions' Unit which is mandatory for the revised (2013) AAT Level 2 Certificate in Accounting.

The book contains a clear text with worked examples and case studies, chapter summaries and key terms to help with revision. Each chapter has a wide range of activities, many in the style of the computer-based assessments used by AAT.

This book covers the areas of financial documents, double-entry, books of prime entry, ledger accounting, cash books, petty cash books and the initial trial balance.

Bookkeeping 1 is a companion text to Osborne Books' *Bookkeeping 2* which covers the AAT Unit 'Control accounts, journals and the banking system'.

Downloadable blank documents for use with this text are available in the Resources section of www.osbornebooks.co.uk.

Osborne Workbooks

Osborne Workbooks contain practice material which helps students achieve success in their assessments. *Bookkeeping 1 Workbook* contains a number of paper-based 'fill in' practice exams in the style of the computer-based assessment. Please visit www.osbornebooks.co.uk for further details and access to our online shop.

1 The accounting system

this chapter covers...

This chapter is a basic introduction to the accounting system of a business and gives an overview of all the topics that will be explained throughout this book.

You may have a general idea of how accounting and finance 'fit into' a business and the reasons why money transactions are critical to its operation, but if you are working in an accounting and finance environment it is important to appreciate fully the way accounting systems work. It is the aim of the course you are studying that you will acquire the knowledge and skills which will enable you to work effectively in an accounting and finance environment.

This chapter describes and explains the basic structure of an accounting system. It covers:

- the range of financial transactions in business, eg buying, selling, making payments
- the way in which financial documents such as invoices are used to record financial transactions
- the ways in which financial transactions are first recorded in the books of the business – using 'books of prime entry', eg a cash book
- the ways in which an accounting system is set up in a business, for example a double-entry system using ledger accounts
- the way in which the accounts are brought together in a summary known as the 'trial balance'
- the ways in which an accounting system can be used to provide information for the business owners and management, for example how much is owed by customers and how much profit has been made

FINANCIAL TRANSACTIONS

All businesses carry out a wide range of financial transactions on a daily basis. These transactions will need documenting and then recording in some form of manual or computerised accounting system. Common transactions include:

selling goods and services

Goods and services can be sold:

- either for immediate payment – known as 'cash' sales, although confusingly this word 'cash' can involve payment by credit or debit card as well as notes and coins, or
- for payment at a later date – these are known as 'credit' sales

making purchases and paying expenses

Examples of purchases and expenses include a wide range of large and small transactions, some more important than others:

- settling purchase invoices, eg paying by cheque or electronically for goods or services supplied during the previous month
- buying an item used in the business, eg a new delivery van, paid for by bank transfer
- buying diesel fuel for the delivery van, using the company credit card
- buying some postage stamps for the office using cash

payments in and out of the bank account

The money received by the business and the money paid out by the business will pass through the bank account, for example:

- cash, cheques and electronic payments received from selling goods and services
- settling the company credit card by direct debit payment from the bank account
- paying the weekly wages through the bank account
- drawing cash out of the bank for use in the office

the importance of keeping track

As you will see from the above examples, recording financial transactions will be a complex process. A business will need to keep track of:

- expenses and purchases

■ wages paid

■ what each customer owes, and when the money is due

■ amounts owed to suppliers, and when the payment is due

■ amounts paid into the bank and out of the bank

If these transactions are not recorded accurately, the owner of the business and other interested organisations such as the bank and the tax authorities will not know how much money the business is making (or losing!).

THE FIVE STAGE ACCOUNTING SYSTEM

The accounting system, which will be set in motion by all the transactions listed on the previous page, can be broken down into five stages. These will be covered in greater detail later in this chapter. These stages (illustrated on the next page) are:

1 A **financial transaction** takes place – a sale, a purchase, a payment

2 The transaction involves a **financial document**, for example an invoice (a sale), a credit note (returned goods), a petty cash voucher (small cash payments).

3 The document is first recorded on paper (or on computer) by the business, for example a day book (for credit transactions) recording sales of goods or goods returned, a cash book recording payments in and out of the bank, or a petty cash book which records small cash payments made (eg buying some stamps for the office).

    These books are known as the **books of prime entry**; this simply means 'the first place a transaction is recorded in the accounting records.'

4 The entries in the books of prime entry, eg the day books, will then need to be transferred to the **ledger accounts** of the business. These are a formal record of the financial transactions and normally involve **double-entry accounts.**

    The double-entry system, which involves two entries for each transaction, a debit entry and a credit entry, is explained in more detail on pages 7-9.

5 The final stage in the accounting system covered in your current studies is the **trial balance**. This is a list of the balances of the double-entry accounts. It is used as a check on the accuracy of the account entries and is also a source of information for the business owners and managers: it will enable them to monitor items such as expenses and what their customers owe, and also to calculate how much profit the business has made. The trial balance is explained in more detail on page 10.

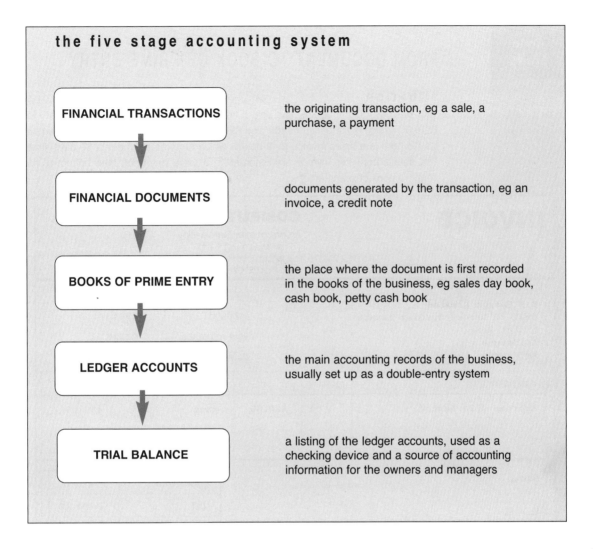

the five stage accounting system

FINANCIAL TRANSACTIONS — the originating transaction, eg a sale, a purchase, a payment

FINANCIAL DOCUMENTS — documents generated by the transaction, eg an invoice, a credit note

BOOKS OF PRIME ENTRY — the place where the document is first recorded in the books of the business, eg sales day book, cash book, petty cash book

LEDGER ACCOUNTS — the main accounting records of the business, usually set up as a double-entry system

TRIAL BALANCE — a listing of the ledger accounts, used as a checking device and a source of accounting information for the owners and managers

We will now explain the last four of these five stages in more detail. The first stage, financial transactions, has already been covered on page 3.

FROM DOCUMENTS TO BOOKS OF PRIME ENTRY

You will need to study a wide variety of financial documents as part of your course. On the next page a Case Study shows how a sales invoice – a **financial document** – is recorded in the sales day book, which is a list of sales invoices issued and a **book of prime entry**. You do not at this stage need to learn all the details of how this record is entered. This will be covered later.

FROM DOCUMENT TO BOOK OF PRIME ENTRY

situation

Your business, Computrade, has sold a laptop computer to R S George Limited, for £576.00 (which is list price of £480 plus £96.00 VAT at 20%). The financial document issued here is a sales invoice (see below) which requires payment in 30 days' time. The details from this invoice are recorded in a sales day book (see bottom of the page), a book of prime entry.

INVOICE

COMPUTRADE

Ardent House, Mercia Way
Newtown, NT1 6TF
Tel 01722 295875 Fax 01722 295611 Email sales@computrade.com
VAT Reg GB 02756 6865 06

invoice to			
R S George Limited **Unit 32 Bruges Trading Estate** **Winter Road** **Maidstone** **ME7 2PH**	invoice no		**2984**
	account		**8934**
	your reference		**CT524**
	date/tax point		**02 04 20-3**

description	quantity	price	unit	total
Extreme 2120 Laptop	1	480.00	each	480.00

terms			
30 days	**goods total**		480.00
E & OE	**VAT**		96.00
	TOTAL		576.00

Sales Day Book					
Date	**Customer**	**Invoice No.**	**Total**	**VAT**	**Net**
20-3			£	£	£
2 April	R S George Limited	2984	576.00	96.00	480.00

FROM BOOKS OF PRIME ENTRY TO LEDGER ACCOUNTS

The next stage in the accounting system is the transfer of entries in the books of prime entry to the ledger accounts. Books of prime entry, as illustrated in the example on the previous page, are listing devices for financial transactions. They include:

- **day books** for
  - credit sales and sales returns, ie transactions involving customers
  - credit purchases and purchases returns, ie transactions involving suppliers
- **cash book** for recording all payments into and out of the bank account
- **petty cash book** for recording all payments into and out of a cash float used for making small purchases and other small payments.

The ledger accounts are the formal bookkeeping records of the business and are kept either in written form or, more often nowadays, on computer. They form the 'core' of the accounting system. Ledger accounts are different to the other accounting records because each transaction requires both debit and credit entries, ie entries in more than one account (normally it is in two accounts).

The flow of accounting information – transaction, book of prime entry, double-entry ledger accounts – is shown below. This gives you an overview of the accounting system. All the stages in this process are fully explained in the chapters that follow.

TRANSACTION	BOOKS OF PRIME ENTRY	LEDGER ACCOUNTS	ACCOUNT ENTRIES
Sales transactions	Sales Day Book	Customer sales	debit credit
	Sales Returns Day Book	Customer returns	debit credit
Purchases transactions	Purchases Day Book	Purchases from Suppliers	debit credit
	Purchases Returns Day Book	Returns to Suppliers	debit credit
Cash and Bank transactions	Cash Book	Payments received Payments made	debit credit
Small Cash transactions	Petty Cash Book	Small cash payments made Cash received	debit credit

LEDGER ACCOUNTS

In this chapter so far we have seen that the accounting system of a business records information from financial transactions and documents (such as invoices and credit notes) into the books of prime entry and then into ledger accounts. It is useful at this point to explain what is meant by 'ledgers' and the way in which they are organised.

Most businesses use an accounting system based on the **double-entry bookkeeping system**, in which financial transactions are recorded in the accounts as **debits** and **credits**. There are two equal entries – debit and credit – of the same amount.

Bookkeeping records are kept in one of two forms: handwritten (manual) records or, increasingly often nowadays, on a computer system such as Sage.

the ledgers

A **ledger** is traditionally a large book into which each business transaction is entered into individual **accounts**.

Because of the large number of accounts involved, there are a number of different individual ledgers, both in manual systems and also in computer systems:

■ **Sales ledger** – each customer is given a personal account which contains records of sales made on credit (ie buy now, pay later), any returned goods and payments received. This account shows the business the amount owed by that particular customer. A customer buying on credit is known in accounting language as a 'trade receivable'.

■ **Purchases ledger** – each supplier is given a personal account which contains records of purchases made on credit (ie buy now, pay later), any returned goods and payments made to the supplier. This account shows the amount owed to that particular supplier (known as a 'trade payable').

■ **General ledger** – this collection of accounts records all other transactions of the business, such as:

- assets – these are items owned, eg premises, cars, computers and also amounts owed to a business

- liabilities – items owed by a business, eg overdrafts and bank loans

- the owner's capital – this includes the amount invested in the business by the owner and also the profits made by the business

- expense items – money going out, eg wages and rent paid

- income items – money coming in, eg sales and rent received

The **general ledger** is sometimes also known as the 'main' ledger or 'nominal' ledger (as in Sage computer accounting programs).

Also note that the term 'the ledger' is sometimes used to describe all the individual ledgers grouped together The ledger structure is shown in the diagram at the bottom of the page.

control accounts ('total' accounts)

Many businesses use **control accounts** to provide them with information about the financial state of the organisation.

Control accounts are 'total' accounts which summarise a number of other accounts. They are set out in the same way as all other ledger accounts. Examples include:

- **sales ledger control account** which contains the totals of all the trade receivable (debtor) accounts in the sales ledger – this tells the business how much is owing from all its customers, a figure that is important for business owners and managers

- **purchases ledger control account** which contains the totals of all the trade payable (creditor) accounts in the purchases ledger – this tells the business how much is owing to all its suppliers at any one time; again this is a figure that is important for anyone running a business

These control accounts are always contained in the general ledger. It is the total of these accounts that is transferred to the trial balance (see next page).

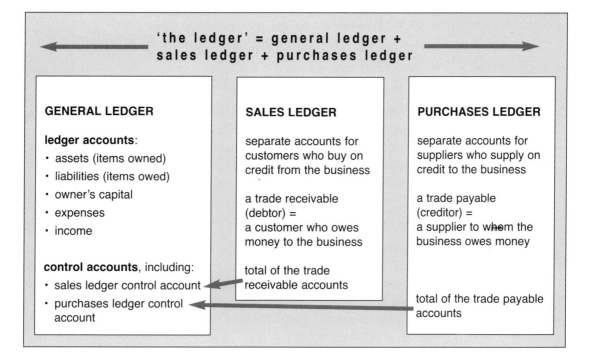

'the ledger' = general ledger + sales ledger + purchases ledger

GENERAL LEDGER

ledger accounts:
- assets (items owned)
- liabilities (items owed)
- owner's capital
- expenses
- income

control accounts, including:
- sales ledger control account
- purchases ledger control account

SALES LEDGER

separate accounts for customers who buy on credit from the business

a trade receivable (debtor) = a customer who owes money to the business

total of the trade receivable accounts

PURCHASES LEDGER

separate accounts for suppliers who supply on credit to the business

a trade payable (creditor) = a supplier to whom the business owes money

total of the trade payable accounts

THE TRIAL BALANCE

format of a trial balance

A trial balance is the important final stage in the accounting system. It brings together the balances of all the ledger accounts in the general ledger, setting them out in two columns – a debit column and a credit column – which when added up should show two equal totals.

A simplified trial balance is shown on the next page. You do not need at this stage to know how all this 'works' but just that it is an important accuracy check in the accounting system.

Note that the trial balance is headed up with

■ the **name** of the business, 'Computrade'

■ the **date** on which it was drawn up – this should be done regularly, eg the end of each month, and always the end of the financial year

what the trial balance shows

The trial balance shows the business owner and managers important and useful information. For example, the trial balance on the next page sets out the account balances of Computrade, it shows that:

■ sales are £58,050

■ £12,500 is owed by the customers (trade receivables)

■ £9,350 is owed to suppliers (trade payables)

■ the wages paid out totalled £44,100

■ the delivery vans are worth £36,000

■ the business has £2,000 in the bank

■ the owner of the business has an investment (capital) worth £105,000

Note that the trade receivables and trade payables figures are 'total' figures and are taken from the sales ledger and purchases ledger control accounts. This makes the trial balance more manageable and meaningful – it would be rather difficult to list all the customer and supplier accounts separately!

the trial balance – what next?

A further stage in the accounting system – which you will deal with in your later studies – is the production of **financial statements** – the **statement of profit or loss** and the **statement of financial position**. Although you will not be assessed on these statements at this level, awareness of them will help you in your current areas of study. They are briefly explained on page 12.

the trial balance

Name of business: Computrade
Trial Balance as at 30 June 20-3

	Debit £	Credit £
Purchases	35,000	
Sales		58,050
Trade receivables	12,500	
Trade payables		9,350
Insurance	1,400	
Rent	6,400	
Wages	44,100	
Bank	2,000	
Office equipment	35,000	
Delivery vans	36,000	
Capital		105,000
	172,400	172,400

names of all the individual ledger accounts

totals of the two money amount columns – note that they add up to the same figure, providing an accuracy check of the accounting system

The next page gives an outline description and explanation of the financial statements of a business: the statement of profit or loss and the statement of financial position.

FINANCIAL STATEMENTS

The financial statements of a business are the **statement of profit or loss** and the **statement of financial position**. They are compiled from the accounting records of the business, mainly from the balances of the ledger accounts which also form the basis of the trial balance.

what the statement of profit or loss shows

The **statement of profit or loss** of a business shows the day-to-day income that the business has received over a given period for goods sold or services provided. It also sets out the **expenses** incurred, including the cost of producing the products and the running expenses.

If the income of the business is greater than the expenses, the business has made a profit. If the income of the business is less than the expenses, the business has made a loss.

what the statement of financial position shows

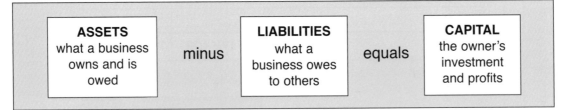

The statement of financial position of a business gives a 'snapshot' of the business at a particular date, eg the end of the financial year, and shows the value of the owner's investment in the business. The statement presents a simple equation, known as the **accounting equation**:

assets (what is owned) minus liabilities (what is owed) = capital (owner's investment)

If a business owner invests £2,000 in a business and buys a computer, he is investing capital of £2,000 and also adding an asset in the form of a computer costing £2,000. The equation will balance because £2,000 has been added to both sides (to assets and to capital). The accounting equation is explained and expanded in full in Chapter 3, pages 57 to 60.

INTERNATIONAL TERMINOLOGY USED IN ACCOUNTING

old and new terms

In your studies of bookkeeping and accounting you will encounter some different ways of expressing common accounting terms.

You will find, at the time of writing this book, that many bookkeepers and accountants use the traditional terminology which originates in the UK.

For example, the traditional way of referring to goods held by a shop or by a manufacturer is the word 'stock'. But you will find that the American term 'inventory' is also used to mean 'stock'.

This new type of terminology is known as **'international accounting terminology'**.

Neither 'stock' nor 'inventory' is in itself right or wrong but there are situations where the international terminology is used instead of the traditional terminology. An example of this are the financial statements produced by the larger limited companies.

The table below shows both the international and traditional UK versions of terms which you are likely to come across in your accounting studies. The table also explains what the terms mean.

international terminology	traditional UK terminology	what it means
inventory	stock	goods held by a business
trade payable	creditor	a supplier you owe money to
trade receivable	debtor	a customer who owes you money
statement of profit or loss	profit and loss account	financial statement calculating profit (or loss) made by a business
statement of financial position	balance sheet	financial statement showing the value of the owner's investment

Chapter Summary

- The accounting system is normally made up of five stages:
  1. financial transactions
  2. financial documents
  3. books of prime entry
  4. ledger accounts
  5. trial balance

- **Financial transactions** are the starting point of the accounting system. They include sales, purchases, expenses, payments in and out of the bank account and small cash (petty cash) transactions.

- Financial transactions normally result in **financial documents**, for example an invoice (for a sale), a credit note (for returned goods), a cheque (for a payment), a petty cash voucher (for a small cash payment).

- In the next stage of the accounting system financial documents are recorded in **books of prime entry**, for example separate day books for sales and sales returns, purchases and purchases returns, the cash book and the petty cash book.

- Next the **ledger accounts** are written up from the books of prime entry. The ledger accounts are normally double-entry accounts, ie two entries are made in the accounts for each transaction – a debit entry and a credit entry.

- As there are so many ledger accounts, **the ledger** is often split into separate ledgers: sales ledger (for customer accounts), purchases ledger (for supplier accounts) and general ledger (all the other accounts, including assets, expenses, income, liabilities, and capital).

- **Control accounts** are 'total' accounts used to summarise important groups of ledger accounts, eg sales ledger control account.

- Finally, the balances of the ledger accounts are transferred to the **trial balance** which is both a checking device and also a source of accounting information for the business owners and managers.

- The **financial statements** of a business – the Statement of Profit or Loss and the Statement of Financial Position – are extracted from the accounts of a business on a regular basis.

Key Terms	**financial document**	a term given to a document which results from a financial transaction, eg an invoice
	'cash' and 'credit' sales	a 'cash' sale is a sale where payment is made straightaway, a 'credit' sale is a sale where payment is made at a later date
	books of prime entry	the place in the books of a business where a financial transaction is recorded for the first time, eg day books, cash book, petty cash book
	day books	a book of prime entry which lists the details of various financial transactions, eg sales, sales returns, purchases and purchases returns
	cash book	the book of prime entry which lists payments in and out of the bank account
	petty cash book	the book of prime entry which lists small cash (notes and coins) business expense payments from an office cash fund
	ledger account	the formal accounting record (often in double-entry format) for financial transactions involving individuals (customers and suppliers) and business assets, expenses, income, liabilities and capital
	double-entry accounts	ledger accounts set up on the double-entry system (ie two entries – a debit and a credit – are made for each transaction)
	the ledger	means literally 'the book' which contains the individual accounts; it is often subdivided into different ledgers, eg sales ledger, purchases ledger, general ledger
	control accounts	'total' accounts contained in the general ledger
	trade receivable	a customer who owes a business money
	trade payable	a supplier owed money by a business
	assets	items owned by a business, eg a delivery van
	liabilities	items owed by a business, eg a bank loan
	capital	the investment made in a business by the owner(s), ie the amount owed to the owner(s) by the business
	trial balance	a list of the balances of the ledger accounts drawn up in two columns (debit and credit) the totals of which should be the same

Activities

1.1 A 'cash sale' in accounting terms is:

(a) a sale involving notes and coins

(b) a sale requiring immediate payment

(c) a sale requiring payment in the future

Which one of these options is correct?

1.2 A financial document is first recorded in an accounting system in a book of prime entry.
True or false?

1.3 The following are all books of prime entry:

(a) cash book, petty cash book, purchases ledger

(b) sales day book, sales returns day book, sales ledger

(c) cash book, petty cash book, sales day book

Which one of these options is correct?

1.4 Transactions recorded in the books of prime entry are then transferred to:

(a) ledger accounts

(b) a trial balance

(c) a petty cash book

Which one of these options is correct?

1.5 A trade receivable is:

(a) a supplier owed money by the business

(b) a customer who owes money to a business

(c) a customer who settles straightaway using cash

Which one of these options is correct?

1.6 In double-entry book-keeping every transaction is recorded using

(a) two debits

(b) two credits

(c) one debit and one credit

Which one of these options is correct?

1.7   The purchases ledger contains the ledger accounts for

(a)   trade receivables

(b)   trade payables

(c)   expenses

Which one of these options is correct?

1.8   A liability of a business is:

(a)   an amount owed by that business

(b)   an item owned by that business

(c)   a cash fund for business expenses

Which one of these options is correct?

1.9   An extract from the trial balance of a shop that sells tiles is shown below.

Name of business: Style & Tile Trial Balance as at 30 June 20-3 (extract)		
	Debit £	**Credit £**
Trade receivables	10,500	
Trade payables		6,720
Advertising	1,400	
Insurance	780	
Wages	52,800	
Bank	3,000	
Shop equipment	22,000	
Delivery vans	28,000	
Capital		155,000

On the basis of the figures shown here, answer the following questions:

(a)   How much do the customers of Style & Tile owe the business?

(b)   How much does Style & Tile owe its suppliers?

(c)   How much does Style & Tile have in the bank?

(d)   How much investment does the owner have in the business?

(e)   Where are the figures for trade receivables and trade payables taken from?

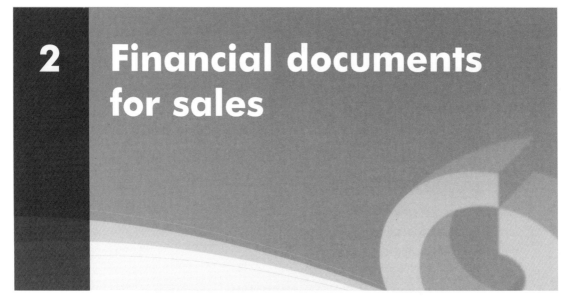

2 Financial documents for sales

this chapter covers...

This chapter examines the procedures involved when a business sells goods or services on credit – which means that payment is made at a later date, possibly a month later.

The important point here is that the business wants to get paid on time and it wants to get the right amount. It can achieve these aims through the efficient use and monitoring of financial documents.

This chapter covers the areas of:

- *the use of business documents – quotation, purchase order, invoice, delivery note, returns note, credit note, statement*

- *the calculation of document totals and discounts*

- *the calculation of Value Added Tax (VAT)*

- *the coding of documents*

- *the checking and authorisation of documents*

Note that the documents explained in this chapter illustrate the traditional paper-based system. There is nowadays a growing trend for electronic documents, eg online orders, invoices, statements and payments. These follow the same principles as the paper-based documents.

FINANCIAL DOCUMENTS

When a business sells goods or services it will use a number of different documents (listed in the diagram below). A single sales transaction of course involves both seller and buyer. In this chapter we look at the situation from the point of view of the **seller** of the goods or services. The transaction from the point of view of the buyer is dealt with in Chapter 6. Documents which are used in the **selling** process include:

- price **quotation** which the seller may be asked to provide
- **purchase order** which the seller receives from the buyer
- **delivery note** which goes with the goods from the seller to the buyer
- **invoice** which lists the goods and tells the buyer what is owed
- **returns note** which is sent with any goods that are being returned
- **credit note** which is sent to the buyer if any refund is due
- **statement** sent by the seller to remind the buyer what is owed

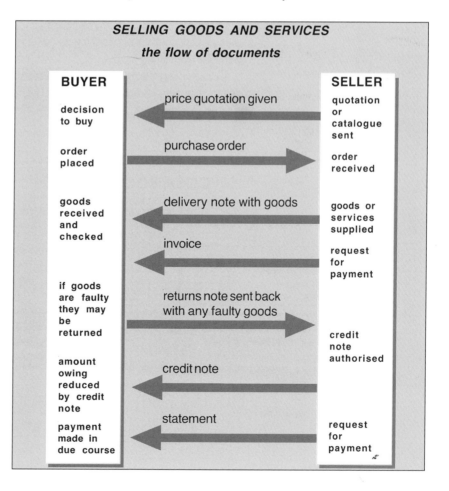

the flow of documents

Before you read the Case Study, make sure you have studied the diagram on the previous page. You will see in the columns representing the buyer and the seller that there are various activities requiring financial documents.

Case Study

COOL SOCKS – A SALES TRANSACTION

situation

Cool Socks Limited manufactures fashion socks in a variety of colours. It supplies a number of different customers, including Trends, a fashion store in Broadfield. In this Case Study, Trends places an order for 100 pairs of socks with Cool Socks. The socks are delivered, but some are found to be faulty, so some of the socks have to be returned. The Case Study looks in detail at the documents involved.

THE PRICE QUOTATION

Before placing the order, the buyer at Trends will need to find out the price of the socks. This can be done by consulting Cool Socks' printed catalogue or website, or by means of a written or telephoned enquiry.

Cool Socks *may* provide a written quotation for the socks if they are requested to do so, although this procedure is more common with higher value orders. A written quotation might look like this:

QUOTATION ────

COOL SOCKS LIMITED

Unit 45 Elgar Estate, Broadfield, BR7 4ER
Tel 01908 765314 Fax 01908 765951 Email toni@cool.u-net.com
VAT REG GB 0745 4672 76

Trends 4 Friar Street Broadfield BR1 3RF	date	19 09 20-3

Thank you for your enquiry of 17 September 20-3. We are pleased to quote as follows:

100 pairs Toebar socks (blue)@ £2.36 a pair, excluding VAT.

M Arnold

Sales Department

PURCHASE ORDER – THE SOCKS ARE ORDERED

The buyer at Trends, once she has accepted the quoted price will post, fax or email the authorised purchase order shown below, or she might send an online order. The order will have been processed manually, or produced on a computer accounting program.

Note the following details:

- each purchase order has a specific reference number (here it is 47609) – this is useful for filing and quoting on later documents such as invoices and statements; this reference number is an example of **coding** in accounting (see page 35)

- the catalogue number of the goods required is stated in the product code column – this number is a further example of coding

- the quantity of the goods required is stated in the quantity column – socks are normally supplied in pairs!

- the description of the goods is set out in full

- the price is not essential, although some purchase orders will include a price

- the purchase order is signed and dated by the person in charge of purchasing – without this authorisation the supplier is unlikely to supply the goods (the order will probably be returned)

Trends   **PURCHASE ORDER**

4 Friar Street
Broadfield
BR1 3RF
Tel 01908 761234 Fax 01908 761987
VAT REG GB 0745 8383 56

Cool Socks Limited, Unit 45 Elgar Estate, Broadfield, BR7 4ER	purchase order no 47609 date 25 09 20-3

product code	quantity	description
45B	100 pairs	Blue Toebar socks @ £2.36 per pair

AUTHORISED   signature.......*D Signer*...date....*25/09/20-3*

DELIVERY NOTE – THE SOCKS ARE DELIVERED

A delivery note is despatched with the goods when the order is ready. It is either processed manually in the office or printed out by a computer accounting program, often at the same time as the invoice (see next page). In this case, the delivery note travels with the socks, and a copy will be signed by Trends on receipt. Note the following details:

- the delivery note has a numerical reference (here it is 68873), useful for filing and later reference if there is a query – this is another example of coding

- the method of delivery is stated – here the delivery is by parcel carrier

- the delivery note quotes the purchase order number – 47609 – this enables the buyer to link the delivery with the original purchase order – this is another example of the use of coding

- the delivery note quotes
  - Cool Socks' catalogue reference 45B as the product code
  - the quantity supplied
  - the description of the goods, but no price – it is not needed at this stage

  these details will be checked against the goods themselves straightaway so that any discrepancies can be reported without delay

- the delivery note will be signed and dated by the person receiving the goods as proof of delivery; nowadays this process can also be carried out electronically – the person receiving the goods will be asked to sign a portable electronic device

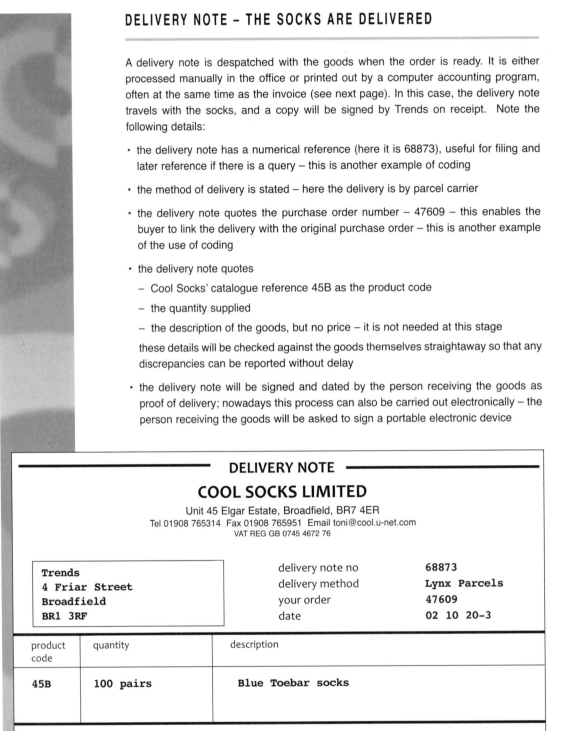

DELIVERY NOTE

COOL SOCKS LIMITED

Unit 45 Elgar Estate, Broadfield, BR7 4ER
Tel 01908 765314 Fax 01908 765951 Email toni@cool.u-net.com
VAT REG GB 0745 4672 76

Trends
4 Friar Street
Broadfield
BR1 3RF

delivery note no	68873
delivery method	Lynx Parcels
your order	47609
date	02 10 20-3

product code	quantity	description
45B	100 pairs	Blue Toebar socks

Received
signature...... *V Williams* ......name (capitals). *V WILLIAMS* ....date. 6/10/20-3

INVOICE – THE SELLER REQUESTS PAYMENT

The invoice is the trading document which is sent by the seller to the buyer stating how much is owed by the buyer of goods or services.

The invoice, like the delivery note, is prepared in the supplier's (seller's) office, and is either processed manually or produced on a computer printer using a computer accounting program.

Invoices produced by different organisations will vary to some extent in terms of detail, but their basic layout will always be the same. The invoice prepared by Cool Socks Limited – illustrated on page 25 – is typical of a modern typed or computer printed document.

An invoice will normally be printed as part of a multiple set of documents which is likely to include a delivery note and a copy invoice for the seller's own records. The copy invoice will normally be filed in numerical order (see 'coding' below). If a computer accounting program is used, the invoice can, of course, be called up on screen, referenced by its invoice number.

Note the following details, and refer to the invoice on page 25.

addresses

The invoice shows the address:

- of the seller of the goods – Cool Socks Limited
- where the invoice should be sent – to Trends
- where the goods are to be sent – if it is different from the invoice address

coding and references

There are a number of important coding references on the invoice:

- the numerical reference of the invoice itself – 787923
- the account number allocated to Trends by the seller – 3993 – for use in the seller's computer accounting program; note that account references can include letters as well – for example another supplier might give Trends the code TR126
- the original reference number on the purchase order sent by Trends – 47609 – which will enable the shop to link the invoice with the original order
- the product code from the seller's catalogue or product list – here it is 45B

Note that coding on a financial document can be:

- numeric – ie just numbers
- alpha-numeric – ie a mixture of letters and numbers

date

The date on the invoice is important because the payment date (here one month) is calculated from it. It is also the transaction date used for VAT (Value Added Tax) purposes (see the next page).

the goods

The invoice must specify accurately the goods supplied. The details – set out in columns in the body of the invoice – include:

- **product code** – this is the catalogue number which appeared on the original purchase order and on the delivery note

- **description** – the goods must be specified precisely

- **quantity** – this should agree with the quantity ordered

- **price** – this is the price of each unit shown in the next column

- **unit** is the way in which the unit is counted and charged for, eg 'boxes' of tights or single items, eg designer dresses, in which case the unit is quoted as 'each'

- **total** is the unit price multiplied by the number of units

- **discount %** is the percentage allowance (often known as 'trade' discount) given to customers who regularly deal with the supplier, ie they receive a certain percentage (eg 10%) deducted from their bill (see page 28 for further explanation of discounts)

- discounts are also given for **bulk purchases** – 'bulk discount' will also be shown in the discount column

- **net** is the amount due to the seller after deduction of trade or bulk discount, and before VAT is added on

totals and VAT

Further calculations are made in the box at the bottom of the invoice:

- **Goods Total** is the amount due to the seller (it is the total of the net column)

- **Value Added Tax (VAT)**, here calculated as 20% of the total after deduction of any cash discount. VAT is added to produce the invoice final total

- **Total** is the VAT plus the Goods Total; it is the amount due to the seller

Note: VAT (Value Added Tax) is a 'sales tax' on the supply of goods and services. It is changed from time-to-time by the Government. In this book a standard VAT rate of 20% is used.

terms

The terms of payment are stated on the invoice. In this case these include:

- **Net monthly** – this means that full payment of the invoice should be made within a month of the invoice date

- **Carriage paid** means that the price of the goods includes delivery

- **E & OE** stands for 'errors and omissions excepted' which means that if there is a error or something left off the invoice by mistake, resulting in an incorrect final price, the supplier has the right to rectify the mistake and demand the correct amount

Another term used (not shown here) is **Settlement Discount** (also known as **Cash Discount**) – a further discount given when payment is made early, eg '2.5% settlement discount for payment within 7 days'. See page 28 for further details.

INVOICE

COOL SOCKS LIMITED

Unit 45 Elgar Estate, Broadfield, BR7 4ER
Tel 01908 765314 Fax 01908 765951 Email toni@cool.u-net.com
VAT Reg GB 0745 4672 76

invoice to

Trends **4 Friar Street** **Broadfield** **BR1 3RF**

invoice no	**787923**
account	**3993**
your reference	**47609**
date/tax point	**02 10 20-3**

deliver to

as above

product code	description	quantity	price	unit	total	discount %	net
45B	**Blue toebar socks**	**100**	**2.36**	**pair**	**236.00**	**0.00**	**236.00**

terms

Net monthly
Carriage paid
E & OE

goods total	**236.00**
VAT	**47.20**
TOTAL	**283.20**

CREDIT NOTE – A REFUND IS DUE TO THE BUYER

A **credit note** is a 'refund' document. It reduces the amount owed by the buyer. The goods, remember, have not yet been paid for. The credit note is prepared by the seller and sent to the buyer. Examples of reasons for a refund by credit note include:

- the goods may have been damaged, lost in transit or they may be faulty
- not all the goods have been sent – this is referred to as 'shortages'
- the unit price on the invoice may be incorrect and the buyer overcharged

In this Case Study, when the staff of Trends unpack the socks in the store room they find that ten pairs are damaged. They telephone Cool Socks to report the problem and Cool Socks authorise the return of the socks for credit. These socks will then be sent back to Cool Socks with a request for credit – ie a reduction in the bill for the 10 damaged pairs – with a document known as a returns note (see page 129). Cool Socks will then issue the credit note for £28.32 shown below. Note the following details:

- the invoice number of the original consignment is quoted
- the reason for the issue of the credit note is stated at the bottom of the credit note – here 'damaged' goods
- the details are otherwise exactly the same as on an invoice

---

CREDIT NOTE

COOL SOCKS LIMITED

Unit 45 Elgar Estate, Broadfield, BR7 4ER
Tel 01908 765314 Fax 01908 765951 Email toni@cool.u-net.com
VAT REG GB 0745 4672 76

to

| Trends |
| 4 Friar Street |
| Broadfield |
| BR1 3RF |

credit note no	12157
account	3993
your reference	47609
our invoice	787923
date/tax point	10 10 20–3

product code	description	quantity	price	unit	total	discount %	net
45B	Blue Toebar socks	10	2.36	pair	23.60	0.00	23.60

Reason for credit
10 pairs of socks received – damaged

GOODS TOTAL	23.60
VAT	4.72
TOTAL	28.32

STATEMENT – THE SELLER REQUESTS PAYMENT

A seller will not normally expect a buyer to pay each individual invoice as soon as it is received: this could result in the buyer having to make a number of payments during the month. Instead, a **statement of account** is sent by the supplier to the buyer at the end of the month. This statement shows what is owed by the buyer to the seller. It contains details of:

* any balances (amounts owing) at the beginning of the month – these appear in the debit column with the wording 'balance b/f' in the details column ('b/f' stands for 'brought forward')
* any payments received from the buyer (credit column)
* invoices issued for goods supplied – the full amount due, including VAT (debit column)
* refunds made on credit notes – including VAT (credit column)
* the running balance and, in the box at the bottom, the final net total of all the items
* the bank details required for making payment by BACS or Faster Payments

The statement issued by Cool Socks to Trends for the period covering the sale and refund is shown below. Note that the balance of £150 owing at the beginning of the month has been paid off in full by a BACS payment on 2 October.

STATEMENT OF ACCOUNT
COOL SOCKS LIMITED
Unit 45 Elgar Estate, Broadfield, BR7 4ER
Tel 01908 765314 Fax 01908 765951 Email toni@cool.u-net.com
VAT REG GB 0745 4672 76

TO

Trends
4 Friar Street
Broadfield
BR1 3RF

account **3993**

date **31 10 20-3**

date	details	debit £	credit £	balance £
01 10 20-3	Balance b/f	150.00		150.00
02 10 20-3	BACS payment 170961		150.00	00.00
02 10 20-3	Invoice 787923	283.20		283.20
10 10 20-3	Credit note 12157		28.32	254.88

Electronic payments: pay Cool Socks Ltd at Albion Bank, Account 11451226, Sort code 904717

TOTAL	254.88

DISCOUNTS

The invoice in the Case Study (see the next page) shows a column for **discount**.

We also saw that the terms at the bottom of the invoice can allow for **settlement discount** (also known as **cash discount**).

We will now explain these terms and show how the discount is calculated.

trade discount and bulk discount

It is common practice for suppliers to give businesses that order from them on a regular basis an agreed discount – a percentage reduction in the invoiced amount. This is known as **trade discount** because it applies to businesses 'in the trade' rather than to the general public. Discount may also be given by sellers to buyers who purchase in large quantities or over certain money amounts (eg over £5,000); this is known as **bulk discount**.

In the example on the next page 10% trade discount has been given to Trends. Note how the discount percentage is shown in the discount column and the net amount is the amount after deduction of the discount.

The calculations on the invoice are as follows:

Step 1	Calculate the total price before discount
	100 x £2.36 = £236.00
Step 2	Calculate the trade discount
	£236.00 x 10% (ie 10/100) = £23.60
Step 3	Calculate the net price before VAT
	£236.00 - £23.60 = £212.40
Step 4	Calculate the VAT
	£212.40 x 20% (ie 20/100) = £42.48
Step 5	Calculate the total invoice price
	£212.40 + £42.48 = £254.88

INVOICE

COOL SOCKS LIMITED
Unit 45 Elgar Estate, Broadfield, BR7 4ER
Tel 01908 765314 Fax 01908 765951 Email toni@cool.u-net.com
VAT Reg GB 0745 4672 76

invoice to

Trends 4 Friar Street Broadfield BR1 3RF	invoice no	787923
	account	3993
	your reference	47609
	date/tax point	02 10 20-3

as above

product code	description	quantity	price	unit	total	discount %	net
45B	Blue toebar socks	100	2.36	pair	236.00	10.00	212.40

terms
Net monthly
Carriage paid
E & OE

goods total	212.40
VAT	42.48
TOTAL	254.88

an invoice with 10% trade discount deducted

settlement (cash) discount

Settlement discount (also known as **cash discount**) is a discount offered by the seller to the buyer to encourage the buyer to settle up straightaway or in a short space of time rather than waiting the thirty or more days specified on the invoice. For example, the terms on the bottom of the invoice may include the phrase: *"Settlement discount of 2.5% for payment within seven days"*. This means that the seller will allow 2.5% off the net invoice price (ie the price before VAT is added on) if the invoice is settled within seven days of the invoice date.

There are two important points to remember:

1. VAT charged on an invoice with settlement (cash) discount offered is calculated on the invoice amount **after** deduction of settlement discount.

2. The invoice total is the sum of this reduced amount of VAT and the goods total **before** deduction of settlement discount.

If we take the Cool Socks invoice on the next page, the calculations for a cash discount of 2.5% are as follows:

Step 1	Calculate the total price before trade discount 100 x £2.36 = £236.00
Step 2	Calculate the trade discount (as before) £236.00 x 10% (ie 10/100) = £23.60
Step 3	Calculate the net price/Goods Total (as before) £236.00 - £23.60 = £212.40
Step 4	NOW calculate the settlement discount £212.40 x 2.5% (ie 2.5/100) = £5.31
Step 5	Calculate the reduced goods total (this is not written on the invoice) £212.40 - £5.31 = £207.09
Step 6	Calculate the VAT on this lower amount £207.09 x 20% (ie 20/100) = £41.41
Step 7	Calculate the total invoice price **(using the goods total before deduction of settlement discount)** £212.40 + £41.41 = £253.81

INVOICE

COOL SOCKS LIMITED
Unit 45 Elgar Estate, Broadfield, BR7 4ER
Tel 01908 765314 Fax 01908 765951 Email toni@cool.u-net.com
VAT Reg GB 0745 4672 76

invoice to

Trends 4 Friar Street Broadfield BR1 3RF	

invoice no	787923
account	3993
your reference	47609
date/tax point	02 10 20-3

as above

product code	description	quantity	price	unit	total	discount %	net
45B	Blue toebar socks	100	2.36	pair	236.00	10.00	212.40

terms

2.5% settlement discount for payment within 7 days, otherwise net monthly

Carriage paid

E & OE

goods total	212.40
VAT	41.41
TOTAL	253.81

an invoice with 10% trade discount deducted and 2.5% settlement discount allowed for quick settlement

VALUE ADDED TAX (VAT) – A 'SALES TAX'

what is Value Added Tax (VAT)?

VAT is a UK sales tax on the selling price charged to buyers.

As we have seen on some of the business documents illustrated in this chapter, VAT is added to the price of items sold after discount has been deducted. VAT is a **sales tax** paid by the consumer and administered and collected by **HM Revenue & Customs**, a Government Department.

Businesses must keep accurate records of VAT paid and collected. This means filing financial documents such as invoices and credit notes for a minimum period of six years. HM Revenue & Customs tax inspectors visit businesses from time-to-time to ensure that VAT is being charged correctly and that there are no VAT 'fiddles' taking place.

some useful VAT calculations

In your studies you are likely to be asked to carry out a variety of calculations involving VAT. Here are some of the more common ones.

what is the VAT to be charged?

If you need to work out the VAT on a given amount you apply the formula:

$$\text{amount} \times \frac{20 \text{ (ie the VAT rate)}}{100} = \text{VAT payable}$$

VAT chargeable on £100 is therefore $£100 \times \frac{20}{100} = £20.00$

Note that when calculating VAT, the VAT total is usually rounded down to the nearest penny; eg VAT of £2.56<u>78</u> becomes £2.5<u>6</u> and not £2.5<u>7</u>.

calculating the VAT when the VAT is included but not shown

If you are given a total amount, for an example a shop till receipt which does not show the VAT amount, you may need to work out both the VAT content and also the amount before VAT is added (the 'VAT exclusive' amount). The VAT content is worked out by using the formula:

$$\frac{\text{VAT percentage} \times \text{amount which includes VAT}}{100 + \text{VAT percentage}} = \text{VAT content}$$

The VAT content can also be found by using the **VAT fraction** provided by HM Revenue & Customs. For a VAT rate of 20%, the VAT fraction is $^1/6$. All you have to do to find out the VAT is to divide the amount including VAT by 6. For example, the VAT included in £12 is $£12 \div 6 = £2$.

AUTHORISING AND CHECKING INVOICES

credit limits

The credit limit of a customer is the maximum amount which the seller will allow the customer to owe at any one time.

Part of the accounting control system of a business is to set credit limits for its established customers and to establish limits for new customers. Each time that an invoice is issued, a check should be made against the credit limit of that customer.

authorisation of invoices

Most invoices issued will be within the credit limit and processed with the authority of the person in charge of invoicing. What if the credit limit will be exceeded? No business will refuse to supply a good customer. It may be that payment will soon come in from the buyer, or the amount involved is relatively small. In these cases the invoice will need authorisation from a more senior person in the accounts department. It is quite possible that a credit limit may have to be raised if a customer is buying more goods or services, and, of course, is paying invoices on time.

the need to check invoices

Few things are more annoying to a buyer than an incorrect invoice – the wrong goods, the wrong price, the wrong discount, and so on. It wastes the buyer's time and may require an adjusting credit note to be issued. It is essential that a number of important details are checked by the accounts staff of the seller before invoices are authorised and sent out.

What will the person need to check? He or she will need to look at:

- the purchase order relating to the invoice (this is very important)
- the seller's own record of any price quoted (eg a printed or online catalogue or a product database)
- the seller's file record of the buyer (either paper-based or on the computer) which should give the credit limit and the discount allowed

the checks to be made

- Is the **correct customer** being invoiced? There are often customers with similar names; the customer coding must be carefully checked.
- Are the goods being sent to the **correct place**? Sometimes the delivery address can be different from the address normally held on file.

- Are the **correct goods** being sent? The product coding on the purchase order must be checked carefully against the description; it is possible that the buyer has quoted an incorrect code
- Is the **quantity** correct?
- Is the **unit** correct? Is it a box of products or an individual item being requested?
- Is the **price** correct?
- Is the **correct discount** percentage being allowed to the customer? Do any special terms apply? The list of discounts or customer file will need to be looked at.
- Are the **calculations** on the invoice correct? This is very important if the invoice has not been produced on a computer. The normal checks for a straightforward invoice with trade discount deducted are:

    quantity x unit price = total before discount

    total before discount x discount % = discount

    total before discount – discount = net total

    net total x VAT % = VAT

    net total + VAT = invoice total

If the invoice is for more than one one product, all the invoice 'lines' must be carefully and individually checked and the addition also checked.

Very important note:

If there is **settlement discount** being offered, the VAT amount must be calculated on the net total **after deduction of settlement discount**, but it must be assumed that discount is not being taken and so the total equals:

    net total **before** deduction of settlement discount plus VAT amount calculated on net total **after** deduction of settlement discount

This does not sound completely logical, but it is correct!

DEALING WITH DISCREPANCIES

Discrepancies on financial documents can occur in the following situations:

- **The discrepancy is found in the internal checking process**, before the document is issued. In this case the document will have to be passed back to the person or section which made the mistake and a new corrected document will have to be issued and authorised; normally the original document reference number can be retained.
- **The buyer finds the discrepancy after the document has been issued**. In this case an apology will have to be made by the seller to the buyer and a correcting document issued; under no circumstances should the buyer alter or correct the document.

CODING SYSTEMS

We have already seen in this chapter that **coding** is widely used in the documentation process. Coding is important for two main reasons:

■ it provides an instant and accurate way of referencing customers, suppliers, individual products, purchase orders

■ it enables documents to be filed in an efficient way so that they can be easily accessed; it is important in any business that documents can be found and referred to easily, either in paper format, or on a computer system

Filing systems are often organised using either an **alphabetic** or a **numeric** coding system:

■ customer files are normally filed alphabetically by name

■ invoices are normally filed numerically by invoice number

Sometimes coding may be **alpha-numeric**, using a mixture of letters and numbers. For example customers who have 'JON' as the first three letters of their name – 'Jones' for example – may be coded JON01, JON02, JON03, and so on. If you think about it, alpha-numeric coding is used widely in everyday life: examples include vehicle registration plates, postcodes, tax codes and National Insurance 'numbers'.

Study the invoice extract shown below and see how many accounting-related codes you can identify and what types they are. The answers are shown at the bottom of the page.

---

invoice (extract)

Simway Ltd 4 High Street Broadfield BR1 2GF		invoice no	82346
		account reference	SIM003
		purchase order	47609
		date/tax point	07 12 20-3

product code	description	quantity	price	unit	total	discount %	net
STPGR	Stapler (green)	10	10.70	each	107.00	10.00	96.30

Alpha-numeric code: account reference SIM003

Numeric codes: invoice number 82346
purchase order number 47609

Alphabetical code: product code STPGR

CODING AT WORK

supplier account codes

Legno Ltd, a timber wholesaler, allocates codes to each of its suppliers. Each code is alpha-numeric, made up of the first three letters of the supplier's name followed by a two digit number to distinguish the suppliers when two or more share the same first three letters. The digits reflect the alphabetical order of the names. For example:

Supplier	Supplier account code	Notes
Jonas Supplies	JON01	*'as' comes before 'at'*
Jonathan UK Ltd	JON02	*'at' comes before 'es'*
Jones Ltd	JON03	

Last week Legno Ltd opened accounts for two new suppliers: Jonty Supplies and Jonsson Ltd.

You are asked to allocate account codes to these suppliers. Apart from the three accounts listed above there are no other accounts starting with the three letters 'JON'.

What would the codes be? The **answer** is shown below:

Supplier	Supplier account code	Notes
Jonsson Ltd	JON04	*'ss' comes after the 'es' of Jones and before the 'ty' of Jonty*
Jonty Supplies	JON05	

sales product codes

Legno Ltd also operates a system which allocates General Ledger account codes to different types of timber sales. These are entered on the sales invoices and credit notes so that the amount can be entered in the correct account. The ledger codes are as follows:

Product type	General Ledger Code
Pine sales	GL4000
Oak sales	GL4001
Beech sales	GL4002
Hardwood sales	GL4003
Ash sales	GL4004

A new trainee asks you to check that he has the right code for an invoice for the sale of oak. He asks if it is GL4002 because that is a code used very frequently on invoices. Is the trainee correct?

Answer: No. The code is incorrect. The code for the sale of oak is GL4001.

FILING – RETENTION OF DOCUMENTS

importance of efficient filing

It is important in any business that documents and other forms of data can be found and referred to easily, either in paper format, or on a computer system. The efficient organisation of a filing system is therefore critical to the efficient operation of that business. If a document cannot be located because it has not been put away, or has been put away in the wrong place, time, money and tempers can be lost.

As we saw in the last section there are methods of numerical and alphabetical coding which can make the sorting and storage of documents and other data easier and more efficient. For example:

- **numerical** filing: financial documents, eg invoices and credit notes
- **alphabetical** filing: customer correspondence

filing retention policy

Over the years businesses are likely to accumulate a large volume of:

- paper-based documents: financial documents, letters, contracts
- electronically based data: emails, database files, spreadsheet files

The question then arises: "For how long should we keep all these records?" The answer is that businesses should have a **retention policy** stating that records are normally kept for **six years, plus the current year**.

The reasons for this are legal requirements. Legislation covering company law, taxation and data protection generally requires that records should be kept for anywhere between three and six years.

Another legal reason is that **after six years** if anyone wants to take legal action against a business, they are prevented from doing so by a principle known as **limitation of action**. That is why all necessary evidence is kept for at least six years.

destruction of filing records

A business should always keep its filing records securely so that people who are not authorised to access the records are prevented from getting hold of confidential information. After the six years has elapsed the records can be destroyed or shredded (paper records), or 'wiped' (data held electronically). This includes the wiping or destruction of a computer's hard disk if a computer is being replaced

Chapter Summary

- When a business sells goods or services on credit it will deal with a number of financial documents. The most important of these are the
  - purchase order
  - delivery note
  - invoice
  - credit note
  - statement

- The seller of the goods or services requests payment by means of an invoice and then reminds the buyer by means of a regular statement of account (normally monthly).

- Discounts – reductions in the selling price – are often given by the seller to the buyer. These include trade discount, bulk discount and settlement discount for early payment. Trade and bulk discounts are deducted by the seller from the invoice total. Settlement discount is deducted by the buyer.

- A refund due to the buyer will be acknowledged and documented by means of a credit note.

- All documents are normally coded (given an alphabetic, numeric or alpha-numeric code) for reference purposes.

- VAT (Value Added Tax), a sales tax payable on most goods and services, is included on the majority of invoices and credit notes.

- All documents should be checked carefully by the seller to make sure that the right goods or services have been supplied, and at the right price. It is essential that items such as discounts, VAT and totals are calculated correctly.

- Financial documents will need to be authorised before they are sent out.

- Any discrepancies found on the documents either by the seller or the buyer should be dealt with promptly.

- Documents are normally filed away for reference purposes. The documents will be coded for easy access and retained for at least six years.

Key Terms		
	purchase order	a document issued by the buyer of goods and services, sent to the seller, indicating the goods or services required
	delivery note	a document sent by the seller to the buyer with the goods, detailing what has been sent
	invoice	a document issued by the seller of goods or services indicating the amount owing and the required payment date
	credit note	a document issued by the seller of the goods or services reducing the amount owed by the buyer
	statement	a document issued by the seller to the buyer summarising invoices, credit notes issued and payments received and stating the amount owed
	trade discount	a percentage reduction in the selling price given by the seller to the buyer because of the trading relationship
	bulk discount	a discount given by the seller to the buyer for bulk purchases, ie purchases over certain quantities or over certain money amounts
	settlement (cash) discount	a percentage reduction in the selling price given to the buyer if the buyer pays within a specified short space of time
	Value Added Tax (VAT)	a government tax on sales, normally calculated on invoices and credit notes
	credit limit	the maximum amount the seller will allow the customer to owe at any one time
	coding	document references using numeric, alphabetic or alpha-numeric identification systems
	document retention policy	the requirement for an organisation to keep documents for a specified minimum period of time, normally six years plus the current year

Activities

2.1 What type of financial document would normally be used when goods are sold on credit:

(a)   to be sent with the goods from the seller to the buyer, and listing the goods sent?

(b)   as a formal notification of the amount owed?

(c)   to remind the buyer of the amount owed to the seller?

(d)   as a formal notification from the seller of a refund made to the buyer?

(e)   to order the goods from the seller in the first place?

2.2 (a)   Explain the term 'trade discount'.

(b)   You supply goods priced at £159.50 to a customer at a trade discount of 30%. What would the total invoice amount be, assuming a VAT rate of 20% and no further discounts?

2.3 Zeta Stationery sells gel pens and has a special sales offer. A box of ten gel pens normally sells at £8.00 (excluding VAT). Zeta Stationery is offering to give a 20% bulk discount for orders of ten boxes or more. One morning it receives the following orders:

(a)   20 boxes ordered by Osborne Electronics Limited

(b)   50 boxes ordered by Helfield College

(c)   5 boxes ordered by Jim Masters

(d)   1,000 boxes ordered by Trigger Trading Limited

Calculate in each case

- the total cost before discount

- the discount

- the cost after discount

- the VAT at the current rate

- the total cost

2.4 Recalculate the totals in Activity 2.3 allowing for a settlement (cash) discount of 2.5%.

2.5 You work as one of three assistants in an accounts office. Your supervisor is off sick. You receive an urgent and large purchase order from a customer and find that the product code and goods description do not match up. The goods have to be despatched on the same day. What is the problem and what would you do about it?

2.6 (a)   Give three examples of coding found on financial documents prepared by a seller.

(b)   Explain why coding is important.

2.7   Invoices filed away by a business are normally retained for at least

(a)   one year plus the current year

(b)   six years plus the current year

(c)   ten years plus the current year

(d)   twenty years plus the current year

Which of these options is correct?

2.8   •   Check the invoice extracts shown below.

•   State what is wrong with them.

•   Calculate the correct final totals.

Note: VAT is rounded down to the nearest penny.

invoice (a)

description	quantity	price	total	discount %	net
Cotton shirts (red)	10	9.50	95.00	20	85.50

goods total	85.50
VAT @ 20%	17.10
TOTAL	102.60

invoice (b)

description	quantity	price	total	discount %	net
'Crazy Surfin' T-shirts (yellow)	50	5.00	225.00	10	202.50

goods total	202.50
VAT @ 20%	40.50
TOTAL	243.00

2.9 You work in the Accounts Department of Pool Cleaning Services Limited, a business which maintains swimming pools, spa baths and jacuzzis.

It is 31 July 20-3 and you are looking through the file for the account of Mr Henry Simpson. Your file shows that you issued an invoice on 8 July (shown below) and a credit note on 14 July for a 10% trade discount which should have been deducted from the invoice (see next page).

You also note from last month's statement that Mr Simpson still owed you £58.75 on 1 July for a call out charge he had not yet paid. You received a cheque for this amount on 4 July.

You are to prepare a statement for Mr H Simpson as at 31 July 20-3. It should show opening and closing balances and transactions for the month. A blank statement is shown on the next page.

INVOICE

Pool Cleaning Services Limited

Unit 5 Neptune Estate, Mereford, MR7 4EF
Tel 01908 352456 Fax 01908 352466 Email mail@poolcleaning-services.com
VAT Reg GB 0745 4872 21

invoice to

H Simpson
45 Bishops Avenue
Marston Hackett
MR7 9JH

invoice no	**10982**
account	**234**
your reference	**verbal**
date/tax point	**08 07 20-3**

description	total	discount	net
Annual swimming pool service, 27 June 20-3	290.00	0.00	290.00

Net Total	290.00
VAT	58.00
TOTAL	348.00

terms
Net monthly

extract from credit note No. 2378 dated 14 July

description		total	discount	net
Annual swimming pool service		29.00	0.00	29.00

Reason for credit
10% discount allowable on invoice
10982

NET TOTAL	29.00
VAT	5.80
TOTAL	34.80

STATEMENT OF ACCOUNT

Pool Cleaning Services Limited

Unit 5 Neptune Estate, Mereford, MR7 4EF
Tel 01908 352456 Fax 01908 352466 Email mail@poolcleaning-services.com
VAT Reg GB 0745 4872 21

TO

account

date

date	details	debit £	credit £	balance £

Electronic payments: pay Pool Cleaning Services Ltd at
Britannia Bank, Account 12397610, Sort code 83 11 20

TOTAL £

3 Double-entry and the accounting equation

this chapter covers...

This chapter describes and explains how double-entry accounts are set up and how they work. It covers:

- *the need for accounts and what they are used for*

- *the way in which double-entry accounts are organised into ledgers*

- *the format of double-entry accounts*

- *the principles of debits and credits*

- *the way in which the bank account fits into the double-entry system*

- *how to write up the double-entry accounts*

- *how to work out whether an entry made in a double-entry account should be a debit or a credit*

- *the way in which double-entry accounts relate to the accounting equation*

- *the operation of the accounting equation*

- *the balancing of double-entry accounts*

important technical note

This book uses the phrase 'bank account' to mean both an account held at a bank and also a ledger account set up by a business to record bank transactions. To avoid confusion all ledger accounts in this book use capital letters for the start of the account name, but the account held at the bank is referred to using small letters. The rule is:

Bank **A**ccount = a ledger account in the books of the business

bank **a**ccount = an account held at a bank

AN INTRODUCTION TO DOUBLE-ENTRY ACCOUNTS

double-entry accounts and the accounting system

As we saw in Chapter 1, double-entry accounts are written up from the books of prime entry which include day books and cash books.

Books of prime entry record financial transactions and are themselves written up from business documents, which include invoices and bank payments. The phrase 'prime entry' means 'the first place where information is entered'. Books of prime entry will be covered in detail in later chapters of this book.

The diagram below shows how the double-entry accounts fit into the earlier stages of the accounting system.

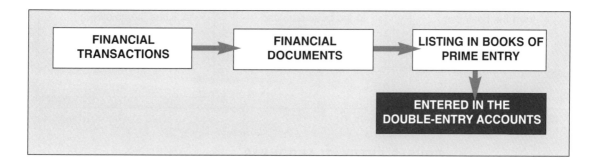

what do double-entry accounts record?

Double-entry accounts form the 'core' of the accounting system. They are a record of financial transactions:

- what is owed on credit by individual customers as a result of sales
- what is owed on credit to individual suppliers as a result of purchases
- income items
- expense items

Double-entry accounts can be:

- accounts for types of income or expenses (sales, purchases, insurance, wages)
- accounts for assets (items owned)
- accounts for liabilities (amounts owed)

In other words, double-entry accounts cover all types of financial transaction.

how are double-entry accounts organised?

Double-entry accounts are grouped for convenience in different **ledgers** (for credit sales, credit purchases, general accounts).

These are shown in the diagram below and will be explained in more detail in later chapters.

All the ledgers grouped together are called '**the ledger**'. The word 'ledger' means 'book'.

'the ledger' = sales ledger & purchases ledger & general ledger

SALES LEDGER

accounts for customers
• who buy on credit
  from the business
• who owe money to
  the business

PURCHASES LEDGER

accounts for suppliers
• who supply on credit
  to the business, and
• to whom the business
  owes money

GENERAL LEDGER

accounts for
• assets (items owned)
• liabilities (items owed)
• owner's capital
• expenses
• income

DOUBLE-ENTRY 'T' ACCOUNTS

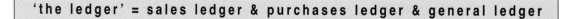

Double-entry accounts are normally set out in the form of a 'T' with the account name at the top; they are known as 'T accounts' – see the example below:

debit (dr)	Account name	credit (cr)

Each account has two sides:

■ a **debit** side (often written as 'dr') on the left

■ a **credit** side (often written as 'cr') on the right

You can remember this using the phrase '**Dr**ive on the left and **Cr**ash on the right'. If you do not normally drive on the left you could use the phrase '**D**ozy **L**ions **C**annot **R**un'.

A simple double-entry transaction makes entries in **two accounts** – a debit entry in one account and a credit entry in the other account.

In the example below a business has paid an insurance premium. The accounts record two aspects of the transaction: the insurance expense and the deduction from the bank account.

The debit entry goes to the Insurance Account and the credit entry to the Bank Account. If you are wondering why the Insurance Account entry is a debit and the Bank Account entry a credit, we will explain the rules over the next few pages.

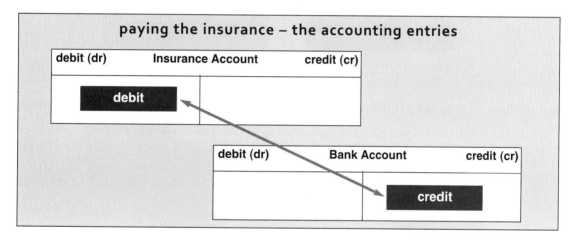

BANK ACCOUNTS – DEBITS AND CREDITS

An organisation such as a business will need to use a bank account. Transactions passing through the account held at the bank – for example, money received, payments made – will need recording in the accounts of the business.

Bank Account in the accounting system of a business (see the previous page) is a separate record of the money paid into and out of the bank.

The problem for the bookkeeper is that the terms 'debit' and 'credit' are used differently by the bank and a business. In fact they are the opposite way round. This can prove confusing when dealing with a bank statement:

■ banks see a **debit** as a **payment out** of a customer's account

■ banks see a **credit** as a **payment into** a customer's account

Businesses, however should always think as follows:

- **money paid into the bank is always a debit** in the accounting system of the business
- **money paid out of the bank is always a credit** in the accounting system of the business

This 'left to right' flow of money in and out of the Bank Account as set up in the ledgers of a business can be seen as follows:

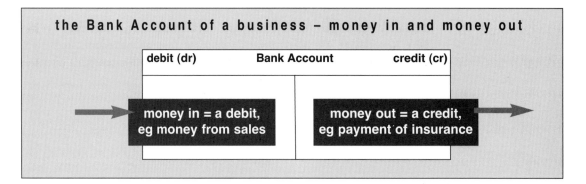

debit or credit?

When a financial transaction is recorded as an entry in the Bank Account of a business as part of the double-entry system, it is easy to work out whether it is a credit or a debit by using the 'money in = debit and money out = credit' rule. It is then straightforward to work out whether the entry in the other account is a debit or credit. The rules are:

- **payment into the bank . . . money in = a debit . . .**

  so the other entry must be a credit

  Example:

  £1,000 received from sales paid into the bank. The entries are:

  Debit: Bank Account £1,000   Credit: Sales Account £1,000

- **payment out of the bank . . . money out = a credit . . .**

  so the other entry must be a debit

  Example:

  £500 insurance premium paid out of the bank account by electronic transfer. The entries are:

  Debit: Insurance Account £500   Credit: Bank Account £500

Note from these two entries quoted above:

- the debit and credit entries are for the same amount
- the debit entry is quoted first and the credit entry is quoted second

Not every double-entry transaction involves the Bank Account, but many do, and it is a very useful starting point for getting to grips with debits and credits. The two transactions we have just explained are illustrated below.

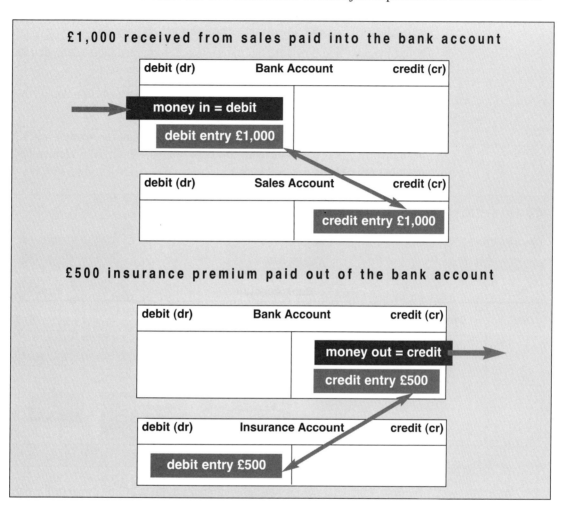

We will now go a step further and illustrate the full format of double-entry accounts and the information that needs to be recorded in the account.

WRITING UP A DOUBLE-ENTRY ACCOUNT

In this chapter the double-entry accounts have so far been displayed as a simple 'T'. This 'T' format is a useful way of displaying the account, but a full double-entry account is more detailed and will have a number of columns. You will need to know how to enter the transaction details in these columns.

As you will see in the example below, there are two lines of detail on the account:

■ the account name and the 'debit' and 'credit' headings at the top; remember that the account name has capital letters at the beginning of each word (see the 'important technical note' on page 44)

■ on the next line down are the transaction column headings (date, details, £); these are the same on the debit and on the credit sides

Study the account format and read the notes about the transaction details that follow.

The transaction here shows how the Bank Account is written up for insurance of £500 paid out from the bank on 30 March 20-3 (remember: payment out of bank = credit entry).

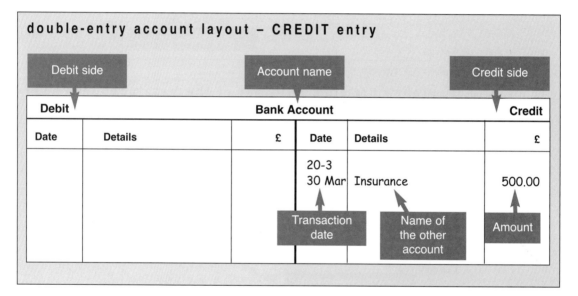

■ **date** – the year date is normally entered on the next line down of the date column and the actual date and transaction details on the following line; note that the month is often abbreviated, here it is '30 Mar' (30 March)

■ **details** – this is the other account that has been used in the double-entry transaction, here the other account is Insurance Account and the entry will be a debit because the Bank Account entry is a credit ('money out = a credit')

■ **£** – this is the **amount** column; obviously the '£' refers to the UK pound, you might also see a $ or a € sign if that is appropriate; occasionally you may also find that £ and pence (or dollars and cents) are separated into two columns

The entry to the Insurance Account for the above transaction is shown on the next page.

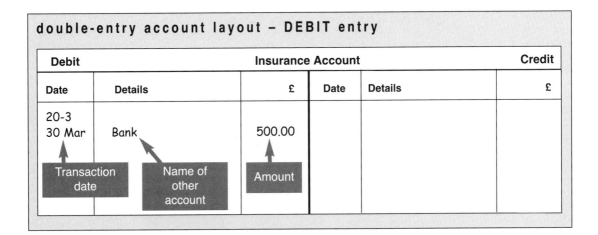

double-entry account layout – DEBIT entry

Debit			Insurance Account		Credit
Date	Details	£	Date	Details	£
20-3 30 Mar	Bank	500.00			

Transaction date

Name of other account

Amount

RULES FOR DEBITS AND CREDITS

So far in this chapter we have seen that:

■ money paid into the bank results in a **debit** entry to Bank Account in the accounting system of the business

■ money paid out of the bank results in a **credit** entry to Bank Account in the accounting system of the business

Bank Account

money in = debit money out = credit

We will now look in more detail at the 'other' accounts involved in the transactions, identifying which are normally debit or credit entries to the accounts.

entries that are always debits

Some postings to the double-entry accounts are always debits because the other account entry is the credit side of Bank Account and the transaction involved is a payment out for something. They include:

■ **purchases** – eg goods bought for selling or materials used for manufacturing items

■ **expenses** – ie expenses incurred in running the business, eg rent, advertising, insurance

■ **assets bought** – items bought for the business, for example computers and vehicles

entries that are always credits

Some postings to the double-entry accounts are **always credits** because the other account entry is the **debit side of Bank Account** and the transaction involved is money coming into the business. They include:

- **sales** – money received for goods sold or services provided
- **capital** – money paid in by the owner
- **loans** – money borrowed from the bank or other sources

Examples of debits and credits are illustrated in the diagram below which uses the simple 'T' account and just shows the account names in order to makes things clearer. Note that:

- money received entries: **debit** Bank Account and **credit** the account recording the amount
- money paid out entries: **credit** Bank Account and **debit** the account recording the expense
- the description entered in each account is the name of the other account in the transaction

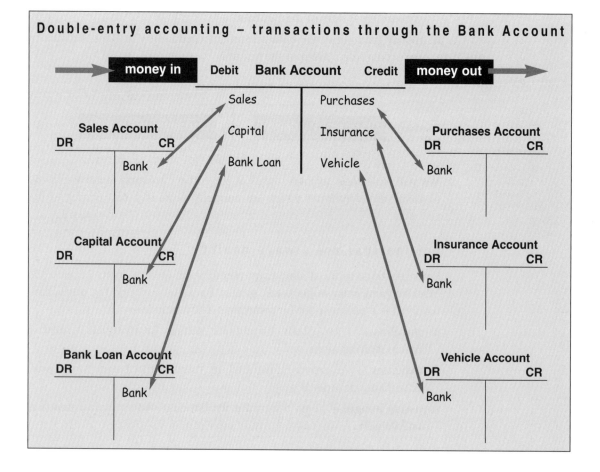

Set out below is a Case Study putting into practice all the double-entry theory covered so far in this chapter, using the full layout of the double-entry accounts.

PRONTA PIZZA – DOUBLE-ENTRY IN PRACTICE

Riccardo has just started a new pizza home delivery business. He has put in capital of £30,000 himself and raised loans of £10,000 from the bank and £10,000 from his brother Carlo. He has paid all this money into a business account at Albion Bank so that he can then pay for all that he needs to start and run the business.

He asks his bookkeeper to enter all the transactions shown in the table below into his cash book (which contains the Bank Account). He then asks the bookkeeper to set up the ledgers and carry out all the necessary double-entry account postings.

payments received and paid into the bank		date of payment
Capital introduced by Riccardo	£30,000	15 January 20-3
Bank loan	£10,000	16 January 20-3
Loan from brother Carlo	£10,000	18 January 20-3
payments paid out of the bank		
Equipment for cooking	£10,000	22 January 20-3
Van for pizza deliveries	£15,000	25 January 20-3
Materials purchased	£3,000	28 January 20-3
Insurance	£2,000	31 January 20-3

Riccardo's Bank Account in the books of Pronta Pizza after these entries have been made is shown below. The 'other' double-entry accounts follow on the next two pages.

Debit				Bank Account		Credit
Date	**Details**	**£**	**Date**	**Details**		**£**
20-3			20-3			
15 Jan	Capital	30,000	22 Jan	Equipment		10,000
16 Jan	Bank loan	10,000	25 Jan	Van		15,000
18 Jan	Carlo Loan	10,000	28 Jan	Purchases		3,000
			31 Jan	Insurance		2,000

money in = debit →   **money out = credit** →

The 'other entries' for payments into the Bank Account – ie credits

Debit			Capital Account		Credit
Date	Details	£	Date	Details	£
			20-3 15 Jan	Bank	30,000

Debit			Bank Loan Account		Credit
Date	Details	£	Date	Details	£
			20-3 16 Jan	Bank	10,000

Debit			Carlo Loan Account		Credit
Date	Details	£	Date	Details	£
			20-3 18 Jan	Bank	10,000

The 'other entries' for payments out of the Bank Account – ie debits

Debit			Equipment Account		Credit
Date	Details	£	Date	Details	£
20-3 22 Jan	Bank	10,000			

Debit			Van Account		Credit
Date	Details	£	Date	Details	£
20-3 25 Jan	Bank	15,000			

Debit			Purchases Account			Credit
Date	Details	£	Date	Details		£
20-3 28 Jan	Bank	3,000				

Debit			Insurance Account			Credit
Date	Details	£	Date	Details		£
20-3 31 Jan	Bank	2,000				

A NOTE ON CASH AND CREDIT TRANSACTIONS

The difference between paying for cash sales and sales made on credit terms is straightforward:

> **cash** payment = paying straightaway

> **credit** terms = paying at a later date

The double-entry bookkeeping described so far in this chapter relates just to **cash transactions**, ie money paid and banked straightaway.

There are also situations where goods are sold or purchased now and paid for later. These **credit transactions** will involve two double-entry transactions:

- the **first** on the date when the sale or purchase is made but no payment is made through the Bank Account – the payment due is entered in a customer or supplier account in the ledgers to record the debt

- the **second** at a later date when payment is made and passes through the Bank Account and the customer or supplier account in the ledgers

These account entries will be covered in detail in Chapter 4 'Accounting for sales and sales returns' and in Chapter 7 'Accounting for purchases and purchases returns'. In conclusion, all you need to note at this stage is:

- a **cash** sale or purchase requires just **one** double-entry transaction

- a **credit** sale or purchase requires **two** double-entry transactions on different dates:

  - the first when the credit sale or credit purchase takes place

  - the second when payment is made for the transaction

DEBITS AND CREDITS – CONCLUSION

'cash' transactions involving the bank account

Study the table below which gives examples of 'cash' double-entry transactions which involve payments in and out of the bank. The column 'money in/out' indicates whether the payments are into or out of the bank.

	money in/out	debit	credit
buying an asset	out	asset account	bank account
receiving a bank loan (liability)	in	bank account	loan account
owner contributing capital	in	bank account	capital account
business paying wages (expense)	out	wages account	bank account
business receiving rent (income)	in	bank account	rent received account
business purchasing materials	out	purchases account	bank account

balances of accounts

So far in this chapter we have concentrated on the rules for debit and credit **entries** made in the double-entry accounts. These rules also extend to the double-entry account **balances**. As we will see at the end of this chapter, double-entry accounts are regularly balanced, in other words the amount that is 'held' in each account is calculated, just as your bank calculates how much money is held in your bank account, and is your bank 'balance'.

debits and credits – the rules

The table set out below shows which accounts normally have **debit** entries and balances and which accounts normally have **credit** entries and balances.

DEBITS	CREDITS
Assets (items bought and owned by by the business)	**Liabilities** (amounts owed by the business, eg loans)
Customer accounts (money due to be paid to the business)	**Supplier accounts** (money due to be paid to suppliers by the business)
Expenses of the business	**Sales and other types of income** received by the business
Purchases	**Capital**

DOUBLE-ENTRY AND THE ACCOUNTING EQUATION

the accounting equation

In Chapter 1 we outlined the final accounts of a business – the Statement of Profit or Loss and the Statement of Financial Position – which are the end result of the accounting process. The Statement of Profit or Loss shows how much profit (or loss) is made and the Statement of Financial Position shows how the assets of a business are financed. The Statement of Financial Position also reflects what is known as the accounting equation:

assets (what a business owns and is owed)

minus   **liabilities (what is owed by the business)**

equals   **capital (the investment of the owner and profits made)**

ASSETS what a business owns and is owed	minus	**LIABILITIES** what a business owes to others	equals	**CAPITAL** the owner's investment and profits

To help explain this equation we will now look at the concept of 'financial position' on a personal basis. If someone asked you what your financial position is, you might say:

'I have a total of £2,000 in the bank and in cash and I am owed £500 by a friend. I owe £100 to my brother.

My financial position is as follows: I have £2,000 plus the £500 owed to me but I have to pay £100 to my brother, so I have £2,400.'

If you then express this in accounting terms (ie assets, liabilities and capital) you can see how the accounting equation works. Study the table below and then the accounting equation on the next page.

	amount	personal situation	accounting term
	£2,000	what you own	an asset
+	£500	what you are owed	an asset
–	£100	what you owe	a liability
=	£2,400	your financial position	capital

ASSETS £2,000 owned + £500 owed to you = £2,500	minus	LIABILITIES what you owe = £100	equals	CAPITAL your financial position = £2,400

the accounting equation and double-entry

The accounting equation is a useful way of looking at the way double-entry accounting works. As we have seen, each business financial transaction is recorded in the accounting system and results in two entries being made in the ledgers – a debit and a credit.

Where the accounting equation becomes relevant is that each equal debit and credit entry will always ensure that the equation will balance.

We will now illustrate this by seeing how example financial transactions . . .

■ are entered in the double-entry accounts as debits and credits

■ alter the accounting equation so that the equation still balances

starting a business by paying money into the bank

You pay £30,000 into the bank as capital to start your business. The account entries are:

Debit: Bank Account £30,000   **Credit: Capital Account £30,000**

Here you are increasing assets by a debit entry of £30,000 and increasing capital by a credit entry £30,000.

The accounting equation (£30,000 – £0 = £30,000) balances:

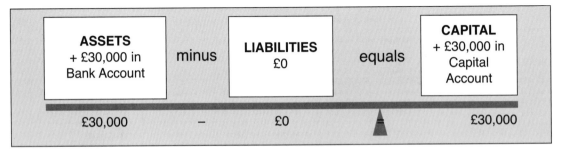

ASSETS + £30,000 in Bank Account	minus	LIABILITIES £0	equals	CAPITAL + £30,000 in Capital Account
£30,000	–	£0		£30,000

2

a bank loan which is paid into the bank account

You receive a bank loan (a liability) of £10,000 which goes straight into the business account at the bank (an asset). The account entries will be:

Debit: Bank Account £10,000   **Credit: Bank Loan Account £10,000**

Here you are **increasing assets** by a debit entry of £10,000 and **increasing liabilities** by a credit entry of £10,000. The accounting equation is now £40,000 (Assets) *minus* £10,000 (Liabilities) = £30,000 (Capital). The equation still balances because the increase in assets (a 'plus') is compensated for by the increase in liabilities (a 'minus') on the same side of the equation.

ASSETS £40,000 in Bank Account	minus	LIABILITIES £10,000 in Bank Loan Account	equals	CAPITAL £30,000 in Capital Account
£30,000 + £10,000 = £40,000	–	£10,000		£30,000

3 **buying a computer (an asset)**

You buy a computer (an asset) for £5,000 using money from the business bank account (also an asset). The account entries will be:

Debit: Computer Account £5,000   **Credit: Bank Account £5,000**

Here you are **increasing assets** by a debit entry of £5,000 to Computer Account and **decreasing assets** by a credit entry of £5,000 to Bank Account. The accounting equation is unchanged and still balances because you have just switched money from one asset (the bank account) to another asset (the computer). It now looks like this:

ASSETS £40,000 Bank Account + Computer Account	minus	LIABILITIES £10,000 in Bank Loan Account	equals	CAPITAL + £30,000 in Capital Account
£40,000 – £5,000 + £5,000 = £40,000	–	£10,000		£30,000

4 **paying off part of the bank loan (a liability)**

You repay £1,000 of the bank loan (a liability) using money from the business bank account (an asset). The account entries will be:

Debit: Bank Loan Account £1,000   **Credit: Bank Account £1,000**

Here you are **decreasing a liability** with a debit entry of £1,000 to the Bank Loan Account and **decreasing an asset** by a credit entry of £1,000 to the Bank Account.

The equation still balances because the decrease in assets is compensated for by the decrease in liabilities on the same side of the equation. The equation now looks like this:

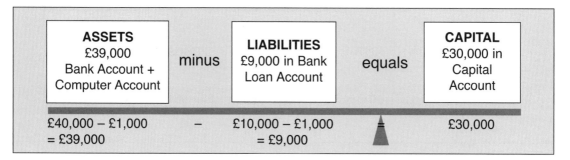

double-entry rules for changes in assets, liabilities and capital

You will see from the four examples on the last three pages that increases and decreases in assets, liabilities and capital follow a strict pattern which ensures that the accounting equation always balances:

- an **increase in an asset** is always a **debit entry**
- a **decrease in an asset** is always a **credit entry**
- an **increase in a liability** is always a **credit entry**
- a **decrease in a liability** is always a **debit entry**
- an **increase in capital** is always a **credit entry** (capital – which includes profit – increases as a business grows and makes a profit)

These rules are set out in the summaries shown below.

asset accounts

examples of assets:

    property
    vehicles
    computers
    inventory
    money due from customers
    money in the bank and cash

entries to the asset account:

DEBIT	CREDIT
asset increase	asset decrease

liability and capital accounts

examples of liabilities:

    bank loans
    bank overdrafts
    loans from other sources
    money due to suppliers

entries to the liability account:

DEBIT	CREDIT*
liability decrease	liability increase

*an increase in capital is also a credit entry

BALANCING ACCOUNTS

It is normal accounting practice to balance double-entry accounts at regular intervals in order to calculate the 'total' of the account. This process provides the owner of the business with valuable information, such as:

- the amount owing to each supplier (trade payable)
- the amount owed by each customer (trade receivable)
- the amount of sales and purchases and expenses
- the amount of VAT due to, or from, HM Revenue & Customs

These accounts are set out in the purchases, sales and general ledgers:

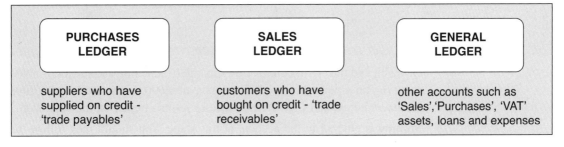

PURCHASES LEDGER	SALES LEDGER	GENERAL LEDGER
suppliers who have supplied on credit - 'trade payables'	customers who have bought on credit - 'trade receivables'	other accounts such as 'Sales', 'Purchases', 'VAT' assets, loans and expenses

We will now explain how to balance accounts from all three ledgers. The principles are the same for all three.

BALANCING A PURCHASES LEDGER ACCOUNT

Set out below is an example of a supplier's account (Donato Wholesale) which has been written up in the purchases ledger of Pronta Pizza (a pizza take-away business) during the month, but has not yet been balanced. Purchases made from the supplier are entered on the credit (right-hand) side of the account and faulty goods returned to the supplier are entered on the debit (left-hand) side of the account.

Dr			Donato Wholesale Account		Cr
20-3	Details	£	20-3	Details	£
14 Jul	Purchases returns	25.00	13 Jul	Purchases	320.00
22 Jul	Purchases returns	75.00	20 Jul	Purchases	80.00
			24 Jul	Purchases	200.00

Now study the way in which this account is balanced:

Dr					Donato Wholesale Account			Cr
20-3	Details		£	20-3	Details			£
14 Jul	Purchases returns		25.00	13 Jul	Purchases			320.00
22 Jul	Purchases returns		75.00	20 Jul	Purchases			80.00
31 Jul	Balance c/d	**1**	500.00	24 Jul	Purchases			200.00
		2	600.00				**2**	600.00
				1 Aug	Balance b/d		**3**	500.00

The debit and the credit columns are separately added up and the totals noted down (eg on a piece of paper). The totals are £600 on the credit side (three purchases items) and £100 (two purchases returns items) on the debit side.

Nothing is entered in the account at this stage. You should then follow the following procedure:

1 The difference between the totals of the two sides (ie £600 – £100 = £500) is the **balance** of the account; this is entered in the account . . .

- in the money column on the side of the smaller total (here the debit side)
- on the next available line down on that side
- with the date of the balancing (here it is 31 July)
- with the words 'Balance c/d', which is an abbreviation of 'Balance carried down' in the details column

2 Both sides of the account are now added up and the totals (which should be identical, and the higher of the two totals calculated earlier) are entered in the money columns on both sides of the account on the same line; here the figure is £600.

A single line is drawn above the totals and a thicker single line (or a double line) underneath the totals.

3 As we have entered an extra £500 on the debit side in Step 1 we need to compensate for this by entering £500 on the credit side of the account, below the totals entered in Step 2. This ensures that the account shows the £500 account balance on the correct side. Note that the date here is not the month-end date (31 July) but the first day of the following month (1 August). The abbreviation 'Balance b/d' used here stands for 'Balance brought down'.

BALANCING A SALES LEDGER ACCOUNT

On the previous page we balanced a purchases ledger account. This showed how much a supplier, Donato Wholesale, is owed by Pronta Pizza at the end of the month. The balance of this account (£500) is on the **credit** side of the account, representing an amount **owed by** a business, a liability.

It therefore follows that if you turn to the Sales Ledger which shows the opposite situation, ie amounts **owed to** Pronta Pizza by a customer, you will then find the balance of a customer account on the **debit** side of the ledger account, because an amount **owed to** a business is always a **debit**.

Study the example below of a balanced customer account – Albion Hotel – and read the notes that follow. You will see that sales are recorded on the left (debit side) and sales returns are on the right (credit side).

Dr			£	20-3	Details	£	Cr
20-3	**Details**		**£**	**20-3**	**Details**		**£**
6 Jul	Sales		200.00	Jul 9	Sales returns		20.00
8 Jul	Sales		50.00	Jul 16	Sales returns		30.00
22 Jul	Sales		150.00	Jul 31	Balance c/d	**1**	350.00
		2	400.00			**2**	400.00
1 Aug	Balance b/d	**3**	350.00				

1 The balance of **£350** is the difference between the total of the debit entries (**£400**, ie £200 + £50 + £150) and the total of the credit entries (**£50**, ie £20 + £30). It is entered on the credit side, ie the side with the lower total.

2 Both sides are added up to produce a total of £400. A single line is drawn above the totals and a thicker single line (or a double line) underneath them.

3 As we have entered an extra £350 on the credit side in Step 1 we need to compensate for this by entering £350 on the debit side of the account, below the totals entered in Step 2. This ensures that the account shows the £350 account balance on the correct side. Note that the date here is not the month-end date (31 July) but the first day of the following month (1 August). The abbreviation 'Balance b/d' used here stands for 'Balance brought down'.

BALANCING GENERAL LEDGER ACCOUNTS

general ledger balances

You can normally rely on the rule that a purchases ledger account has a balance brought down on the credit side and a sales ledger account has a balance brought down on the debit side.

The rule with General Ledger accounts is that some usually have debit balances and some usually have credit balances:

- **debit account balances** = where **money is spent by the business**, ie spent on purchases, money refunded because of returns, expenses paid

- **credit account balances** = where **money is received by the business**, ie from sales, refunds and other items of income

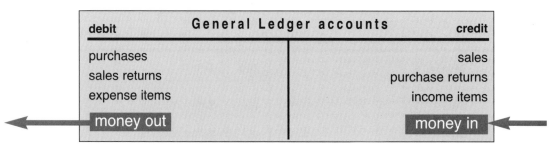

The balancing process is exactly the same as with the purchases ledger and sales ledger accounts, although it is common for the transaction entries to be on one side only.

The account below shows weekly payments for £250 recorded in the Rent Paid Account of a business. As you can see, these entries are all debits. If by any chance there was a refund of rent, it would be entered on the credit side and would reduce the final debit balance by that amount.

Dr					Rent Paid Account			Cr
20-3	**Details**			**£**	**20-3**	**Details**		**£**
1 Feb	Bank			250.00	28 Feb	Balance c/d		1,000.00
8 Feb	Bank			250.00				
15 Feb	Bank			250.00				
22 Feb	Bank			250.00				
				1,000.00				1,000.00
1 Mar	Balance b/d			1,000.00				

Chapter Summary

- Double-entry accounts are an integral part of the accounting system of a business and are written up from books of prime entry.

- Double-entry accounts form the core of the accounting system and record items such as income, expenses, amounts owed by customers, amounts owing to suppliers, assets, liabilities and capital.

- Double-entry accounting requires that two entries are made in the accounts for each transaction – a debit and a credit in separate accounts.

- Double-entry accounts are normally set up in the form of a 'T' with debit entries on the left and credit entries on the right.

- Double-entry accounts are organised in different ledgers (books): sales ledger (customer credit accounts), purchases ledger (supplier credit accounts) and general ledger (the rest of the accounts, including Bank Account).

- Money amounts received are recorded on the left-hand side of the Bank Account (debits) and payments made are recorded on the right-hand side (credits). This rule helps you work out your debits and credits: if the transaction is a bank payment made (credit) the other entry must be a debit; if the transaction is a bank receipt (debit) the other entry is a credit.

- The table below is a guide to which entries are debits and which entries are credits:

Debits	Credits
Purchases	Sales
Expenses	Income
Assets	Liabilities
Money owed by credit customers	Money owed to credit suppliers
	Capital

- The Accounting Equation relates directly to double-entry bookkeeping:

    Assets − Liabilities = Capital

    All double-entry transactions will change the figures in the Accounting Equation, but will ensure that it always balances. The changes in the assets, liabilities and capital in the Accounting Equation follow these rules:

Debits	Credits
Increases in assets	Increases in liabilities
	Increases in capital
Decreases in liabilities	Decreases in assets

- Ledger accounts are regularly balanced to provide information about the financial activity of a business. Purchases Ledger account balances are normally credit, Sales Ledger balances are normally debit and General Ledger balances can be either debit or credit.

Key Terms		
	books of prime entry	the first place in the accounting records of a business where financial transactions are recorded, using details from business documents
	day book	a book of prime entry which lists the details of various financial transactions, eg Sales Day Book (a list of sales invoices) and Cash Book (compiled from bank transactions)
	cash book	the book of prime entry which lists payments in and out of an account at the bank; it can also act as the 'Bank Account' ledger account in the double-entry system
	double-entry	an accountng system which normally involves two entries for each transaction – a debit and a credit
	ledger accounts	double-entry accounts for financial transactions involving individuals (credit customers and credit suppliers), assets, purchases, expenses, income, liabilities and capital
	the ledger	means literally 'the book' which contains the individual ledger accounts; it is normally subdivided into different categories: – sales ledger (customer accounts) – purchases ledger (supplier accounts) – general ledger (all other accounts)
	statement of financial position	one of the final accounts of a business; it shows the owner's capital in the business (investment and profits) calculated as total assets (items owned and amounts owed to the business) minus total liabilities (amounts owed by the business)
	accounting equation	total assets – total liabilities = capital This calculates the total capital of the business (ie the owner's investment and profits made) in terms of assets and liabilities – in other words, the financial position of the business owner; it always balances if the double-entry bookkeeping is carried out correctly (see also the last bullet point in the Chapter Summary on the previous page)
	account balancing	the process of calculating the difference between the totals of the debit and credit columns of a ledger account in order to provide information to management about the financial activity of the business

Activities

3.1   Which is the main source for the writing up of the double-entry accounts? Select one option.

(a) the ledgers

(b) financial documents

(c) books of prime entry

(d) the trial balance

3.2   The ledger which contains the accounts of customers who buy on credit is the:

(a) general ledger

(b) sales ledger

(c) purchases ledger

Which one of these options is correct?

3.3   The rule for entries in the Bank Account in the cash book is:

(a) money in is a debit, money out is a credit

(b) money out is a debit, money in is a credit

(c) the debit entries and credit entries always add up to the same amount

Which one of these options is correct?

3.4   The table below lists transactions recorded in a Bank Account in the cash book of a business. Tick the appropriate column to indicate whether the entry will be a debit or a credit in the cash book.

	debit ✔	credit ✔
Payment of wages		
Cash received from sales		
Payment of an invoice by a credit customer		
Payment of an insurance premium		
Loan received from a finance company		
Loan repayment made		
Bank charges		

3.5 The table below lists transactions passed through the bank account of a business, and then recorded in the cash book of the business. Write the name of the two accounts involved in the double-entry in the correct column. The first example is completed to show what is required. The name of the account which is not the Bank Account is shown in bold type.

	debit	credit
Payment of **wages**	Wages	Bank
Payment of **insurance**		
Money received from **sales**		
Purchases made		
Loan received from the bank		
Loan repayment		
Telephone bill paid		
Rates bill paid		
Rent received from office let out		

3.6 The Bank Account shown below has been written up by the bookkeeper, but someone still has to carry out the double-entry in the appropriate other accounts.

You have been asked to do this for her, using the blank accounts set out on the next page, completing the account name, date, details and amount for each entry. Enter the accounts in date order.

You may photocopy the blank accounts on the next page if you wish or download a copy from www.osbornebooks.co.uk.

Debit			Bank Account			Credit
Date	**Details**	**£**	**Date**	**Details**		**£**
20-3			20-3			
1 May	Sales	975.00	6 May	Telephone		265.00
11 May	Sales	456.70	12 May	Insurance		678.00
14 May	Bank loan	5,000.00	15 May	Purchases		2760.90

Debit			....Account		Credit
Date	Details	£	Date	Details	£

Debit			....Account		Credit
Date	Details	£	Date	Details	£

Debit			....Account		Credit
Date	Details	£	Date	Details	£

Debit			....Account		Credit
Date	Details	£	Date	Details	£

Debit			....Account		Credit
Date	Details	£	Date	Details	£

3.7   Some account **balances** are debit balances and some account balances are credit balances. Complete the table below by entering the following words in bold type in the correct column.

Purchases   Capital   Expenses   Liabilities   Supplier Accounts (ie money owed to suppliers)

Customer Accounts (ie money owed by customers)   **Assets, Sales, Income**

Debit balances	Credit balances

3.8   Some account **entries** are normally debits and some are normally credits.

Tick the appropriate column in the table below, indicating whether the type of account listed in the left-hand column normally requires a debit entry or a credit entry.

	debit ✔	credit ✔
Asset bought by the business		
Liability (eg bank loan taken out)		
Capital introduced by the owner		
Sales made by the business		
Purchases made by the business		
Expenses of the business		
Customer who owes the business money		
Supplier who is owed money by the business		

3.9   Which is the correct formula for the accounting equation? Select one option.

(a)   Liabilities – Assets = Capital

(b)   Assets – Liabilities = Capital

(c)   Assets + Liabilities = Capital

(d)   Assets + Capital = Liabilities

3.10   Insert the correct figures in the blank boxes in the accounting equation table below.

Assets £	Liabilities £	Capital £
120,000	45,000	
	61,000	95,000
265,500	86,500	
88,000		50,000
	37,500	90,000
345,700		209,000

3.11   An increase or a decrease in an asset or liability or capital will result in either a debit or a credit to the asset, liability or capital accounts.

Indicate with a tick in the table what type of entry – debit or credit – will be brought about by the increase or decrease described in the column on the left.

Transaction	Debit ✔	Credit ✔
Increase in capital account		
Increase in liability account		
Decrease in asset account		
Decrease in liability account		
Increase in asset account		

3.12 Enter the transactions set out below in double-entry accounts.

All the transactions pass through the Bank Account, so you will have to write the entries in the Bank Account and also work out what the 'other' accounts will be. No credit sales or purchases are involved.

You can draw up your own accounts, photocopy the accounts on page 69, or download blank accounts from the Osborne Books website (www.osbornebooks.co.uk).

Date	Transaction
20-4	
3 Feb	Paid in capital of £10,000
4 Feb	Received bank loan of £25,000
6 Feb	Sales of £1,340
10 Feb	Purchases of £750
14 Feb	Paid rates of £450
15 Feb	Purchases of £2,760
18 Feb	Sales of £860
21 Feb	Paid for advertising costing £138
25 Feb	Sales of £2,640
28 Feb	Paid wages of £3,560

3.13 You are working as a bookkeeper for Sphere Sports which acts a distributor for footballs and tennis balls. You have been handed the ledgers and asked to balance the four accounts shown on the next two pages. The date is 31 March 20-3.

(a)

Dr	Solo Supplies Account (Purchases Ledger)					Cr
20-3	Details	£	20-3	Details	£	
			23 Mar	Purchases	248.00	
			25 Mar	Purchases	78.75	
			30 Mar	Purchases	180.00	

(b)

Dr	Atletico Supplies Account (Purchases Ledger)				Cr
20-3	**Details**	**£**	**20-3**	**Details**	**£**
23 Mar	Purchases returns	80.00	24 Mar	Purchases	120.00
26 Mar	Purchases returns	70.00	27 Mar	Purchases	360.00
			30 Mar	Purchases	170.00

(c)

Dr	Trajan Sports Account (Sales Ledger)				Cr
20-3	**Details**	**£**	**20-3**	**Details**	**£**
23 Mar	Sales	450.00	24 Mar	Sales returns	80.00
26 Mar	Sales	70.00	30 Mar	Sales returns	70.00
27 Mar	Sales	180.00			

(d)

Dr	Office Expenses Account (General Ledger)				Cr
20-3	**Details**	**£**	**20-3**	**Details**	**£**
4 Mar	Bank	75.20			
6 Mar	Bank	191.00			
8 Mar	Bank	34.65			
15 Mar	Bank	63.46			

4 Accounting for sales and sales returns

this chapter covers...

This chapter focuses on using the accounting system to record the details of sales and sales returns.

Having looked in the previous chapter at the documents and procedures involved in selling on credit we will now take the financial documents of sales invoices and credit notes for sales and record them in books of prime entry (day books) and in the bookkeeping system of general ledger and sales ledger.

We will be using two books of prime entry:

■ sales day book

■ sales returns day book

Information from these day books will then be transferred into the bookkeeping system using accounts in general ledger and sales ledger.

The chapter also covers the methods of coding, used to trace transactions through the accounting system

Notes:

■ In this chapter we focus on the accounting for credit sales and sales returns transactions. Cash sales will be seen when we study the cash book in Chapters 9 and 10.

■ We use the international financial reporting standards term 'trade receivable' to mean a person who owes money to a business; normally this is a customer. You may also in your studies come across the traditional term 'debtor' which means exactly the same thing.

THE ACCOUNTING SYSTEM

We have seen earlier in Chapter 1 (page 4) that the accounting system comprises a number of stages of recording and presenting financial transactions:

■ financial documents

■ books of prime entry (eg day books)

■ double-entry bookkeeping

■ trial balance

In this chapter we look at how financial documents for credit sales and sales returns transactions are recorded in the books of prime entry, together with the entries to be made in the double-entry bookkeeping accounts. Later in the book we will see how a list of the balances of the double-entry accounts is used to form the trial balance (Chapter 12).

ACCOUNTING FOR CREDIT SALES AND SALES RETURNS

In accounting, the term 'sales' means: **the sale of goods in which the business trades**.

This means that an office stationery shop will record as sales things such as photocopier paper, ring binders, etc – the income from the goods in which the business trades is described as **revenue income**. By contrast, if the shop sells off its old cash till when it is replaced with a new one, this is not recorded as sales but, instead, is accounted for as the sale of an asset – such income is described as **capital income**.

'Sales returns' are when goods previously sold on credit are returned to the business by its customers.

The diagram on the next page shows the order in which the accounting records are prepared for credit sales and sales returns transactions. You will see that the steps are:

■ start with a **financial document**, either a sales invoice or a credit note issued

■ enter it in the appropriate **book of prime entry** (the first accounting book in which the financial document is recorded and summarised), either sales day book or sales returns day book

■ transfer the information from the book of prime entry into the double-entry accounts in the **general ledger**

■ transfer the information from the book of prime entry into the accounts of trade receivables – ie the customers – in the **sales ledger**

accounting for credit sales and sales returns

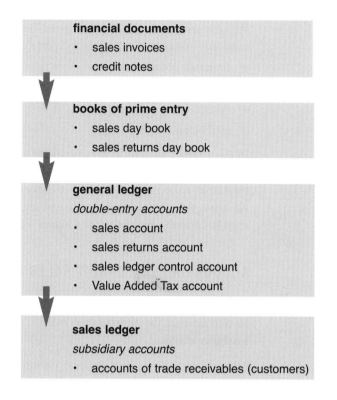

We will now look in more detail at the mechanics of the books of prime entry and the double-entry bookkeeping system. We shall then apply the accounting system to the recording of credit sales and sales returns.

BOOKS OF PRIME ENTRY

The books of prime entry include a number of **day books** which list money amounts and other details taken from financial documents.

The day books used for credit sales and sales returns are:

- sales day book
- sales returns day book

These are called books of prime entry because they are the first place in the accounting system where financial documents are recorded. Note that books of prime entry are not part of double-entry bookkeeping, but are used to give totals which are then entered into the accounts.

The reasons for using books of prime entry are:

■ the totals from the books of prime entry can be checked before they are entered into the ledger accounts

■ the use of books of prime entry for a large number of regular transactions, such as sales, means that there are fewer transactions to enter into the double-entry accounts

■ the work of the accounts department can be divided up – one person can enter transactions in the books of prime entry, while another can concentrate on the double-entry accounts

A sales day book is written up as shown below, with sample entries which will have been taken from individual sales invoices:

Sales Day Book						SDB21
Date	Details	Invoice number	Account code	Total	VAT*	Net
20-4				£	£	£
5 Jan	Doyle & Co Ltd	901	SL058	144	24	120
8 Jan	Sparkes & Sons Ltd	902	SL127	192	32	160
13 Jan	T Young	903	SL179	96	16	80
15 Jan	A-Z Supplies Ltd	904	SL003	240	40	200
21 Jan	Sparkes & Sons Ltd	905	SL127	144	24	120
31 Jan	Totals for month			816	136	680
				GL1200	GL2200	GL4100

* VAT = 20 per cent

Notes:

■ Sales day book is prepared from financial documents – sales invoices issued to customers.

■ The code 'SDB21' at the top of the day book is used for cross-referencing to the bookkeeping system: here it indicates that this is page 21 of the sales day book (SDB).

■ The **account code** column cross-references here to 'SL' – the Sales Ledger – followed by the account number of the trade receivable (customer).

■ The **total** or **gross** column records the amount of each financial document, ie after VAT has been included.

■ The code 'GL' beneath the totals amounts refers to the account numbers in the General Ledger.

■ Sales day book is totalled at appropriate intervals – daily, weekly, or monthly (as here) – and the total of the **net** column tells the business the amount of credit sales for the period.

■ The amounts from sales day book are recorded in the ledger accounts.

a note on day books and Value Added Tax

When a business is VAT-registered, VAT is charged on invoices and credit notes issued to customers. When writing up day books from VAT invoices and credit notes:

■ enter the total amount of the invoice or credit note into the 'total' column

■ enter the VAT amount in the VAT column

■ enter the net amount of the invoice or credit note, before VAT is added, in the 'net' column

Later in this chapter we shall see how the VAT columns from the sales and sales returns day books are entered into the double-entry accounts.

WRITING UP THE SALES DAY BOOK

The sales day book lists the credit sales made by a business. Following the issue of an invoice for each transaction, the sales day book is prepared from sales invoices, as seen on the previous page. In order to write up the sales day book, we take the sales invoices that have been checked and authorised and enter the details:

■ date of invoice

■ name of customer

■ sales invoice number

■ cross reference to the customer's account number in the sales ledger, eg 'SL058'

■ enter the total amount of the invoice into the total or gross column

■ enter the VAT amount shown on the invoice

■ enter the net amount of the invoice (often described as 'goods or services total'), before VAT is added

The next step in the accounting process is to make entries in the ledger accounts contained in the general ledger and in the sales ledger.

GENERAL LEDGER AND SALES LEDGER

Within an accounting system there are often a number of ledger sections – for example general ledger, sales ledger and purchases ledger. In accounting for sales transactions we will make use of the following ledgers:

■ **general ledger** (also often referred to as the main or nominal ledger) containing sales account, sales returns account, sales ledger control account, Value Added Tax account, together with other accounts kept by the business

■ **sales ledger**, which is a subsidiary ledger to general ledger, and contains the accounts of the trade receivables

The diagram shown below illustrates the way in which ledgers and accounts are used in connection with sales:

GENERAL LEDGER	SALES LEDGER
• **sales account** – to record sales invoices issued • **sales returns account** – to record credit notes issued • **sales ledger control account** – to record the total amount of trade receivables • **Value Added Tax account** – to record the VAT amounts of credit sales and sales returns	ledger containing the separate subsidiary accounts for each **trade receivable**, ie customers who owe money to the business

Notes:

■ **General ledger** also contains a number of other accounts, for example accounts for items such as purchases, expenses, receipts and payments, and also the assets and liabilities of the business.

■ **Sales ledger** is a subsidiary ledger to general ledger because it gives a detailed breakdown of the amount of the sales ledger control account in the general ledger. It does this by showing the separate accounts for each trade receivable of the business: these accounts are called **subsidiary accounts** because they provide a record of individual amounts owed by each trade receivable. The total of these accounts should always equal the balance (total amount) of the sales ledger control account.

ACCOUNTING SYSTEM FOR CREDIT SALES

The accounting system for credit sales fits together in the following way:

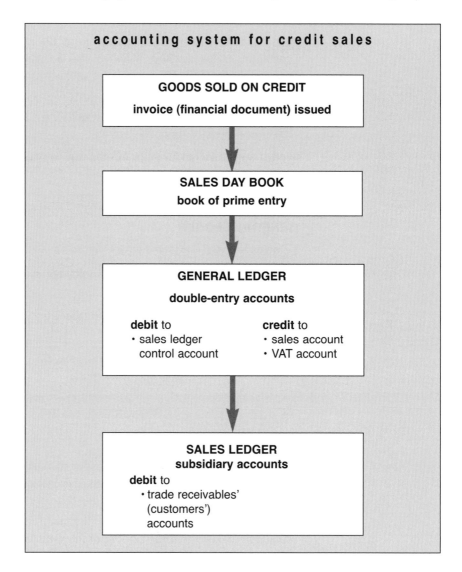

We will now look in more detail at the sales day book and the accounting system for credit sales.

In the examples which follow we will assume that the business is registered for Value Added Tax, and therefore VAT is charged on invoices issued to customers.

The VAT rate used in the examples is 20%.

BOOKKEEPING FOR CREDIT SALES

After the sales day book has been written up and totalled, the information from it is transferred to the double-entry system in the general ledger.

The completed sales day book is shown below, followed by the accounts in the general ledger which record the credit sales transactions listed in the sales day book.

Sales Day Book						SDB21
Date	Details	Invoice number	Account code	Total	VAT	Net
20-4				£	£	£
5 Jan	Doyle & Co Ltd	901	SL058	144	24	120
8 Jan	Sparkes & Sons Ltd	902	SL127	192	32	160
13 Jan	T Young	903	SL179	96	16	80
15 Jan	A-Z Supplies Ltd	904	SL003	240	40	200
21 Jan	Sparkes & Sons Ltd	905	SL127	144	24	120
31 Jan	Totals for month			816	136	680
				GL1200	GL2200	GL4100

GENERAL LEDGER

Dr	**Sales Ledger Control Account** (GL1200)	Cr
20-4 £	20-4	£
31 Jan Sales Day Book SDB21 816		

Dr	**Value Added Tax Account** (GL2200)	Cr
20-4 £	20-4	£
	31 Jan Sales Day Book SDB21	136

Dr	**Sales Account** (GL4100)	Cr
20-4 £	20-4	£
	31 Jan Sales Day Book SDB21	680

Note that from the sales day book on the previous page:

■ the total of the total column, £816, has been debited to sales ledger control account (which records the asset of receivables)

■ the total of the VAT column, £136, has been credited to VAT account (which has given value)

■ the total of the net column, £680, has been credited to sales account (which has given value)

■ each entry in the general ledger is cross-referenced back to the page number of the sales day book; here the reference is 'SDB21'.

The last step is to record the amount of sales made to each trade receivable. We do this by recording the sales invoices in sales ledger as follows:

SALES LEDGER

Dr		**A-Z Supplies Ltd** (SL003)		Cr
20-4		£	20-4	£
15 Jan	Sales SDB21	240		

Dr		**Doyle & Co Ltd** (SL058)		Cr
20-4		£	20-4	£
5 Jan	Sales SDB21	144		

Dr		**Sparkes & Sons Ltd** (SL127)		Cr
20-4		£	20-4	£
8 Jan	Sales SDB21	192		
21 Jan	Sales SDB21	144		

Dr		**T Young** (SL179)		Cr
20-4		£	20-4	£
13 Jan	Sales SDB21	96		

Notes:

■ the sales day book (see page 81) incorporates an account code column, used to cross-reference each transaction to the account of each trade receivable in the sales ledger (SL); this enables a particular transaction to be traced from financial document (invoice issued), through the book of prime entry (sales day book), to the receivable's account

■ each entry in the sales ledger is cross-referenced back to the page number of the sales day book; here the reference is 'SDB21'.

subsidiary accounts

The accounts in sales ledger are prepared following the principles of double-entry bookkeeping. However, they are **subsidiary accounts,** which means they are used to provide a note of how much each trade receivable owes to the business.

As such they are not part of double-entry but are represented in the general ledger by sales ledger control account. This means that, here, the £816 debit entry is split up in the sales ledger between the four trade receivables' subsidiary accounts. Note that subsidiary accounts are often referred to as **memorandum accounts**.

ACCOUNTING SYSTEM FOR SALES RETURNS

Sales returns (or returns in) are when goods previously sold on credit are returned to the business by its customers. A credit note (see page 26) is the financial document issued by a business when it makes a refund to a customer who has bought goods on credit. A credit note reduces the amount owed by the trade receivable.

The accounting procedures for sales returns involve:

■ **financial documents** – credit notes issued to customers

■ **book of prime entry** – sales returns day book

■ **double-entry accounts** – general ledger (sales returns account, which records the total net amount of credit notes issued, Value Added Tax account, which records the VAT amount of sales returns, and sales ledger control account, which records the asset of trade receivables)

■ **sales ledger** – the subsidiary accounts for each individual trade receivable of the business

The accounting system for sales returns is shown in the diagram on the next page.

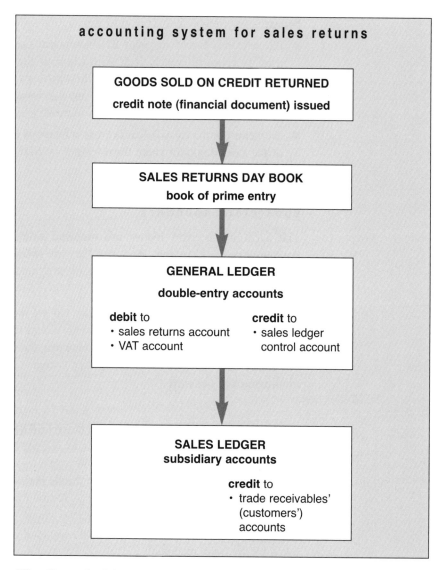

We will now look in more detail at the sales returns day book and the double-entry accounts for sales returns. Note that the business is registered for Value Added Tax.

SALES RETURNS DAY BOOK

The sales returns day book uses virtually the same layout as the sales day book seen on page 81 of this chapter. It operates in a similar way, storing up information about sales returns transactions until such time as a transfer is made into the double-entry accounts system. The financial documents for sales returns day book are credit notes issued to customers.

The sales returns day book is written up as follows, with sample entries:

	Sales Returns Day Book					SRDB5
Date	Details	Credit note no	Account code	Total	VAT*	Net
20-4				£	£	£
15 Jan	T Young	702	SL179	48	8	40
27 Jan	A-Z Supplies Ltd	703	SL003	144	24	120
31 Jan	Totals for month			192	32	160
				GL1200	GL2200	GL4110

* VAT = 20 per cent

Notes:

■ The sales returns day book is prepared from credit notes (or copies of credit notes) issued to customers.

■ The day book is totalled at appropriate intervals – weekly or monthly.

■ The VAT-inclusive amounts from the total column are credited to the trade receivables' individual subsidiary accounts in sales ledger.

■ The total of the VAT column is transferred to the debit of the VAT account in general ledger.

■ The total of the net column tells the business the amount of sales returns for the period. This amount is transferred to the debit of sales returns account in general ledger.

■ The total or gross column records the amount of each credit note issued, ie after VAT has been included. This amount is transferred to the credit of sales ledger control account in general ledger.

BOOKKEEPING FOR SALES RETURNS

After the sales returns day book has been written up and totalled, the information from it is transferred into the double-entry system.

The accounts in the general ledger to record the transactions from the above sales returns day book (including any other transactions already recorded on these accounts) are as follows (see next page):

GENERAL LEDGER

Dr	**Sales Ledger Control Account** (GL1200)		Cr
20-4	£	20-4	£
31 Jan Sales Day Book SDB21 816		31 Jan Sales Returns Day Book SRDB5	192

Dr	**Value Added Tax Account** (GL2200)		Cr
20-4	£	20-4	£
31 Jan Sales Returns Day Book SRDB5	32	31 Jan Sales Day Book SDB21	136

Dr	**Sales Returns Account** (GL4110)		Cr
20-4	£	20-4	£
31 Jan Sales Returns Day Book SRDB5	160		

The last step is to record the amount of sales returns from each trade receivable. We do this by recording the sales returns in the subsidiary accounts for each trade receivable in the sales ledger as follows:

SALES LEDGER

Dr	**A-Z Supplies Ltd** (SL003)		Cr
20-4	£	20-4	£
15 Jan Sales SDB21	240	27 Jan Sales Returns SRDB5	144

Dr	**T Young** (SL179)		Cr
20-4	£	20-4	£
12 Jan Sales SDB21	96	15 Jan Sales Returns SRDB5	48

THE USE OF ANALYSED SALES DAY BOOKS

As well as the layout of the day books we have seen so far in this chapter, a business can use analysed day books whenever it needs to analyse its sales and sales returns between:

■ different types of goods sold, eg paint, wallpaper, brushes, or services supplied

■ different departments, eg a store with departments for furniture, carpets and curtains, hardware

For example, a business with two different types of sales – sales type 1 and sales type 2 – will write up its sales day book as follows:

Sales Day Book								SDB48
Date	Details	Invoice number	Account code	Total	VAT*	Net	Sales type 1	Sales type 2
20-4				£	£	£	£	£
9 Aug	DIY Limited	1478	SL059	240	40	200	200	–
12 Aug	T Lane	1479	SL108	144	24	120	100	20
16 Aug	Comet Traders Limited	1480	SL038	336	56	280	100	180
23 Aug	Southern Ltd	1481	SL211	192	32	160	160	–
31 Aug	Totals for month			912	152	760	560	200
				GL1200	GL2200		GL4160	GL4170

* VAT = 20 per cent

Analysed sales day books and sales returns day books can be adapted to suit the particular needs of a business. Thus, there is not a standard way in which to present the books of prime entry – the needs of the user of the information are all important. By using analysed day books, the owner of the business can see how much has been sold by types of goods and services, or by departments.

Notes:

■ The account code column is to 'SL' (Sales Ledger) and the customer's account number.

■ The code 'GL' beneath the totals amounts refers to the account numbers in General Ledger.

■ The analysis columns – here sales type 1 and sales type 2 – show the amount of sales net of VAT (ie before VAT is added).

■ The analysis columns analyse the net amount – by products sold or services supplied – from sales invoices.

METHODS OF CODING IN ACCOUNTING SYSTEMS

As a business grows, methods of coding need to be used to trace transactions through the accounting system, ie through financial documents, books of prime entry, double-entry bookkeeping and the trial balance. There are a number of different systems of coding in use:

- **alphabetical**, where letters are used, eg 'ABC'
- **numeric**, where numbers are used, eg '123'
- **alpha-numeric**, where both letters and numbers are used, eg 'ABC123'

Uses of coding in the stages of the accounting system are:

financial documents

- each document, eg invoice, credit note, is numbered
- goods listed on invoices have reference number or letters, eg catalogue reference, which, if a computer accounting system is used, will enable the business to analyse sales by product

books of prime entry

- each page of the day books is numbered
- the number of the document, eg invoice, credit note is recorded
- the code of the trade receivables or trade payables account is recorded, eg 'SL' for sales ledger, followed by the account number or short name (see below)

ledger accounts

- the accounting system is divided into sections: general ledger, sales ledger, and purchases ledger
- general ledger accounts are numbered and are often arranged in a particular order, for example

0100 – 1399	Assets
2100 – 2399	Liabilities
3100 – 3399	Capital
4100 – 4399	Sales
5100 – 5399	Purchases
6100 – 6399	Expenses

- each account in the sales ledger is coded eg 'SL058' (or some accounting systems use an abbreviated name, or short name, eg the account of Peterhead Trading Company might be coded as 'PETER')
- alternatively, in sales ledger an alpha-numeric code – such as 'PET001' – is used; this comprises the first three letters of the customer's name followed by three numbers indicating the first (001) second (002) third (003) etc account use of the same first letter (here 'PET001' is coded as the first account to use 'P').

Case Study

WYVERN TRADERS – CREDIT SALES AND RETURNS

To bring together the material covered in this chapter, we will look at a comprehensive Case Study which makes use of:

- **books of prime entry**
  - sales day book
  - sales returns day book
- **general ledger accounts**
  - sales account
  - sales ledger control account
  - sales returns account
  - Value Added Tax account
- **sales ledger accounts**
  - trade receivables' subsidiary accounts

The Chapter Summary (pages 92 and 93) also includes diagrams which summarise the procedures for recording credit sales and sales returns transactions in the accounting system.

situation

Wyvern Traders is a wholesaler of stationery and office equipment. The business is registered for VAT. The VAT rate is 20%. The following are the credit sales and sales returns transactions for April 20-4:

20-4	
2 Apr	Sold goods to P Woodhouse, £200 + VAT, invoice no 2416
9 Apr	P Woodhouse returns goods, £80 + VAT, we issue credit note no 12
14 Apr	Sold goods to Blackheath Limited, £80 + VAT, invoice no 2417
21 Apr	Blackheath Limited returns goods, £40 + VAT, we issue credit note no 13
26 Apr	Sold goods to P Woodhouse, £160 + VAT, invoice no 2418

The day books, general ledger and sales ledger accounts are illustrated on the next two pages: arrows indicate the transfers from the day books to the individual accounts. Note that some accounts have been repeated on both pages in order to show, on the same page, the accounts relating to a particular day book: in practice a business would keep all the transactions together in one account.

Sales Day Book						SDB30
Date	Details	Invoice number	Account code	Total	VAT	Net
20-4				£	£	£
2 Apr	P Woodhouse	2416	SL248	240	40	200
14 Apr	Blackheath Ltd	2417	SL027	96	16	80
26 Apr	P Woodhouse	2418	SL248	192	32	160
30 Apr	Totals for month			528	88	440
				GL1200	GL2200	GL4100

GENERAL LEDGER

Dr   **Sales Ledger Control Account** (GL1200)   Cr

Date	Details	£	Date	Details	£
20-4			20-4		
30 Apr	Sales Day Book SDB30	528			

Dr   **Value Added Tax Account** (GL2200)   Cr

Date	Details	£	Date	Details	£
20-4			20-4		
			30 Apr	Sales Day Book SDB30	88

Dr   **Sales Account** (GL4100)   Cr

Date	Details	£	Date	Details	£
20-4			20-4		
			30 Apr	Sales Day Book SDB30	440

SALES LEDGER

Dr   **Blackheath Ltd** (SL027)   Cr

Date	Details	£	Date	Details	£
20-4			20-4		
14 Apr	Sales SDB30	96			

Dr   **P Woodhouse** (SL248)   Cr

Date	Details	£	Date	Details	£
20-4			20-4		
2 Apr	Sales SDB30	240			
26 Apr	Sales SDB30	192			

Sales Returns Day Book						SRDB4
Date	Details	Credit note number	Reference	Total	VAT	Net
20-4				£	£	£
9 Apr	P Woodhouse	12	SL248	96	16	80
21 Apr	Blackheath Ltd	13	SL027	48	8	40
30 Apr	Totals for month			144	24	120
				GL1200	GL2200	GL4110

GENERAL LEDGER

Dr   **Sales Ledger Control Account** (GL1200)   Cr

Date	Details	£	Date	Details	£
20-4			20-4		
30 Apr	Sales Day Book SDB30	*528	30 Apr	Sales Returns Day Book SRDB4	144

Dr   **Value Added Tax Account** (GL2200)   Cr

Date	Details	£	Date	Details	£
20-4			20-4		
30 Apr	Sales Returns Day Book SRDB4	24	30 Apr	Sales Day Book SDB30	*88

Dr   **Sales Returns Account** (GL4110)   Cr

Date	Details	£	Date	Details	£
20-4			20-4		
30 Apr	Sales Returns Day Book SRDB4	120			

SALES LEDGER

Dr   **Blackheath Ltd** (SL027)   Cr

Date	Details	£	Date	Details	£
20-4			20-4		
14 Apr	Sales SDB30	*96	21 Apr	Sales Returns SRDB4	48

Dr   **P Woodhouse** (SL248)   Cr

Date	Details	£	Date	Details	£
20-4			20-4		
2 Apr	Sales SDB30	*240	9 Apr	Sales Returns SRDB4	96
26 Apr	Sales SDB30	*192			

* transactions entered previously

The diagrams below and on the next page summarise the material we have studied so far in this chapter. They show the procedures for recording transactions in the accounting system for credit sales and sales returns.

Further chapter summary points follow on page 94.

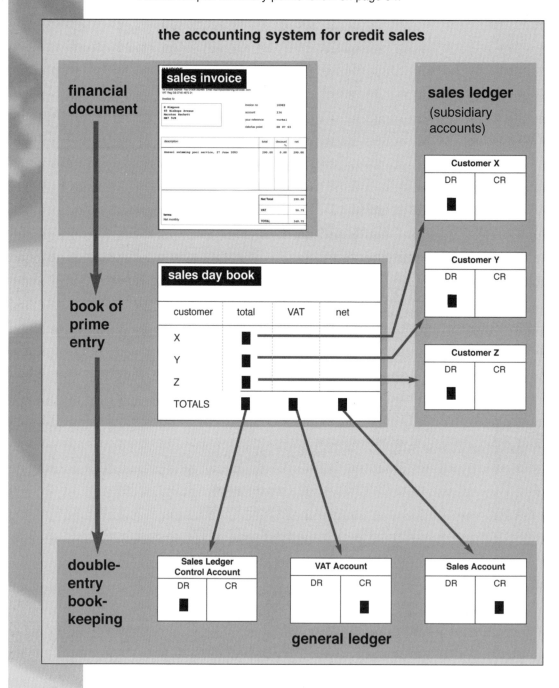

the accounting system for credit sales

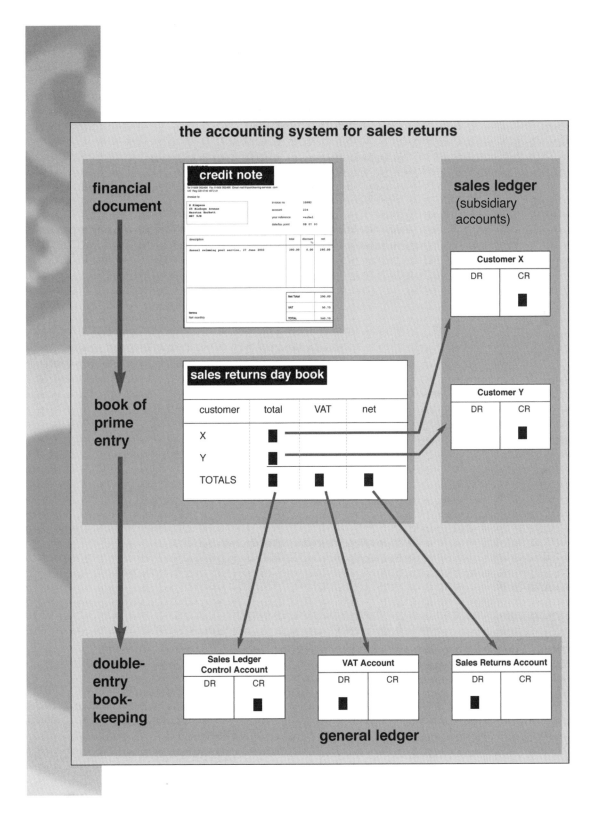

the accounting system for sales returns

financial document

book of prime entry

double-entry book-keeping

sales ledger (subsidiary accounts)

general ledger

■ The accounting system comprises a number of specific stages of recording and presenting financial transactions:
- financial documents
- books of prime entry (eg day books)
- double-entry bookkeeping
- trial balance

■ The financial documents relating to credit sales are:
- sales invoices
- credit notes issued

■ Sales day book is the book of prime entry for credit sales. It is prepared from sales invoices sent to customers.

■ Sales returns day book is the book of prime entry for sales returns. It is prepared from credit notes issued to customers.

■ Analysed sales and sales returns day books are used when a business wishes to analyse its sales between different departments or different types of goods sold or services supplied.

■ Recording credit sales in the double-entry system uses:
- financial documents, sales invoices
- book of prime entry, sales day book
- double-entry accounts in the general ledger
- subsidiary accounts in the sales ledger

■ Recording sales returns in the double-entry system uses:
- financial documents, credit notes issued to customers
- book of prime entry, sales returns day book
- double-entry accounts in the general ledger
- subsidiary accounts in the sales ledger

Key Terms		
	financial documents	source documents for the accounting records
	books of prime entry	the first accounting books in which transactions are recorded
	coding	cross-referencing methods used to trace transactions through the accounting system
	ledger	section of an accounting system, eg general ledger, sales ledger, purchases ledger

sales	the sale of goods in which the business trades
revenue income	income from the goods in which the business trades
capital income	income from items other than the goods in which the business trades, eg a shop selling its old cash till
sales returns	goods previously sold on credit which are returned to the business by its customers
sales day book	book of prime entry prepared from sales invoices
sales returns day book	book of prime entry prepared from credit notes issued to customers
analysed sales day book	day books which incorporate analysis columns, for example between
	– different departments
	– different types of goods sold, or services supplied
general ledger	ledger section which includes
	– sales account
	– sales returns account
	– sales ledger control account
	– Value Added Tax account
sales ledger	subsidiary ledger section which contains the subsidiary accounts of the trade receivables (customers)
subsidiary account	a subsidiary ledger (eg sales ledger) account which provides a record of individual amounts (eg owing by trade receivables to the business)

Activities

4.1   Which one of the following is a book of prime entry?
   (a)   sales day book
   (b)   sales account
   (c)   sales ledger account of T Smith
   (d)   Value Added Tax account
   Answer (a) or (b) or (c) or (d)

4.2   Which one of the following is in the right order?
   (a)   sales invoice; sales day book; sales account; sales ledger control account; customer's account
   (b)   sales day book; sales ledger control account; customer's account; sales account; sales invoice
   (c)   sales day book; sales invoice; customer's account; sales account; sales ledger control account
   (d)   sales account; sales ledger control account; customer's account; sales invoice; sales day book
   Answer (a) or (b) or (c) or (d)

4.3   Explain in note format:
   (a)   the principles of recording a credit sales transaction in the accounting system
   (b)   the principles of recording a sales returns transaction in the accounting system

---

For Activities 4.4 and 4.5:

•   work in pounds and pence, where appropriate

•   the rate of Value Added Tax is to be calculated at 20% (when calculating VAT amounts, you
     should ignore fractions of a penny, ie round down to a whole penny)

•   use a coding system incorporating the following:

sales day book	– SDB50	general ledger account numbers	
sales returns day book	– SRDB18	sales ledger control account	– GL1200
		sales account	– GL4100
sales ledger account numbers		sales returns account	– GL4110
A Cox	– SL032	Value Added Tax account	– GL2200
Dines Stores	– SL048		
E Grainger	– SL055		
M Kershaw	– SL090		
D Lloyd	– SL095		
Malvern Stores	– SL110		
Pershore Retailers	– SL145		
P Wilson	– SL172		

4.4 Wyvern Wholesalers sells office stationery to other businesses in the area. During April 20-5 the following credit transactions took place:

20-5

  2 Apr   Sold goods to Malvern Stores £55 + VAT, invoice no 4578 issued

  5 Apr   Sold goods to Pershore Retailers £65 + VAT, invoice no 4579 issued

  7 Apr   Sold goods to E Grainger £28 + VAT, invoice no 4580 issued

  9 Apr   Sold goods to P Wilson £58 + VAT, invoice no 4581 issued

12 Apr   Sold goods to M Kershaw £76 + VAT, invoice no 4582 issued

14 Apr   Sold goods to D Lloyd £66 + VAT, invoice no 4583 issued

19 Apr   Sold goods to A Cox £33 + VAT, invoice no 4584 issued

22 Apr   Sold goods to Dines Stores £102 + VAT, invoice no 4585 issued

23 Apr   Sold goods to Malvern Stores £47 + VAT, invoice no 4586 issued

26 Apr   Sold goods to P Wilson £35 + VAT, invoice no 4587 issued

29 Apr   Sold goods to A Cox £82 + VAT, invoice no 4588 issued

You are to:

(a)   Enter the above transactions in Wyvern Wholesaler's sales day book for April 20-5, using the format shown below.

(b)   Record the accounting entries in Wyvern Wholesaler's general ledger and sales ledger. (You will need to retain the ledger accounts for use with Activity 4.5.)

Sales Day Book						SDB50
Date	Details	Invoice number	Account code	Total £	VAT £	Net £

4.5 The following details are the sales returns of Wyvern Wholesalers for April 20-5. They are to be:

(a) entered in the sales returns day book for April 20-5, using the format shown below.

(b) recorded in the general ledger and sales ledger (use the ledgers already prepared in the answer to Activity 4.4)

20-5

8 Apr   Pershore Retailers returns goods £20 + VAT, credit note no 572 issued

12 Apr   E Grainger returns goods £28 + VAT, credit note no 573 issued

16 Apr   D Lloyd returns goods £33 + VAT, credit note no 574 issued

28 Apr   Malvern Stores returns goods £20 + VAT, credit note no 575 issued

30 Apr   A Cox returns goods £40 + VAT, credit note no 576 issued

Sales Returns Day Book						SRDB18
Date	Details	Credit note number	Account code	Total £	VAT £	Net £

4.6 You are employed by Johnson Limited as an accounts assistant. The business has a manual accounting system. Double-entry takes place in the general ledger; individual accounts of trade receivables are kept as subsidiary accounts in the sales ledger. The VAT rate is 20%.

Notes:

- show your answer with a tick, words or figures, as appropriate
- coding is not required

(a) The following credit transactions all took place on 30 June 20-9 and have been entered into the sales day book as shown below. No entries have yet been made into the ledger system.

Sales day book

Date 20-9	Details	Invoice number	Total £	VAT £	Net £
30 June	Bowne Ltd	610	960	160	800
30 June	Jamieson & Co	611	4,944	824	4,120
30 June	Pottertons	612	3,888	648	3,240
30 June	Wells plc	613	2,928	488	2,440
	Totals		12,720	2,120	10,600

What will be the entries in the general ledger?

General ledger

Account name	Amount £	Debit ✓	Credit ✓

What will be the entries in the sales ledger?

Sales ledger

Account name	Amount £	Debit ✓	Credit ✓

(b)   The following credit transactions all took place on 30 June 20-9 and have been entered into the sales returns day book as shown below. No entries have yet been made into the ledger system.

Sales returns day book

Date 20-9	Details	Credit note number	Total £	VAT £	Net £
30 June	Lloyd & Co	CN 47	576	96	480
30 June	Wyvern Stores	CN 48	1,248	208	1,040
	Totals		1,824	304	1,520

What will be the entries in the general ledger?

General ledger

Account name	Amount £	Debit ✓	Credit ✓

What will be the entries in the sales ledger?

Sales ledger

Account name	Amount £	Debit ✓	Credit ✓

4.7 The following is taken from the coding lists used at a business called Fashion Trading.

Customer	Sales ledger account code
Allens Stores	ALL001
Dart Enterprises	DAR001
Dennis & Co	DEN002
Eden Contracts	EDE001
Ginger Trading	GIN001
Jarvis & Co	JAR001
New Wave Fashions	NEW001
Number 1 Store	NUM002
Riverside Trading	RIV001
Toast Ltd	TOA001
Ye Olde Stores	YEO001

You are to set up the sales ledger account codes for the new customers shown below.

Customer	Sales ledger account code
Dymock Trading Co	
Hedgehog Fashions	
Jones & Co	

4.8 Sales invoices have been prepared and partially entered in the sales day book, as shown below.

(a) Complete the entries in the sales day book by inserting the appropriate figures for each invoice

(b) Total the last five columns of the sales day book

Sales day book

Date 20XX	Details	Invoice number	Total £	VAT £	Net £	Sales type 1 £	Sales type 2 £
30 June	Yanez & Co	1621		240			1,200
30 June	Napier Stores	1622	1,920			1,600	
30 June	Beale Ltd	1623	768		640		640
	Totals						

5 Process payments from customers

this chapter covers...

The earlier chapters of this book have explained how a business sets about selling its goods and services on credit, issuing invoices, credit notes and statements which help to ensure that the right money is received at the right time. The entry of these sales transactions into the book-keeping system has also been described.

This chapter will now explain the next stage in the process – the way in which a business will process a payment received from a customer who has bought goods on credit. It will continue the Case Study in Chapter 2 in which Cool Socks, a manufacturer of fashion socks, sold socks to Trends, a fashion store.

A payment sent by a business such as Trends in settlement of sales transactions will need to be checked and verified against documentation including:

- the remittance advice sent by the buyer and any payment sent by the buyer

- sales invoices and credit notes issued by the seller

- the statement of account sent by the seller

- the record of what is owing in the buyer's account in the sales ledger of the seller

In checking this documentation the seller will have to look out for any discrepancies which may be the result of an error made by the buyer, for example:

- an overpayment

- an underpayment

- the buyer taking settlement discount when the period for early payment has expired, or even when it is not offered

FINANCIAL DOCUMENTS – SOME REVISION

When a business makes a sale on credit terms it uses a number of financial documents which are sent to the buyer, these include:

■ the **invoice**, which sets out the details of the sales transaction, including
  – the date
  – the sales price and any discount given and VAT (sales tax) added
  – the total due
  – the date when payment is required (which is often 30 days after the date of the invoice)

■ the **credit note**, which is used if any refund is due and can be deducted from the amount owing to the seller – for example a deduction made for faulty goods

■ the **customer statement**, which sets out all the invoices and credit notes issued and any payments received over a set period (often a month), all resulting in a final amount due to be paid

FINANCIAL DOCUMENTS – REMITTANCE ADVICE

A further financial document which is important to the payment process is the **remittance advice**. This is an advice which can be posted, faxed or emailed, stating that a certain amount of money has been sent by a credit customer in settlement of an account. A remittance advice is used:

■ to advise the sending of a payment **direct to the seller's bank account** electronically through the banks' computer systems using **BACS** (useful for bulk payments such as payroll) or by the more recently introduced **Faster Payments** (useful for individual payments), or . . .

■ **to accompany a cheque** – a practice which is becoming less common as more businesses and individuals make payments elecronically and online

These two types of remittance advice are illustrated on the next two pages. The remittance advices both relate to payments made to Cool Socks, the business introduced as a Case Study in Chapter 2. You will see that they both contain references. These are:

■ the buyer's purchase order reference

■ the seller's invoice number

Other details include the amount being sent and the means of payment, ie a cheque enclosed or a payment direct to the bank account of the seller through using BACS or Faster Payments electronic transfer systems.

remittance advice for a direct bank-to-bank electronic payment

REMITTANCE ADVICE			FROM: Trends 4 Friar Street Broadfield BR1 3RF
TO Cool Socks Limited Unit 45 Elgar Estate, Broadfield, BR7 4ER			06 11 20-3

Your ref	Our ref		Amount
787923	47609	FASTER PAYMENTS TRANSFER	254.88
			TOTAL 254.88

THIS HAS BEEN PAID BY FASTER PAYMENTS TRANSFER DIRECTLY INTO YOUR BANK ACCOUNT AT ALBION BANK NO 11451226 SORT CODE 90 47 17

Cool Socks' sales invoice number

Trends' purchase order number

details of Cool Socks' bank account

the amount being sent

electronic payment remittance advice

- This remittance advice relates to a Faster Payments bank transfer made by Trends in payment of their account with Cool Socks Limited. The advice has been emailed from Trends' accounts department.

- The details do not include the invoice amount or the credit note amount, but only the final payment made. An alternative to this is to list the various documents (invoices, credit notes) which make up the payment. This method is shown on the remittance advice on the next page.

- The bank account details on the advice set out Cool Socks' bank account number and sort code in full. Some remittance advices may not provide the account number in full for security reasons.

- Cool Socks will need to check its bank statement in due course to see if the payment has been received.

checks to be made

Cool Socks needs to check a number of details on this advice against the sales documentation and the sales ledger account of the customer making payment. This is to make sure that there are no errors or discrepancies and that the right amount has been sent for the right transactions. This process is explained in full in the Case Study on pages 106 to 109.

remittance advice sent with a cheque payment

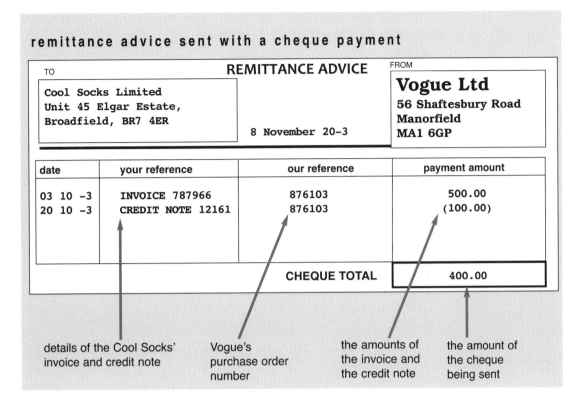

	REMITTANCE ADVICE		
TO		**FROM**	
Cool Socks Limited Unit 45 Elgar Estate, Broadfield, BR7 4ER	8 November 20–3	**Vogue Ltd** 56 Shaftesbury Road Manorfield MA1 6GP	

date	your reference	our reference	payment amount
03 10 –3 20 10 –3	INVOICE 787966 CREDIT NOTE 12161	876103 876103	500.00 (100.00)
		CHEQUE TOTAL	400.00

details of the Cool Socks' invoice and credit note

Vogue's purchase order number

the amounts of the invoice and the credit note

the amount of the cheque being sent

remittance advice sent with a cheque

- This remittance advice is for a payment from Vogue Limited – a cheque for £400 – sent together through the post to Cool Socks.
- The advice shows the amounts of an invoice (£500) and a credit note (£100) taken account of when calculating the £400 payment.
- These details will help Cool Socks in their checking process which will involve the sales documentation and the sales ledger account for Vogue Limited.
- At the time of writing, cheques are becoming a less common means of settling customer accounts, but they are still popular with smaller and more traditional businesses.
- If a customer's cheque is received in payment, it will need to be checked carefully to make sure it is correctly written out and has all the necessary details on it.

checking the cheque

A **cheque** has to be in writing and signed by the customer paying the money. A cheque tells the customer's bank to pay a specified amount to a person or an organisation, know as the '**payee**.'

There are a number of important basic checks that a business needs to carry out when it receives a cheque as payment:

■ is the cheque signed? – it is invalid if it is not

■ is the payee's name correct? – it cannot be paid into the bank if it is not

■ is the cheque in date? – a cheque becomes invalid after six months

■ is the amount in words and figures the same?

The cheque below shows all these details:

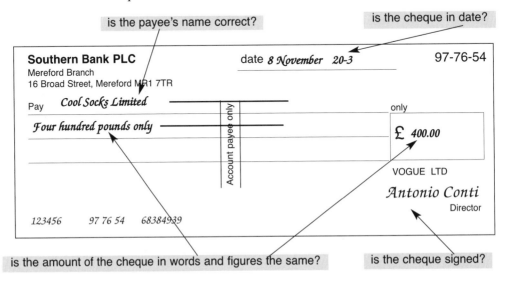

If the business (Cool Socks) accepting payment by cheque does not 'check' these details before paying it in, the bank (Southern Bank) may refuse to pay it and will return it to Cool Socks' bank. But if everything is in order, the amount of the cheque will be deducted from Vogue Ltd's bank account.

Now read the Case Study which follows. Note the internal checks that are made by Cool Socks when Trends settles its account.

Case Study

COOL SOCKS – PROCESSING THE PAYMENT

situation

Cool Socks Limited, a manufacturer of fashion socks, supplies Trends, a fashion store in Broadfield. In this Case Study, Trends sends a payment and remittance advice, which is checked by Cool Socks for errors and discrepancies.

The financial documents issued so far by Cool Socks are an invoice for socks supplied (see next page), a credit note for £28.32 (not illustrated) for some faulty socks returned and a statement of account sent to Trends at the end of the month (see page 108).

The amount due is £283.20 (invoice amount) minus £28.32 (credit note amount) = £254.88.

── INVOICE ──

COOL SOCKS LIMITED
Unit 45 Elgar Estate, Broadfield, BR7 4ER
Tel 01908 765314 Fax 01908 765951 Email toni@cool.u-net.com
VAT Reg GB 0745 4672 76

invoice to

Trends **4 Friar Street** **Broadfield** **BR1 3RF**	

deliver to

as above

invoice no	**787923**
account	**3993**
your reference	**47609**
date/tax point	**02 10 20-3**

product code	description	quantity	price	unit	total	discount %	net
45B	Blue toebar socks	100	2.36	pair	236.00	0.00	236.00

terms

Net monthly
Carriage paid
E & OE

goods total	236.00
VAT	47.20
TOTAL	283.20

STATEMENT OF ACCOUNT

COOL SOCKS LIMITED

Unit 45 Elgar Estate, Broadfield, BR7 4ER
Tel 01908 765314 Fax 01908 765951 Email toni@cool.u-net.com
VAT REG GB 0745 4672 76

TO

| Trends
4 Friar Street
Broadfield
BR1 3RF | account | 3993 |
| | date | 31 10 20-3 |

date	details	debit £	credit £	balance £
01 10 20-3	Balance b/f	150.00		150.00
02 10 20-3	BACS payment 170961		150.00	00.00
02 10 20-3	Invoice 787923	283.20		283.20
10 10 20-3	Credit note 12157		28.32	254.88

Electronic payments: pay Cool Socks Ltd at Albion Bank, Account 11451226, Sort code 904717

TOTAL	254.88

Notes on the statement and the ledger account

The statement of account illustrated above has four entries. The first two relate to full payment of last month's account (£150), and can be ignored. The last two relate to this Case Study and are highlighted by the grey boxes:

- the third entry is the invoice for £283.20 issued on 2 October to Trends
- the last entry is the credit note for £28.32 issued on 10 October to Trends

The amount owed by Trends to Cool Socks (the account balance) is £254.88.

These entries have also been entered by Cool Socks in the double-entry accounting system, in the **sales ledger account** for Trends shown below.

Debit	Sales Ledger: Trends Account						Credit	
20-3	Details	£	p	20-3	Details	£	p
1 Oct	Balance b/d	150	00	2 Oct	Bank	150	00
2 Oct	Sales	283	20	10 Oct	Sales returns	28	32

receipt of the remittance advice

On 6 November Cool Socks received a remittance advice by email (see below) from Trends stating that £254.88 has been paid into the bank account of Cool Socks Limited by using a Faster Payments transfer.

What checks should Cool Socks make to make sure the payment of £254.88 is correct and valid?

REMITTANCE ADVICE

FROM: Trends
4 Friar Street
Broadfield BR1 3RF

TO
Cool Socks Limited
Unit 45 Elgar Estate, Broadfield, BR7 4ER

06 11 20-3

Your ref	Our ref		Amount
787923	47609	FASTER PAYMENTS TRANSFER	254.88

TOTAL 254.88

THIS HAS BEEN PAID BY FASTER PAYMENTS TRANSFER DIRECTLY INTO YOUR BANK ACCOUNT AT ALBION BANK NO 11451226 SORT CODE 90 47 17

---

solution

The following checks could be made by the accounts staff of Cool Socks.

Question Are the remittance advice references correct?

Answer Check the original documentation. The answer is 'Yes'.

- Invoice number 787923 (see page minus 2) agrees with the 'Your ref 787923' of the remittance advice.
- The Trends purchase order number 47609 (to be found in the Cool Socks filing system) is quoted on the remittance advice.

Question Is the remittance advice amount of £254.88 correct? Answer is 'Yes'.

Answer Invoice value £283.20 minus credit note value £28.32 = £254.88

This can be verified from the statement issued by Cool Socks on 31 October and also from the sales ledger account of Trends in the books of Cool Socks. Both (see opposite page) show the two figures (£283.20 and £28.32) which result in the total owing figure of £254.88.

Note that Cool Socks would not need to carry out all these checks, but a minimum requirement is likely to be:
- a check of the documentation references (especially the invoice number), and
- a calculation of the amount paid – from figures obtained from the customer statement issued or from the sales ledger account

DEALING WITH DISCREPANCIES

The Case Study on the previous four pages has explained the checks that should be made by the seller when a remittance advice is received from a credit customer. In this example, all was correct. Normally this is the case, but there are situations where references do not tie up or, more often, the amount is wrong. These **discrepancies** can occur when:

- there is an **underpayment** – not enough money has been received
- there is an **overpayment** – too much money has been received
- the buyer has made a mistake when deducting **settlement discount**

We will deal with each of these in turn.

underpayments

There are number of reasons why a credit customer may not send enough money when settling an account. These are described below, together with the action that should be taken in each case by the seller.

reason   the customer has made a genuine mistake with the figures

solution   the seller should contact the customer (by telephone or email), and politely explain the problem; the customer should be asked for an adjusting payment or advised that it will be adjusted for in the next statement

reason   the customer has not paid all the due invoices because there is a dispute over one of them

solution   the seller should contact the customer and attempt to resolve the problem; if necessary the matter may have to be referred to a line manager

overpayments

There are a number of reasons why a credit customer may send too much money when settling an account. This is not a common experience! These reasons are described below and appropriate solutions are suggested.

reason   the customer has made a genuine mistake with the figures

solution   the seller should contact the customer and explain the situation; the ideal solution for the seller is to keep the extra money and wait for the next statement to make the necessary adjustment; it is possible that the customer may want the money (it may be a large amount), in which case an adjusting payment may need to be made

reason   the customer has ignored a credit note or has paid an invoice twice in error

solution   the seller should contact the customer and explain the situation; the ideal solution for the seller is to retain the extra money and wait for the next statement to make the necessary adjustment, unless the customer urgently needs the money, in which case an adjusting payment will need to be made promptly

discrepancies with settlement discount

Settlement discount is an 'early payment discount' where a seller allows a customer to deduct a percentage discount from the invoice total if payment is made within a specified period of time, eg seven days.

Settlement discount is explained on pages 28-29. If you are unsure about this rather complicated procedure you should read these pages again. The main problem with settlement discount is that it is not normally calculated and taken into account on the invoice itself, but the calculation is left to the customer. This is where errors can occur. When a business offers settlement discount, it is set out in the 'Terms' section at the bottom of the invoice, eg:

Settlement discount of 2.5% for payment within 7 days of the invoice date.

If the goods total before VAT is £100, the discount available if the invoice is paid within 7 days of the invoice is (£100 x 2.5)/100 = £2.50.

The correct total amount actually payable is therefore:

£100 minus £2.50	=	£97.50
plus VAT @ 20% on £97.50	=	£19.50
	=	£117.00

To confuse the issue, the final total of the invoice sent to the customer is:

goods total before discount is taken	=	£100.00
plus VAT on £97.50 (not on £100)	=	£19.50
	=	£119.50

As you can see from this, there is plenty of room for customer error:

■ the amount of discount calculated by the customer may be incorrect

■ the customer may take the discount after the seven days has elapsed

■ the customer may take a discount when it is not being offered at all

In each of these three cases, the seller will have to contact the customer and explain the nature of the discrepancy. Examples of these errors are shown in the Case Study which follows on the next page.

SETTLEMENT DISCOUNT DISCREPANCIES

situation

You work in the accounts department of Cool Socks Limited. The company offers to some (but not all) customers a settlement discount of 2.5% on invoices which are paid within 7 days of the invoice date.

When settlement discount is made available, the 'Terms' section at the bottom of the invoice always states:

"Settlement discount of 2.5% for payment within 7 days of the invoice date."

The date is 25 November and you have to check three invoices which have had settlement discount deducted by the customer. Your line manager asks you to report and correct any discrepancies you can find. The current VAT rate is 20%.

Invoice 1 – payment amount received £1,120.62

Dated 22 November. Terms indicate that 2.5% settlement discount is available for payment within 7 days. Goods total is £1,000 and discount deducted is £50. VAT on the invoice is £195.

Invoice 2 – payment amount received £458.25

Dated 8 November. Terms indicate that 2.5% settlement discount is available for payment within 7 days. Goods total is £400 and the discount deducted is £10. VAT is £78.

Invoice 3 – payment amount received £287.50

Dated 22 November. There is no mention of a 2.5% settlement discount in the 'Terms' section of the invoice. Goods total is £250 and VAT is £50. Cash discount of £6.25 has been taken by the customer.

---

solution

Answers

Invoice 1: the discount deducted is calculated at 5% (£50) and should be at 2.5% (£25). The payment should be £975 + VAT £195 = £1,170.

Invoice 2: the 7 day period for deduction of settlement discount has expired and therefore no discount should be deducted. The payment should have been £400 + VAT of £78 = £478. Note that the VAT is calculated on the £390 and not on the £400, whether or not the discount is taken.

Invoice 3: there is no settlement discount available on this invoice but, despite this, the customer has taken 2.5% (£6.25). The payment should have been £300.

Chapter Summary

■ When a customer who has bought goods or services on credit makes payment of the account, the customer will send a **remittance advice** to the seller.

■ Payment may be received by cheque or electronically through BACS or Faster Payments, the bank computer-based payment transfer systems.

■ When a remittance advice is received it must be checked carefully against the sales documentation held by the seller and the customer's account in the seller's sales ledger. The amount received must be the correct amount. The documentation checked includes invoices, credit notes and the remittance advice itself.

■ If a cheque is received it must be checked to ensure that it is valid.

■ If payment is made through BACS or Faster Payments, the bank statement must be checked in due course to confirm that the payment has been received.

■ Discrepancies relating to payments received can be caused by:

  – **underpayments** – a disputed invoice may not have been included

  – **overpayments** – a credit note may have been ignored or an invoice paid twice

  – problems with **settlement discount** – discount rate incorrect, discount period expired, no discount available

■ In all cases the discrepancies must be communicated to the customer so that an appropriate adjustment can be made.

Key Terms

remittance advice	an advice received from a customer telling the seller that a payment has been made
BACS	Bankers Automated Clearing Services – a bank computer-based system which makes payment direct from one bank account to another – often used for bulk payments
Faster Payments	a bank electronic payment system which makes transfers direct from one bank account to another – often used for individual payments
settlement discount	a percentage reduction in the selling price given to the buyer if the buyer pays within a specified short space of time; this discount is also known as 'cash' discount

Activities

5.1 A business which receives a remittance advice from a customer is likely to check it against the following documents or accounts:

(a)   delivery note, invoice, customer statement

(b)   delivery note, invoice, sales ledger account

(c)   invoice, purchase order, customer statement

(d)   invoice, sales ledger account, customer statement

Which of the above options is correct?

5.2 On an invoice which offers settlement discount:

(a)   the settlement discount calculation is always shown

(b)   the settlement discount percentage is shown

(c)   the VAT (sales tax) is worked out on the goods total before the settlement discount is deducted

(d)   the final invoice total takes into account the settlement discount deducted

Which of the above options is correct?

5.3 On the next three pages are set out remittance advices and associated documents.

You are to check the remittance advices against the documents and

1   identify and describe any discrepancies that you find

2   suggest the action that could be taken by the supplier in each case

5.3 (a)

remittance advice sent to the seller

REMITTANCE ADVICE	FROM: Trends 4 Friar Street Broadfield BR1 3RF

TO
Cool Socks Limited
Unit 45 Elgar Estate, Broadfield, BR7 4ER   06 12 20-3

Your ref	Our ref		Amount
788101	47645	BACS TRANSFER	490.00
		TOTAL	490.00

THIS HAS BEEN PAID BY BACS CREDIT TRANSFER DIRECTLY INTO YOUR BANK ACCOUNT AT ALBION BANK NO 11451226 SORT CODE 90 47 17

statement sent by the seller to the customer

STATEMENT OF ACCOUNT
COOL SOCKS LIMITED
Unit 45 Elgar Estate, Broadfield, BR7 4ER
Tel 01908 765314 Fax 01908 765951 Email toni@cool.u-net.com
VAT REG GB 0745 4672 76

TO
Trends
4 Friar Street
Broadfield
BR1 3RF

account   3993

date   30 11 20-3

date	details	debit £	credit £	balance £
01 11 20-3	Balance b/f	249.57		249.57
02 11 20-3	Payment received		249.57	00.00
02 10 20-3	Invoice 788101	490.00		490.00
10 10 20-3	Credit note 12189		49.00	441.00
			TOTAL	441.00

5.3 (b)

remittance advice sent to the seller

TO		REMITTANCE	FROM
Cool Socks Limited Unit 45 Elgar Estate, Broadfield, BR7 4ER		**REMITTANCE** **ADVICE** 8 December 20-3	**Vogue Ltd** 56 Shaftesbury Road Manorfield MA1 6GP

date	your reference	our reference	payment amount
03 11 -3	INVOICE 788106	876213	500.00
15 11 -3	INVOICE 788256	876287	220.10
20 11 -3	CREDIT NOTE 12218	876287	(22.01)
		TOTAL	698.09

sales ledger account of the customer in the accounting records of the seller

Debit				Vogue Limited			Credit	
20-3	**Details**	**£**	**p**	**20-3**	**Details**	**£**	**p**	
3 Nov	Sales	500	00	10 Oct	Sales returns	22	01	
15 Nov	Sales	220	10					
17 Nov	Sales	625	85					

5.3 (c)

BACS remittance advice sent to the seller

REMITTANCE ADVICE	FROM: RTC Fashions 85 Fish Street Stourminster ST1 8RT

TO
Chico Importers
34 Oldfield Street, London EC1 6TR

03 12 20-3

Your ref	Our ref		Amount
10956	1078	FASTER PAYMENTS TRANSFER Invoice 10956 less 5% settlement discount	638.40
		TOTAL	638.40

THIS HAS BEEN PAID BY FASTER PAYMENT DIRECTLY INTO YOUR BANK ACCOUNT AT HRBC BANK ACCOUNT NO xxxx6534 SORT CODE 40 47 17

invoice sent by the seller

INVOICE

CHICO IMPORTERS

34 Oldfield Street, London EC1 6TR
Tel 0208765322 Fax 0208765564 Email sales@chicoimporters.com
VAT Reg GB 0745 4672 76

invoice to

RTC Fashions 85 Fish Street Stourminster ST1 8RT	invoice no	10956
	account	834
	your reference	1078
	date/tax point	5 11 20-3

product code	description	quantity	price	unit	total	discount %	net
5674R	T shirts (red)	200	3.50	each	700.00	20.00	560.00

terms		goods total	560.00
Net monthly Carriage paid		VAT	112.00
		TOTAL	672.00

6 Process documents from suppliers

this chapter covers...

In Chapter 2 we described the financial documents prepared by a **seller** of goods and services on credit. This chapter looks at the situation from the purchaser's point of view and describes the procedures and documents involved when goods and services are **bought** on credit.

The chapter covers the following areas:

■ the use of financial documents for the purchase of goods and services – purchase invoice, delivery note, goods received note, credit note

■ the checking of the supplier's documents received against the purchaser's documents

■ the calculation of document totals, including discounts and VAT (sales tax)

■ the coding and filing of documents

■ the checking and authorisation of documents

■ dealing with discrepancies

This chapter covers the treatment of documents until payment is made. The processes of calculating and making payment are covered in Chapter 8.

BUSINESS DOCUMENTS – THE PURCHASER'S POINT OF VIEW

When a business **sells** goods and services its main concern is that it provides what has been ordered and that it gets paid on time. When a business **orders** goods and services, on the other hand, it will want to ensure that:

■ the correct goods and services are provided – on time

■ they are charged at the right price

The traditional procedure is for the purchaser to accumulate on file – often stapled together – a series of documents which will be checked against each other as they are produced or come into the office, eg copy purchase order, delivery note, goods received note, invoice, credit note, statement, and so on. These will often be kept in a 'pending invoices' file until payment is made, when they will go into a 'paid invoices' file - as shown in the diagram below.

This chapter covers the treatment of documents until payment is made. Calculating and making payment is covered in Chapter 8.

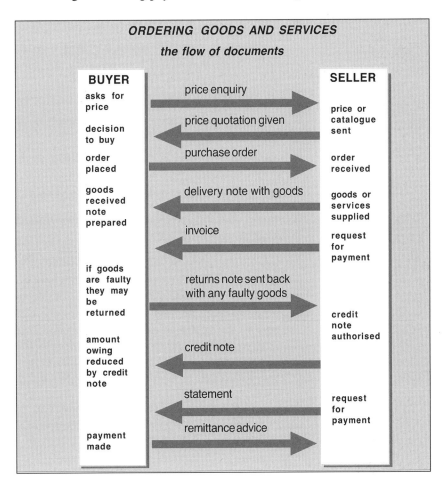

ORDERING PROCEDURES

the traditional method

The diagram on the previous page shows the traditional method of ordering goods and services: a purchase order is issued, the goods (or services) are delivered (or provided) and an invoice is sent which is eventually paid by the customer. There are of course, many variations on this procedure, and nowadays buying and selling and payment increasingly takes place online.

In this book and in your studies the emphasis is on the traditional method of ordering and paying because the principles of this method underlie all the other methods. You should however be aware of the other methods as you are likely to encounter them in your day-to-day work.

other ordering methods – paper based

Businesses can order goods and services in a variety of other ways:

- filling in a catalogue order form and posting it to the seller with payment
- telephoning a company which is selling to you for the first time to ask them to issue you with a 'pro-forma invoice' for the goods or service you need; when you receive this invoice document, you will send it back with payment and the goods or service will be supplied by return
- faxing off a catalogue order form and quoting the company debit card or credit card details
- telephoning an order and quoting the company debit or credit card details

other ordering methods – electronically based

Electronic ordering has been made possible through EDI (Electronic Data Interchange) and e-commerce.

EDI (Electronic Data Interchange) is a method of connecting businesses by computer link so that documents such as purchase orders and invoices can be electronically generated and payments made electronically when they are due. EDI has been running for many years, the electronic links are private and secure; the system is expensive to set up. Supermarkets, for example, commonly use EDI.

e-commerce

E-commerce is a loose term which is short for 'electronic commerce'. It covers selling and buying on the internet, both business-to-business and also by individual personal customers.

documents for purchases

This chapter concentrates on the traditional method of purchasing using paper documents. This is not to say that electronic methods are any different; they are very much based on the same principles. The documents we will describe are:

- purchase order
- delivery note
- goods received note
- purchase invoice

When a business purchases goods, it is important that the accounting system includes checks and controls to ensure that:

- the correct goods have been received in an acceptable condition
- the correct terms (including discounts) and price have been applied
- the goods are paid for once only (paying for goods twice does occur!)

PURCHASE ORDER

A purchaser, when the price of the product has been agreed, normally issues a **purchase order**. It is essential that this purchase order is **authorised** by the appropriate person. This authority may be shown on the document in the form of a signature and date. Some businesses will insist that more senior staff in the buying department sign larger orders. A business keeps a copy of every purchase order it issues and often files them in numerical order (each order has a numerical code). The purchase order for Blue Toebar socks from the Cool Socks Case Study in Chapter 2 is shown below.

Trends		**PURCHASE ORDER**	
4 Friar Street Broadfield BR1 3RF Tel 01908 761234 Fax 01908 761987 VAT REG GB 0745 8383 56			
Cool Socks Limited, Unit 45 Elgar Estate, Broadfield, BR7 4ER		purchase order no date	47609 25 09 20-3
product code	quantity	description	
45B	100 pairs	Blue Toebar socks	
AUTHORISED signature...... *D Signer* ....date.. *25/09/20-3*			

DELIVERY NOTE

When the goods ordered are despatched by the seller they will normally be accompanied by a **delivery note**.

The delivery note shown below was described in the Cool Socks Case Study in Chapter 2. The main features are as follows:

- The delivery note has a numerical reference (here it is 68873), useful for filing and later reference if there is a query.

- The method of delivery is stated – here the delivery is by parcel carrier.

- The delivery note quotes the purchase order number – 47609 – this enables the buyer to 'tie up' the delivery with the original purchase order.

- The delivery note quotes:
  - Cool Socks' catalogue reference 45B as the product code
  - the quantity supplied
  - the description of the goods, but no price – it is not needed at this stage

  These details will be checked against the goods themselves straightaway so that any discrepancies can be reported without delay.

  If the business purchasing the goods uses a **goods received note** (see next page) this will be completed at this stage.

- The delivery note will be signed and dated by the person receiving the goods as proof of delivery. This signature process can also be carried out electronically – the person receiving the goods will be asked to sign a portable electronic device.

DELIVERY NOTE

COOL SOCKS LIMITED

Unit 45 Elgar Estate, Broadfield, BR7 4ER
Tel 01908 765314 Fax 01908 765951 Email toni@cool.u-net.com
VAT REG GB 0745 4672 76

Trends	delivery note no	68873
4 Friar Street	delivery method	Lynx Parcels
Broadfield	your order	47609
BR1 3RF	date	02 10 20-3

product code	quantity	description
45B	100 pairs	Blue Toebar socks

Received
signature...... *V Williams* ......name (capitals). *V WILLIAMS* ......date *05/10/20-3*

GOODS RECEIVED NOTE

Some businesses use an internal document known as a **goods received note (GRN)**. The buyer records on this document the receipt of the goods and the details set out on the delivery note or advice note sent by the supplier.

The GRN is essentially a checklist on which is recorded:

- the name of the supplier
- the quantity and details of the goods ordered
- the purchase order number
- the name of the carrier and any carrier reference number

As the goods are received and checked in, the GRN is ticked and signed to indicate that the right quantity and description of goods has been received.

The GRN forms part of the payment authorisation process: only when a completed and correct GRN is approved by the Accounts Department can the relevant invoice be paid.

Shown below is the goods received note relating to the Case Study in Chapter 2 in which the shop 'Trends' ordered some fashion socks from Cool Socks Limited.

Note that the receipt of the 100 pairs of socks has been recorded, and also the fact that 10 pairs are damaged.

Trends		**GOODS RECEIVED NOTE**
Supplier		
Cool Socks Limited, Unit 45 Elgar Estate, Broadfield, BR7 4ER	GRN no date	1871 (05 10 20-3

quantity	description	order number
100 pairs	Blue Toebar socks	47609

carrier	Lynx Parcels	consignment no 8479347

received by *V Williams*		checked by *R Patel*
condition of goods (please tick and comment)	good condition damaged ✔ (10 pairs) shortages	**copies to** Buyer ✔ Accounts ✔ Stockroom ✔

PURCHASE INVOICE

You will already be very familiar with the **purchase invoice** because it is the **sales invoice** sent out by the person selling the goods or services. In the Chapter 2 Case Study the sales invoice sent out by Cool Socks becomes the purchase invoice received by Trends, the buyer:

INVOICE

COOL SOCKS LIMITED
Unit 45 Elgar Estate, Broadfield, BR7 4ER
Tel 01908 765314 Fax 01908 765951 Email toni@cool.u-net.com
VAT Reg GB 0745 4672 76

invoice to

Trends 4 Friar Street Broadfield BR1 3RF	

invoice no	787923
account	3993
your reference	47609
date/tax point	02 10 20-3

deliver to

as above

product code	description	quantity	price	unit	total	discount %	net
45B	Blue toebar socks	100	2.36	pair	236.00	0.00	236.00

terms
Net monthly
Carriage paid
E & OE

goods total	236.00
VAT	47.20
TOTAL	283.20

CHECKING INVOICE, DELIVERY NOTE AND PURCHASE ORDER

Now that you are familiar with all the purchase documents we will explain the checking process that will need to be made by the purchaser. This involves two separate procedures carried out in the Accounts Department:

■ checking the documents – the invoice, delivery note (or GRN) and copy purchase order – with each other

■ checking the calculations on the invoice

We will deal with these in separate stages, starting with the checking of the documents:

check 1 – goods received and delivery note

When the goods are received they should be checked against the delivery note – the quantities should be counted and the condition of the goods checked and noted on a GRN if required. Any discrepancies or damage should be notified immediately to the supplier so that replacements can be sent or the buyer credited with the value of the missing or damaged goods (ie the amount due reduced by the issue of a credit note).

check 2 – delivery note and purchase order

The delivery note should then be checked in the Accounts Department against a copy of the original purchase order (see illustration on page 121):

■ supplier catalogue number – has the right type of goods been delivered?

■ quantity – has the right number been delivered?

■ specifications – are the goods delivered to the same specifications as those ordered?

■ purchase order reference number – do the goods relate to the purchase order being examined?

If all is in order, the delivery note will be filed with the copy purchase order under the purchase order reference number, ready for checking against the invoice when it arrives.

check 3 – invoice, delivery note and purchase order

When the invoice eventually arrives from the supplier, it should be checked against the delivery note and the purchase order (which should be filed together). The specific points to look at are:

■ **invoice and delivery note**
Are the details of the goods on the invoice and delivery note the same? The product code, description and quantity of the goods should agree.

■ **invoice and purchase order**

Has the correct price been charged? The unit price quoted by the supplier or obtained from the supplier's catalogue will be stated on the purchase order, and should agree with the unit price stated on the invoice. If there is a difference, it should be queried with the supplier.

student task

Look at the invoice below and the purchase order and delivery note on the next page. They all relate to the same transaction. Can you spot any discrepancies? The answers are set out at the bottom of this page.

INVOICE

Stourford Office Supplies

Unit 12, Avon Industrial Estate, Stourford, SF5 6TD
Tel 01807 765434 Fax 01807 765123 Email stourford@stourford.co.uk
VAT Reg GB 0745 4001 76

invoice to

Martley Machine Rental Limited 67 Broadgreen Road Martley MR6 7TR	invoice no **652771** account **MAR435** your reference **47780** date/tax point **31 03 20-3**

deliver to

as above

product code	description	quantity	price	unit	total	discount %	net
3564748	80gsm white Supalaser	15	3.50	ream	52.00	0.00	52.00

terms

Net monthly

Carriage paid

E & OE

goods total	52.00
VAT	10.04
TOTAL	41.96

The purchase order and delivery note agree, but the invoice has a number of discrepancies:

- the order reference differs (47700 and 47780)
- the product code differs (3564749 and 3564748)
- the product description differs (100 gsm and 80 gsm)
- the price differs (£4.00 and £3.50 per ream)

Martley Machine Rental   **PURCHASE ORDER**

67 Broadgreen Road
Martley
MR6 7TR
Tel 01908 546321 Fax 01908 546335
VAT REG GB 0745 8383 56

Stourford Office Supplies Unit 12 Avon Industrial Estate Stourford SF5 6TD	purchase order no date	47700 13 03 20-3

product code	quantity	description	
3564749	15 reams	100gsm white Supalaser paper	@ £4.00 per ream

AUTHORISED   signature.......... *C Farmer* ....date.... *13 March 20-3* ......

catalogue number	quantity	order specifications	purchase order reference number

─────────────── **DELIVERY NOTE** ───────────────

Stourford Office Supplies

Unit 12, Avon Industrial Estate, Stourford, SF5 6TD
Tel 01807 765434 Fax 01807 765123 Email stourford@stourford.co.uk
VAT Reg GB 0745 4001 76

Martley Machine Rental Ltd 67 Broadgreen Road Martley MR6 7TR	delivery note no delivery method your order date	26754 Puma Express 47700 27 03 20-3

product code	quantity	description
3564749	15 reams	100gsm white Supalaser paper

Received

signature.............. *G Hughes* ....print name (capitals).... *G HUGHES* ....date *31.03.20-3*

details to check on the purchase order and delivery note

CHECKING THE CALCULATIONS ON THE INVOICE

Another important step is for the Accounts Department to check the calculations on the invoice. If any one of these calculations is incorrect, the final total will be wrong, and the invoice will have to be queried with the supplier, so accurate checking is essential. The checks to be made are:

quantity x unit price The quantity of the items multiplied by the unit price must be correct. The result – the total price or 'price extension' – is used for the calculation of any trade discount applicable.

trade or bulk discount Any trade or bulk discount – allowances given to approved trade customers or for bulk purchases – must be deducted from the total price worked out. Trade or bulk discount is calculated as a percentage of the total price, eg a trade discount of 20% on a total price of £150 is calculated:

£150 x $\frac{20}{100}$ = £30

The net price charged (before VAT) is therefore

£150 – £30 = £120 = net total

settlement discount Any settlement (cash) discount – an allowance sometimes given for quick payment – is deducted from the net total before VAT is calculated. Settlement discount, when it is offered, is usually included as one of the terms at the bottom of the invoice. It is not deducted from the invoice total, so it will be up to the buyer to settle early and to adjust the invoice total down.

VAT Value Added Tax (a sales tax) in this book is calculated at 20%. To calculate VAT, the total after the deduction of any settlement discount is treated as follows

Total x $\frac{20}{100}$ = VAT amount

If you are using a calculator, all you need to do is to multiply the total by 0.2 to give the VAT, which is then added to the total.

Note that fractions of a penny are ignored. If the total price is £55.78, the VAT will be:

$$£55.78 \times 0.2 = £11.156$$

£11.156 then loses the last digit – the fraction of a penny – to become £11.15.

For the purpose of your studies you must assume that the calculations on all invoices must be checked. In practice, computerised invoicing performs the calculations automatically, and in principle should be correct.

Now check the calculations on the invoice on page 126. You should be able to detect a large number of errors:

- quantity x unit price should be £52.50, not £52.00

- the VAT is wrongly calculated £52.00 x 0.2 = £10.40, not £10.04 (it would be £10.50 on £52.50)

- the VAT has been deducted instead of added: the total should be £52.50 + £10.50 = £63.00

RETURNS – CHECKING CREDIT NOTES

A purchaser will sometimes have to return faulty or incorrect goods and request a credit note from the seller to reduce the amount owed.

Note that a purchaser should never for this reason change figures on an invoice – this would cause havoc with the accounting records! When goods are sent back they are normally returned with a **returns note** which sets out all the details of the goods.

Trends		**RETURNS NOTE**	
4 Friar Street			
Broadfield			
BR1 3RF			
Tel 01908 761234 Fax 01908 761987			
VAT REG GB 0745 8383 56			
Cool Socks Limited, Unit 45 Elgar Estate, Broadfield, BR7 4ER		returns note no 2384 date 08 10 20-3	
product code	quantity	description	
45B	10 pairs	Blue Toebar socks	
REASON FOR RETURN: *faulty goods, credit requested*			
SIGNATURE *R SINGH*		DATE *10 10 20-3*	

When the goods are received back by the seller and checked, a **credit note** will be issued to reduce the amount owing. The credit note from the Cool Socks Case Study is illustrated below.

CHECKING THE CREDIT NOTE

When the **credit note** is received by the purchaser it will have to be checked carefully to make sure that the quantity of goods, the price, discount and VAT are correctly calculated. It will be checked against the **goods received note** if one has been issued (not all businesses do), or the returns note or other internal records to make sure that the discrepancy has been properly resolved – ie has full credit been given for damaged/missing/incorrect goods?

If the credit note is correct, the document will be entered into the accounting records and then filed with (stapled to) the appropriate copy purchase order, delivery note, invoice, GRN or copy returns note, awaiting the arrival of the statement.

CREDIT NOTE

COOL SOCKS LIMITED

Unit 45 Elgar Estate, Broadfield, BR7 4ER
Tel 01908 765314 Fax 01908 765951 Email toni@cool.u-net.com
VAT REG GB 0745 4672 76

to

Trends 4 Friar Street Broadfield BR1 3RF		

credit note no	12157
account	3993
your reference	47609
our invoice	787923
date/tax point	13 10 20-3

product code	description	quantity	price	unit	total	discount %	net
45B	Blue Toebar socks	10	2.36	pair	23.60	0.00	23.60

Reason for credit
10 pairs of socks received damaged
(Your returns note no. R/N 2384)

GOODS TOTAL	23.60
VAT	4.72
TOTAL	28.32

Trends		**GOODS RECEIVED NOTE**	

Supplier

Cool Socks Limited, Unit 45 Elgar Estate, Broadfield, BR7 4ER	GRN no date	1871 05 10 20-3

quantity	description	order number
100 pairs	Blue Toebar socks	47609

carrier   Lynx Parcels   consignment no   8479347

received by *V Williams*	checked by *R Patel*	
condition of goods (please tick and comment)	good condition damaged ✔ (10 pairs) shortages	**copies to** Buyer ✔ Accounts ✔ Stockroom ✔

goods received note – details to check

If you compare the **credit note** on the opposite page and the **goods received note** shown above you will see that the following details can be checked:

■ the identity of the goods returned – here it is blue Toebar socks

■ the quantity returned – ten pairs of socks in this case

■ the purchase order reference number – here it is 47609

As you will see, all is correct and so it is in order for Trends to make payment for this transaction on the due date.

The processes for preparing for payment of purchasers' accounts will be dealt with in full in Chapter 8.

CODING PURCHASES INVOICES AND CREDIT NOTES

the need to code

When a business processes invoices and credit notes received from suppliers it will usually code them so that they can be entered into the accounting system quickly and easily. This will be very useful, for example, if a computer accounting system is used. Normally two different sets of codes will be used

- a **supplier account** code which will identify the supplier of the goods or services – this code may be alphabetic, alpha-numeric or numeric; if letters are involved they usually relate to the first few letters of the name of the supplier
- a **general ledger account** code which will identify the account which will be debited in the accounting system – it normally relates to the type of purchases made or expenses paid; it may be alpha-numeric or numeric

You will see from the purchases invoice and credit note on the opposite page that the codes may be entered in boxes imprinted onto the document by a rubber stamp used by the buyer (see the grey arrows indicating the boxes).

using the account code lists

The business will keep account lists to hand so that accounts staff can quickly look up the appropriate code. As noted above, these will be for

- supplier accounts
- general ledger accounts, eg categories of purchases

Extracts from these two types of account lists are shown below, Note that the account names are sorted in alphabetical order:

Supplier	Supplier code
Jarma Supplies	JA006
John Taylor Limited	JO004
Labtech Limited	LA001
Liverpool Kitware	LI001

Item	General Ledger code
Shades	5045
T-shirts	5060
Trainers	5100
Trousers	5210

The **invoice** on the next page has therefore been given the following codes:

Supplier code JA006 for Jarma Supplies

General ledger code 5060 for Max T-shirts purchased

The **credit note** on the next page has been given the following codes:

Supplier code LA001 for Labtech Limited

General ledger code 5045 for Monaco shades purchased

INVOICE

JARMA SUPPLIES
Advent House, Otto Way
New Milton, SR1 6TF
Tel 01722 295875 Fax 01722 295611 Email sales@johnsonthreads.co.uk
VAT Reg GB 01982 6865 06

invoice to

RT Fashionware
34, Tennyson High Road
Maidstone
ME4 5EW

invoice no	7736
account	94122
your reference	675
date/tax point	01 04 20-7

description	quantity	price	unit	total
Max T-shirts (red)	200	3.00	each	600.00

terms

30 days

Carriage paid

E & OE

Supplier a/c reference	general ledger a/c number
JA006	5060

goods total	600.00
VAT	120.00
TOTAL	720.00

coding details entered on sellers' documents by the purchaser, RT Fashionware

CREDIT NOTE

LABTECH LIMITED
Unit 7 Roughway Estate,
Martley Road, Cookford, CO1 9GH
Tel 01843 265432 Fax 01843 265439 Email accounts@fabtech.co.uk
VAT Reg GB 0877 9333 06

to

RT Fashionware
34, Tennyson High Road
Maidstone
ME4 5EW

credit note no	976
account	94122
your reference	47601
date/tax point	12 04 20-7

description	quantity	price	unit	total
Monaco shades 2744	5	30.00	each	150.00

reason for credit:

lenses damaged

supplier a/c reference	general ledger a/c number
LA001	5045

goods total	150.00
VAT	30.00
TOTAL	180.00

Chapter Summary

- When a business orders goods or services on credit, it may do so using a manual paper-based system or by using an electronic system (either EDI or e-commerce).

- When a business orders goods on credit using a manual paper-based system it is likely to deal with a number of financial documents:
  - the purchase order
  - the delivery note
  - the goods received note
  - the purchase invoice

- It is important that a series of checks are made to the financial documents to ensure that the goods or services provided are the correct ones, charged at the right price. The checks will involve calculations and references.

- If a discrepancy is found, it should be noted and the seller contacted so that the account of the purchaser can be credited and the amount owing reduced accordingly.

- Purchases invoices and credit notes should be coded with the supplier account and general ledger account codes for types of purchases so that they can easily be entered into the accounting system.

Key Terms

EDI	Electronic Data Interchange (EDI) is an electronic system of ordering goods and services using secure private computer links
e-commerce	buying and selling on the Internet by businesses and personal customers
purchase order	a document issued and authorised by the buyer of goods and services, sent to the seller, indicating the goods or services required
delivery note	a document listing and accompanying the goods sent to the purchaser
goods received note	a document used by purchasers to record receipt of inventory and any returns made
purchases invoice	a document issued by the seller of goods or services to the purchaser indicating the amount owing and the required payment date
returns note	a document sent to the supplier with any faulty goods
credit note	a document issued by the seller of goods or services to the purchaser reducing the amount owing

Activities

6.1 What type of business document would normally be used when goods are bought on credit

(a) to order the goods from the seller?

(b) to accompany goods sent from the seller?

(c) to record the receipt and any discrepancies relating to the goods at the buyer's premises?

(d) to advise the buyer in the first instance of the amount of money due?

(e) to advise the buyer that a reduction is being made in the buyer's account for faulty goods supplied?

6.2 What is the difference between a delivery note and a goods received note?

6.3 Which documents would normally be checked by the buyer against the purchase order? Answer (a) or (b) or (c) or (d).

(a) the delivery note and the invoice

(b) the invoice and the returns note

(c) the goods received note and the returns note

(d) the returns note and the delivery note

6.4 What document would a buyer expect to receive from a seller if goods which were delivered in a damaged condition have been returned to the seller?

6.5 Eduservice, an educational consultancy business, ordered some USB sticks from Compusupply Limited on purchase order 53659 for the IT Department at Martley College in Broadfield. The goods were delivered to the Eduservice office at 45 The Ridings, Broadfield on 3 February.

You work in the Eduservice office as an accounts assistant. Part of your job is to deal with all the documents.

You have today (5 February 20-3) received an invoice from Compusupply. You are not happy with the service you are receiving from this company and are thinking of going elsewhere for a supplier.

Shown on the next two pages are:

• an extract from an email from Compusupply agreeing the level of trade discount given

• the original purchase order

• the invoice you receive

You are to write an email to Compusupply setting out the errors that have been made. Address the email to sales@compusupply.co.uk and sign it off with your own name as an accounts assistant. The date is 5 February 20-3.

Extract of email dated 1 November 20-02 from Compusupply to Eduservice

"In view of our long-standing trading relationship we are happy to increase the trade discount we allow your company from 10% to 15% from 1 November 20-2.

Kind regards

James Watts
Credit Controller
Compusupply"

EDUSERVICE	PURCHASE ORDER
45 The Ridings Broadfield BR2 3TR Tel 01908 333691	

TO

Compusupply Limited Unit 17 Elgar Estate, Broadfield, BR7 4ER	purchase order no 53659 date 27 January 20–3

product code	quantity	description
4573	10	Opus 1GB USB sticks @ £95 per box of ten Please deliver to: J Wales, IT Department Martley College, Fairacre, Broadfield BR5 7YT

Authorised   signature......*J Wales*......................................date...*27.1.20-3*........

INVOICE

COMPUSUPPLY LIMITED
Unit 17 Elgar Estate, Broadfield, BR7 4ER
Tel 01908 765756 Fax 01908 765777 Email sales@compusupply.co.uk
VAT Reg GB 0745 4689 13

invoice to

Eduservice 45 The Ridings Broadfield BR2 3TR	

invoice no	20424
account	242
your reference	53659
date/tax point	30.01.20-3

deliver to

as above

product code	description	quantity	price	unit	total	discount %	net
4574	Opus 2GB USB sticks	10	125.00	(box of 10)	125.00	10	112.50

goods total	112.50
VAT	22.50
TOTAL	135.00

terms
Net monthly
Carriage paid
E & OE

6.6   **(a)**   John Smith & Co, a stationery shop, ordered 20 boxes of gel pens from Helicon Stationery Supplies on purchase order 17643 (see below).

The goods were delivered to John Smith & Co on 4 December 20-4, but the order was short by 2 boxes and only 18 boxes were delivered. This was noted in a goods received note (see the next page). The problem was advised to Helicon Supplies by email on 4 December and a credit note requested. The credit note was issued on 10 December and sent to John Smith & Co. (see the next page).

You are to check the three documents and write the text of an email from John Smith & Co to Helicon pointing out any discrepancies you find. Use your own name. The date is 12 December.

      (b)   John Smith & Co code all purchase invoices and credit notes with a supplier code and a general ledger code. Extracts from the two coding lists are shown below.

You are to state the supplier and general ledger codes which are to be used on the credit note on the next page.

Supplier	Supplier code
French & Co	FR002
Gemax Supplies	GE004
Helicon Stationery	HE001
JSTAT Ltd	JS001

Item	General Ledger code
Paper	5005
Pens	5010
Pension costs	5201
Power costs	7210

John Smith & Co   PURCHASE ORDER

7 Buttermere Road
Broadfield BR6 3TR
Tel 01908 761234 Fax 01908 761987
email info@johnsmith&co.co.uk
VAT REG GB 0745 8383 56

Helicon Stationery Supplies 91 High Street, Broadfield, BR7 4ER	purchase order no	17643
	date	25 11 20–4

product code	quantity	description
919BK	20 boxes of 10	Gel Pens (Black)

AUTHORISED   signature......*D Smith*..date....*25/11/20-4*

John Smith & Co

GOODS RECEIVED NOTE

GRN no.   302

supplier   Helicon Stationery Supplies

date   4 December 20-4

order ref.	quantity	description
17643	20 boxes of 10	Gel pens (black)

received by....*D Patel*...checked by.......*R T Fraser*.................

condition of goods   condition - *good*

damages - *none*

shortages √ *18 out of 20 boxes received*

CREDIT NOTE

HELICON STATIONERY SUPPLIES

91 HIGH STREET, BROADFIELD, BR7 4ER
Tel 01908 129426 Fax 01908 129919
email sales@heliconstationery.co.uk
VAT REG GB 0622 838370

to

John Smith & Co
7 Buttermere Road
Broadfield BR6 3TR

credit note no	234672
account	2984
your reference	17644
date/tax point	10 December 20-4

product code	description	quantity	price	unit	total	discount %	net
909BK	Rollerball pens (black)	3	8.00	box	24.00	10	19.20

reason for credit
Shortages

supplier a/c reference	general ledger a/c number

goods total	19.20
VAT @ 20%	3.84
TOTAL	23.04

7 Accounting for purchases and purchases returns

this chapter covers...

This chapter focuses on using the accounting system to record the details of purchases and purchases returns.

Having looked in the previous chapter at the documents and procedures involved in buying on credit we will now take the financial documents of purchases invoices and credit notes for purchases and record them in books of prime entry (day books) and in the bookkeeping system of general ledger and purchases ledger.

We will be using two books of prime entry:

■ *purchases day book*

■ *purchases returns day book*

Information from these day books will then be transferred into the bookkeeping system using accounts in general ledger and purchases ledger.

Notes:

■ *In this chapter we focus on accounting for credit purchases and purchases returns transactions. Cash purchases transactions will be seen when we study the cash book in Chapters 9 and 10.*

■ *We use the international standards term 'trade payable' to mean a person who is owed money by a business; normally this is a supplier. You may also in your studies come across the traditional term 'creditor' which means exactly the same thing.*

THE ACCOUNTING SYSTEM

We have seen in Chapter 1 (page 4) that the accounting system comprises a number of stages of recording and presenting financial transactions:

- financial documents
- books of prime entry (eg day books)
- double-entry bookkeeping
- trial balance

In this chapter we look at how financial documents for credit purchases and purchases returns transactions are recorded in the books of prime entry, together with the entries to be made in the double-entry bookkeeping accounts. Later in the book we will see how a list of the balances of the double-entry accounts is used to form the initial trial balance (Chapter 12).

ACCOUNTING FOR CREDIT PURCHASES AND RETURNS

In accounting, the term 'purchases' means **the purchase of goods with the intention that they should be resold at a profit**.

This means that an office stationery shop will record as purchases those items – such as photocopier paper, ring binders – which it buys with the intention of resale at a profit. Such purchases – together with the running costs of the business, eg wages, heating and lighting, telephone – are described as **revenue expenditure**. Other asset items purchased in connection with the running of the business – eg buildings, shop fittings – are recorded not as purchases but, instead, are accounted for as the purchase of an asset, ie buildings, shop fittings – such expenditure is described as **capital expenditure**.

'Purchases returns' are when goods previously bought on credit are returned by the buyer to the supplier.

The diagram on the next page shows the order in which the accounting records are prepared for credit purchases and purchases returns transactions. You will see that the steps are:

- start with a **financial document**, either a purchases invoice or a credit note received
- enter it in the appropriate **book of prime entry** (the first accounting book in which the financial document is recorded and summarised), either purchases day book or purchases returns day book

■ transfer the information from the book of prime entry into the double-entry accounts in the **general ledger**

■ transfer the information from the book of prime entry into the subsidiary accounts of trade payables in the **purchases ledger**

accounting for credit purchases and purchases returns transactions

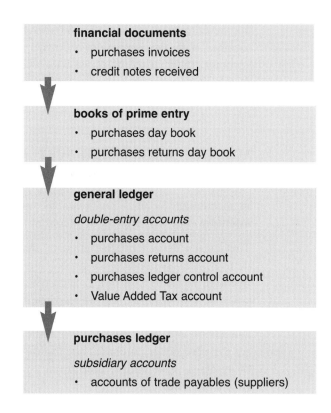

We will now look in more detail at the use of the books of prime entry and the double-entry bookkeeping system for credit purchases and purchases returns. These are very similar to the system already used for credit sales and sales returns in Chapter 4 and you may wish to refer to the sections of Chapter 4 which cover books of prime entry (pages 76-78), and methods of coding in accounting systems (page 88).

ACCOUNTING SYSTEM FOR CREDIT PURCHASES

The accounting system for credit purchases fits together in the following way:

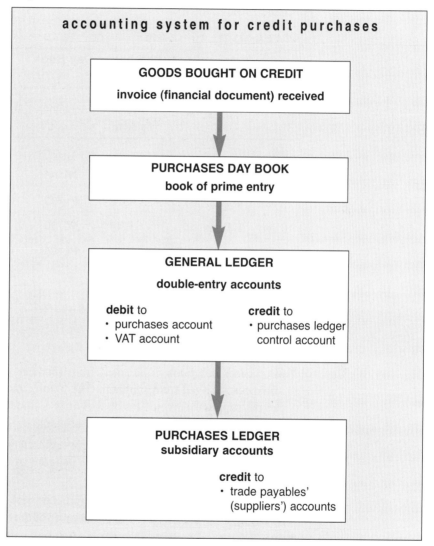

We will now look in more detail at the purchases day book and the accounting system for credit purchases.

In the examples which follow we will assume that the business is registered for Value Added Tax and that VAT is charged on invoices received from suppliers.

The VAT rate used in the examples is 20%.

PURCHASES DAY BOOK

The purchases day book is a collection point for accounting information on the credit purchases of a business and is set out in the following way (with sample entries shown):

Purchases Day Book						PDB57
Date	Details	Invoice number	Account code	Total	VAT*	Net
20-4				£	£	£
5 Jan	P Bond Ltd	1234	PL125	96	16	80
9 Jan	D Webster	A373	PL730	144	24	120
16 Jan	P Bond Ltd	1247	PL125	48	8	40
20 Jan	Sanders & Sons	5691	PL495	192	32	160
31 Jan	Totals for month			480	80	400
				GL2350	GL2200	GL5100

* VAT = 20 per cent

Notes:

- Purchases day book is prepared from financial documents – purchases invoices received from suppliers. The invoice number used is either that of the supplier's invoice (as above) or is a unique number given to each invoice by the buyer's accounts department.

- The code 'PDB57' is used for cross-referencing to the bookkeeping system: here it indicates that this is page 57 of the purchases day book (PDB).

- The **account code** column cross-references here to 'PL' – the Purchases Ledger – followed by the account number of the trade payable (supplier).

- The **total** or **gross** column records the amount of each financial document, ie after VAT has been included.

- The code 'GL' beneath the totals amounts refers to the account numbers in General Ledger.

- Purchases day book is totalled at appropriate intervals – daily, weekly or monthly (as here) – and the total of the **net** column tells the business the amount of credit purchases for the period.

■ The amounts from purchases day book are recorded in the ledger accounts.

In order to write up the purchases day book, we take purchases invoices – that have been checked and authorised – for the period and enter the details:

■ date of invoice

■ name of supplier

■ purchase invoice number, using either the supplier's invoice number, or a unique number given to each invoice by the buyer's accounts department

■ cross-reference to the supplier's account number in the purchases ledger, eg 'PL125'

■ enter the total amount of the invoice into the 'total' column

■ enter the VAT amount shown on the invoice – don't be concerned with any adjustments to the VAT for the effect of any settlement (cash) discounts, simply record the VAT amount shown

■ enter the net amount of the invoice (often described as 'goods or services total'), before VAT is added

BOOKKEEPING FOR CREDIT PURCHASES

After the purchases day book has been written up and totalled, the information from it is transferred to the double-entry system in general ledger. The accounts in general ledger to record the transactions from the purchases day book on the previous page are as follows:

GENERAL LEDGER

Dr	**Value Added Tax Account** (GL2200)		Cr
20-4	£	20-4	£
31 Jan Purchases Day Book PDB57	80		

Dr	**Purchases Ledger Control Account** (GL2350)		Cr
20-4	£	20-4	£
		31 Jan Purchases Day Book PDB57	480

Dr	**Purchases Account** (GL5100)		Cr
20-4	£	20-4	£
31 Jan Purchases Day Book PDB57	400		

Note that from the purchases day book:

■ total of the total column, £480, has been credited to purchases ledger control account (which records the liability to trade payables)

■ the total of the VAT column, £80, has been debited to VAT account (which has gained value)

■ the total of the net column, £400, has been debited to purchases account (which has gained value)

■ each entry in general ledger is cross-referenced back to the page number of the purchases day book; here the reference is to 'PDB57'

The last step is to record the amount of purchases made from each individual trade payable. We do this by recording the purchases invoices in the purchases ledger as follows:

PURCHASES LEDGER

Dr	P Bond Limited (PL125)		Cr
20-4	£	20-4	£
		5 Jan Purchases PDB57	96
		16 Jan Purchases PDB57	48

Dr	Sanders & Sons (PL495)		Cr
20-4	£	20-4	£
		20 Jan Purchases PDB57	192

Dr	D Webster (PL730)		Cr
20-4	£	20-4	£
		9 Jan Purchases PDB57	144

Notes:

■ The purchases day book incorporates a reference column, used to cross-reference each transaction to the account of each supplier in the purchases ledger (PL); this enables a particular transaction to be traced from financial document (invoice received), through the book of prime entry (purchases day book), to the supplier's account.

■ Each entry in the purchases ledger is cross-referenced back to the page number of the purchases day book; here the reference is 'PDB57'.

subsidiary accounts

The accounts in purchases ledger are prepared following the principles of double-entry bookkeeping. However, they are **subsidiary accounts** which means they are used to provide a note of how much each trade payable is owed by the business.

Subsidiary accounts are not part of double-entry but are represented in the general ledger by purchases ledger control account. This means that, here, the £480 credit entry is split up in the purchases ledger between the three suppliers' subsidiary accounts. Note that subsidiary accounts are often referred to as **memorandum accounts**.

ACCOUNTING SYSTEM FOR PURCHASES RETURNS

Purchases returns (or returns out) are when goods previously bought on credit are returned by the business to its suppliers. A credit note (see page 26) is requested and, when received, it is entered in the accounting system to reduce the amount owing to the trade payable.

The accounting procedures for purchases returns involve:

■ **financial documents** – credit notes received from suppliers

■ **book of prime entry** – purchases returns day book

■ **double-entry accounts** – general ledger (purchases returns account, which records the total net amount of credit notes received, Value Added Tax account, which records the VAT amount of purchases returns, and purchases ledger control account, which records the liability to trade payables)

■ **purchases ledger** – the subsidiary accounts for each individual trade payable of the business

The way in which the accounting system for purchases returns fits together is shown in the diagram on the next page.

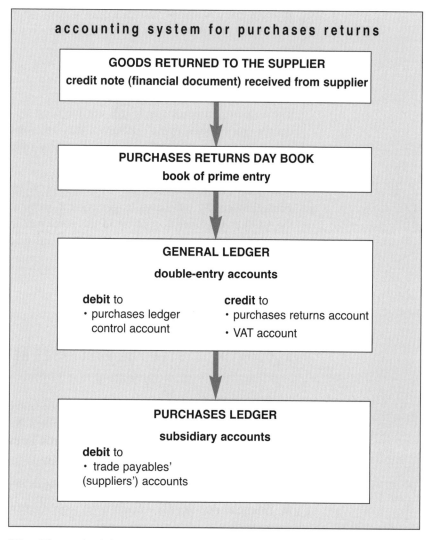

We will now look in more detail at the purchases returns day book and the double-entry accounts for purchases returns. Note that the business is registered for Value Added Tax.

PURCHASES RETURNS DAY BOOK

The purchases returns day book uses virtually the same layout as the purchases day book seen earlier in this chapter. It operates in a similar way, storing up information about purchases returns transactions until such time as a transfer is made into the double-entry accounts system. The prime documents for purchases returns day book are credit notes received from suppliers.

The purchases returns day book is written up as follows, with sample entries:

Purchases Returns Day Book						PRDB3
Date	Details	Credit note no	Account code	Total	VAT*	Net
20-4				£	£	£
20 Jan	D Webster	123	PL730	48	8	40
27 Jan	Sanders & Sons	406	PL495	96	16	80
31 Jan	Totals for month			144	24	120
				GL2350	GL2200	GL5110

* VAT = 20 per cent

Notes:

- The purchases returns day book is prepared from credit notes received from suppliers. The credit note number used is either that of the supplier's credit note (as above) or is a unique number given to each credit note by the buyer's accounts department.
- The day book is totalled at appropriate intervals – weekly or monthly.
- The VAT-inclusive amounts from the total column are debited to the trade payables' individual accounts in the purchases ledger.
- The total of the VAT column is transferred to the credit of the VAT account in the general ledger.
- The total of the net column tells the business the amount of purchases returns for the period. This amount is transferred to the credit of purchases returns account in the general ledger.
- The total or gross column records the amount of each credit note received, ie after VAT has been included. This amount is transferred to the debit of purchases ledger control account in general ledger.

BOOKKEEPING FOR PURCHASES RETURNS

After the purchases returns day book has been written up and totalled, the information from it is transferred into the double-entry system. The accounts in the general ledger to record the transactions from the above purchases returns day book (including any other transactions already recorded on these accounts) are as follows:

GENERAL LEDGER

Dr		Value Added Tax Account (GL2200)		Cr
20-4		£	20-4	£
31 Jan	Purchases Day Book PDB57	80	31 Jan Purchases Returns Day Book PRDB3	24

Dr		Purchases Ledger Control Account (GL2350)		Cr
20-4		£	20-4	£
31 Jan	Purchases Returns Day Book PRDB3	144	31 Jan Purchases Day Book PDB57	480

Dr		Purchases Returns Account (GL5110)		Cr
20-4		£	20-4	£
			31 Jan Purchases Returns Day Book PRDB3	120

The last step is to record the amount of purchases returns made to each trade payable. We do this by recording the purchases returns in the subsidiary accounts for each trade payable in the purchases ledger as follows:

PURCHASES LEDGER

Dr		Sanders & Sons (PL495)		Cr
20-4		£	20-4	£
27 Jan	Purchases Returns PRDB3	96	20 Jan Purchases PDB57	192

Dr		D Webster (PL730)		Cr
20-4		£	20-4	£
20 Jan	Purchases Returns PRDB3	48	9 Jan Purchases PDB57	144

THE USE OF ANALYSED PURCHASES DAY BOOKS

Businesses use analysed day books whenever they wish to analyse purchases and purchases returns between different categories of purchases:

- goods bought for resale, often split between types of goods purchased, eg in a clothes shop between ladies wear and mens wear

- purchases made by different departments, eg within a department store

For example, a business with two different types of purchases – purchases type 1 and purchases type 2 – will write up its purchases day book as follows:

Purchases Day Book								PDB86
Date	Details	Invoice number	Account code	Total	VAT*	Net	Purchases type 1	Purchases type 2
20-4				£	£	£	£	£
2 Sep	Fashions Limited	1401	PL087	144	24	120	70	50
4 Sep	Eastern Telephones	1402	PL061	240	40	200	–	200
8 Sep	Mercian Models	1403	PL102	336	56	280	280	–
12 Sep	Media Advertising	1404	PL092	720	120	600	–	600
15 Sep	Style Limited	1405	PL379	480	80	400	100	300
19 Sep	Wyvern Motors	1406	PL423	192	32	160	–	160
30 Sep	Totals for month			2,112	352	1,760	450	1,310
				GL2350	GL2200		GL5160	GL5190

* VAT = 20 per cent

Analysed purchases day books and purchases returns day books can be adapted to suit the particular needs of a business. Thus there is not a standard way in which to present the books of prime entry – the needs of the user of the information are all important. By using analysed day books, the owner of the business can see how much has been bought by types of purchases, or by departments.

Notes:

- In this purchases day book each purchases invoice has been given a unique number (starting at 1401) by the buyer's accounts department.

- The account code column is to 'PL' (Purchases Ledger) and the supplier's account number.

- The code 'GL' beneath the totals amounts refers to the account numbers in General Ledger.

- The analysis columns – here purchases type 1 and purchases type 2 – show the amount of purchases net of VAT (ie before VAT is added).

- The analysis columns analyse the net amount – by type of expenditure – from purchases invoices.

WYVERN TRADERS – PURCHASES AND RETURNS

To bring together the material covered in this chapter, we will look at a comprehensive Case Study which makes use of

- **books of prime entry**
  - purchases day book
  - purchases returns day book
- **general ledger accounts**
  - purchases account
  - purchases ledger control account
  - purchases returns account
  - Value Added Tax account
- **purchases ledger accounts**
  - trade receivables' subsidiary accounts

The Chapter Summary (pages 155 and 156) includes diagrams which summarise the procedures for recording credit purchases and purchases returns transactions in the accounting system.

situation

Wyvern Traders is a wholesaler of stationery and office equipment. The business is registered for VAT. The VAT rate is 20%. The following are the credit purchases and purchases returns transactions for April 20-4:

20-4	
1 Apr	Purchased goods from Midland Supplies, £120.00 + VAT, their invoice no 12486
9 Apr	Returned goods to Midland Supplies, £40.00 + VAT, credit note no 104 received
14 Apr	Purchased goods from Swan Equipment, £80.00 + VAT, their invoice no P076
28 Apr	Purchased goods from Swan Equipment, £160.00 + VAT, their invoice no P102
30 Apr	Returned goods to Swan Equipment, £80.00 + VAT, credit note no X102 received

The day books, general ledger and purchases ledger accounts are illustrated on the next two pages: arrows indicate the transfers from the day books to the individual accounts. Note that some accounts have been repeated on both pages in order to show, on the same page, the accounts relating to a particular day book: in practice a business would keep all the transactions together in one account.

Purchases Day Book — PDB19

Date	Details	Invoice number	Account code	Total	VAT	Net
20-4				£	£	£
1 Apr	Midland Supplies	12486	PL045	144	24	120
14 Apr	Swan Equipment	P076	PL112	96	16	80
28 Apr	Swan Equipment	P102	PL112	192	32	160
30 Apr	Totals for month			432	72	360
				GL2350	GL2200	GL5100

GENERAL LEDGER

Purchases Ledger Control Account (GL2350)

Dr Date	Details	£	Cr Date	Details	£
20-4			20-4		
			30 Apr	Purchases Day Book PDB19	432

Value Added Tax Account (GL2200)

Dr Date	Details	£	Cr Date	Details	£
20-4			20-4		
30 Apr	Purchases Day Book PDB19	72			

Purchases Account (GL5100)

Dr Date	Details	£	Cr Date	Details	£
20-4			20-4		
30 Apr	Purchases Day Book PDB19	360			

PURCHASES LEDGER

Midland Supplies (PL045)

Dr Date	Details	£	Cr Date	Details		£
20-4			20-4			
			1 Apr	Purchases	PDB19	144

Swan Equipment (PL112)

Dr Date	Details	£	Cr Date	Details		£
20-4			20-4			
			14 Apr	Purchases	PDB19	96
			28 Apr	Purchases	PDB19	192

Purchases Returns Day Book						PRDB7
Date	Details	Credit note number	Account code	Total	VAT	Net
20-4				£	£	£
9 Apr	Midland Supplies	104	PL045	48	8	40
30 Apr	Swan Equipment	X102	PL112	96	16	80
30 Apr	Totals for month			144	24	120
				GL2350	GL2200	GL5110

GENERAL LEDGER

Dr   **Purchases Ledger Control Account** (GL2350)   Cr

Date	Details	£	Date	Details	£
20-4			20-4		
30 Apr	Purchases Returns Day Book PRDB7	144	30 Apr	Purchases Day Book PDB19	*432

Dr   **Value Added Tax Account** (GL2200)   Cr

Date	Details	£	Date	Details	£
20-4			20-4		
30 Apr	Purchases Day Book PDB19	*72	30 Apr	Purchases Returns Day Book PRDB7	24

Dr   **Purchases Returns Account** (GL5110)   Cr

Date	Details	£	Date	Details	£
20-4			20-4		
			30 Apr	Purchases Returns Day Book PRDB7	120

PURCHASES LEDGER

Dr   **Midland Supplies** (PL045)   Cr

Date	Details	£	Date	Details	£
20-4			20-4		
9 Apr	Purchases Returns PRDB7	48	1 Apr	Purchases PDB19	*144

Dr   **Swan Equipment** (PL112)   Cr

Date	Details	£	Date	Details	£
20-4			20-4		
30 Apr	Purchases Returns PRDB7	96	14 Apr	Purchases PDB19	*96
			28 Apr	Purchases PDB19	*192

* transactions entered previously

Further chapter summary points follow on page 157.

Chapter Summary

The diagrams on the next two pages summarise the material we have studied in this chapter. They show the procedures for recording transactions in the accounting system for credit purchases and purchases returns.

Further chapter summary points follow on page 157.

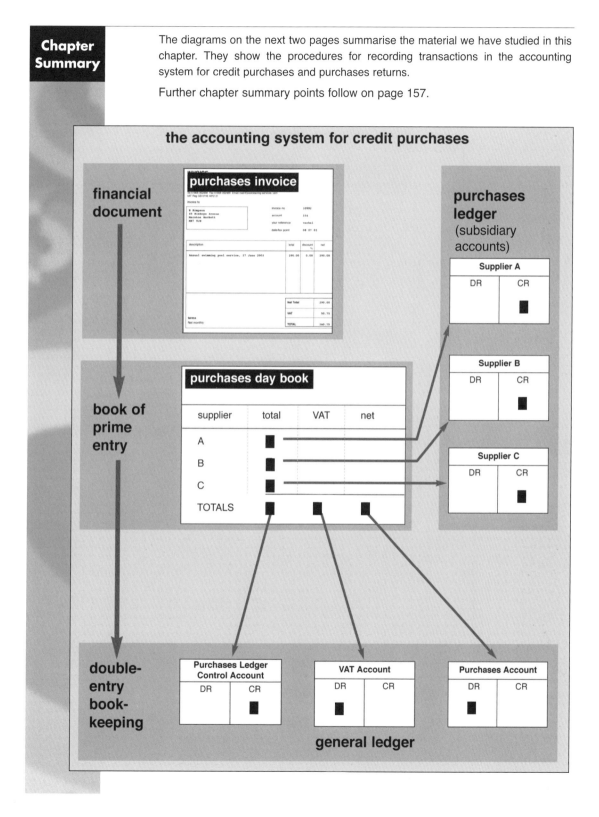

the accounting system for credit purchases

financial document

purchases invoice

book of prime entry

purchases day book

supplier	total	VAT	net
A			
B			
C			
TOTALS			

purchases ledger (subsidiary accounts)

Supplier A

DR	CR

Supplier B

DR	CR

Supplier C

DR	CR

double-entry book-keeping

Purchases Ledger Control Account

DR	CR

VAT Account

DR	CR

Purchases Account

DR	CR

general ledger

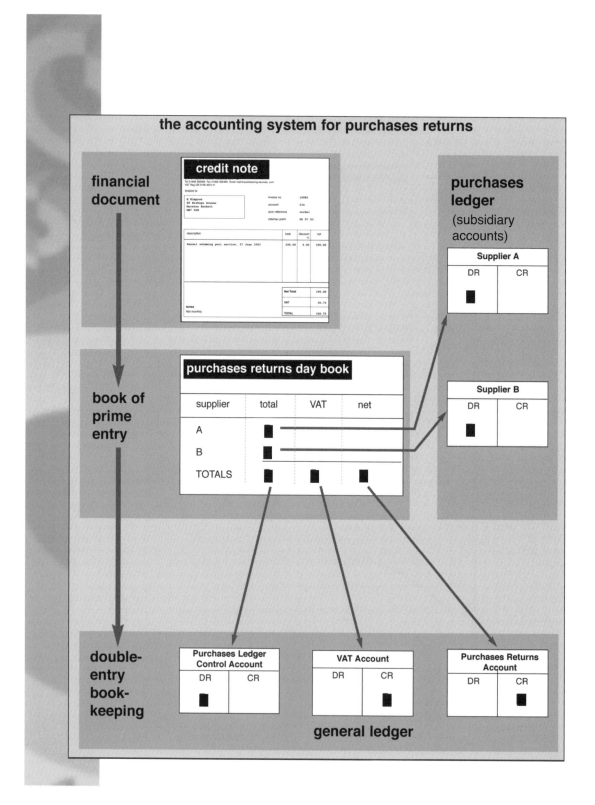

the accounting system for purchases returns

financial document

credit note

book of prime entry

purchases returns day book

supplier	total	VAT	net
A	■		
B	■		
TOTALS	■	■	■

purchases ledger
(subsidiary accounts)

Supplier A

DR	CR
■	

Supplier B

DR	CR
■	

double-entry book-keeping

Purchases Ledger Control Account

DR	CR
■	

VAT Account

DR	CR
	■

Purchases Returns Account

DR	CR
	■

general ledger

■ The accounting system comprises a number of specific stages of recording and presenting financial transactions:
  - financial documents
  - books of prime entry (eg day books)
  - double-entry bookkeeping
  - trial balance

■ The financial documents relating to credit purchases are:
  - purchases invoices
  - credit notes received

■ Purchases day book is the book of prime entry for credit purchases. It is prepared from purchases invoices received from suppliers.

■ Purchases returns day book is the book of prime entry for purchases returns. It is prepared from credit notes received from suppliers.

■ Analysed purchases and purchases returns day books are used when a business wishes to analyse its purchases between different types of expenditure.

■ Recording credit purchases in the double-entry system uses:
  - financial documents, purchases invoices
  - book of prime entry, purchases day book
  - double-entry accounts in the general ledger
  - subsidiary accounts in the purchases ledger

■ Recording purchases returns in the double-entry system uses:
  - financial documents, credit notes received from suppliers
  - book of prime entry, purchases returns day book
  - double-entry accounts in the general ledger
  - subsidiary accounts in the purchases ledger

purchases — the purchase of goods with the intention that they should be resold at a profit

revenue expenditure — the cost of purchases and running costs of the business

capital expenditure — the cost of asset items other than for resale, purchased in connection with the running of the business, eg buildings, shop fittings

purchases day book — book of prime entry prepared from purchases invoices

purchases returns — goods purchased on credit which are returned to the supplier

purchases returns day book — book of prime entry prepared from credit notes received from suppliers

analysed day books — day books which incorporate analysis columns, for example between
- goods bought for resale, often split between different types of goods
- purchases made by different departments

general ledger — ledger section which includes
- purchases account
- purchases returns account
- purchases ledger control account
- Value Added Tax account

purchases ledger — subsidiary ledger section which contains the subsidiary accounts of the trade payables (suppliers)

subsidiary account — a subsidiary ledger (eg purchases ledger) account which provides a record of individual amounts (eg owing by the business to trade payables)

Activities

7.1 Which one of the following is a book of prime entry?

(a) purchases account

(b) Value Added Tax account

(c) purchases returns day book

(d) purchases ledger account of M Ostrowski

Answer (a) or (b) or (c) or (d)

7.2 Which one of the following is in the right order?

(a) purchases returns day book; purchases ledger control account; credit note issued; purchases returns account; supplier's account

(b) purchases returns account; supplier's account; purchases ledger control account; purchases returns day book; credit note issued

(c) purchases returns day book; purchases returns account; purchases ledger control account; supplier's account; credit note issued

(d) credit note issued; purchases returns day book; purchases returns account; purchases ledger control account; supplier's account

Answer (a) or (b) or (c) or (d)

7.3 Which one of the following are the correct general ledger entries for a purchases returns transaction?

(a) debit purchases ledger control; debit VAT; credit purchases returns

(b) debit purchases ledger control; credit purchases returns; credit VAT

(c) debit purchases returns; debit VAT; credit purchases ledger control

(d) debit purchases returns; credit purchases ledger control; credit VAT

Answer (a) or (b) or (c) or (d)

7.4 Explain in note format:

(a) the principles of recording a credit purchases transaction in the accounting system

(b) the principles of recording a purchases returns transaction in the accounting system

For Activities 7.5 and 7.6:

- work in pounds and pence, where appropriate
- the rate of Value Added Tax is to be calculated at 20% (when calculating VAT amounts, you should ignore fractions of a penny, ie round down to a whole penny)
- use a coding system incorporating the following:

purchases day book	– PDB36
purchases returns day book	– PRDB11

purchases ledger account numbers	
AMC Enterprises	– PL520
S Green	– PL574
I Johnstone	– PL604
Mercia Manufacturing	– PL627
L Murphy	– PL659
Severn Supplies	– PL721

general ledger account numbers	
purchases ledger control account	– GL2350
purchases account	– GL5100
purchases returns account	– GL5110
Value Added Tax account	– GL2200

7.5   During April 20-5, Wyvern Wholesalers had the following credit transactions:

20-5

2 Apr	Purchased goods from Severn Supplies £250 + VAT, invoice no 6789
5 Apr	Purchased goods from I Johnstone £210 + VAT, invoice no A241
9 Apr	Purchased goods from L Murphy £185 + VAT, invoice no 2456
15 Apr	Purchased goods from Mercia Manufacturing £180 + VAT, invoice no X457
19 Apr	Purchased goods from AMC Enterprises £345 + VAT, invoice no AMC 456
26 Apr	Purchased goods from S Green £395 + VAT, invoice no 2846

You are to:

(a)   Enter the above transactions in Wyvern Wholesaler's purchases day book for April 20-5, using the format shown on the next page.

(b)   Record the accounting entries in Wyvern Wholesaler's general ledger and purchases ledger.

(Note that you will need to retain these ledger accounts for use with Activity 7.6)

Purchases Day Book						PDB36
Date	Details	Invoice number	Account code	Total £	VAT £	Net £

7.6 The following are the purchases returns of Wyvern Wholesalers for April 20-5. They are to be:

(a) entered in the purchases returns day book for April 20-5, using the format shown on the next page

(b) recorded in the general ledger and purchases ledger (use the ledgers already prepared in the answer to Activity 7.5)

20-5

7 Apr Returned goods to Severn Supplies £50 + VAT, credit note no 225 received

14 Apr Returned goods to L Murphy £80 + VAT, credit note no X456 received

21 Apr Returned goods to AMC Enterprises £125 + VAT, credit note no 3921 received

29 Apr Returned goods to S Green £68 + VAT, credit note no SG247 received

Purchases Returns Day Book						PRDB11
Date	Details	Credit note number	Account code	Total £	VAT £	Net £

7.7 You are employed by Hussein Limited as an accounts assistant. The business has a manual accounting system. Double-entry takes place in the general ledger; individual accounts of trade payables are kept as subsidiary accounts in the purchases ledger. The VAT rate is 20%.

Notes:
- show your answer with a tick, words or figures, as appropriate
- coding is not required

(a) The following credit transactions all took place on 30 April 20-4 and have been entered into the purchases day book as shown below. No entries have yet been made into the ledger system.

Purchases day book

Date 20-4	Details	Invoice number	Total £	VAT £	Net £
30 April	Seng Ltd	4517	1,152	192	960
30 April	Peall & Co	2384	2,832	472	2,360
30 April	Knightons	A761	4,176	696	3,480
30 April	Galeazzi plc	7248	1,488	248	1,240
	Totals		9,648	1,608	8,040

What will be the entries in the general ledger?

General ledger

Account name	Amount £	Debit ✓	Credit ✓

What will be the entries in the purchases ledger?

Purchases ledger

Account name	Amount £	Debit ✓	Credit ✓

(b) The following credit transactions all took place on 30 April 20-4 and have been entered into the purchases returns day book as shown below. No entries have yet been made into the ledger system.

Purchases returns day book

Date 20-4	Details	Credit note number	Total £	VAT £	Net £
30 April	Martin & Co	381	1,056	176	880
30 April	Wentworth Stores	C48	672	112	560
	Totals		1,728	288	1,440

What will be the entries in the general ledger?

General ledger

Account name	Amount £	Debit ✓	Credit ✓

What will be the entries in the purchases ledger?

Purchases ledger

Account name	Amount £	Debit ✓	Credit ✓

7.8   The following is taken from the coding lists used at a business called Fashion Trading.

Supplier	Purchases ledger account code
Bingham Fashions	BIN001
Bourne Stores	BOU002
Elite Trading	ELI001
Green Dragon	GRE001
Guest & Co	GUE002
High Society	HIG001
Modes Ltd	MOD001
Myers Trading	MYE002
Treetop Stores	TRE001
Wragby Ltd	WRA001
Zeta & Co	ZET001

You are to set up the purchases ledger account codes for the new suppliers shown below.

Supplier	Purchases ledger account code
Bridon Ltd	
Foster & Co	
Hirst & Co	

7.9 Purchases invoices have been prepared and partially entered in the purchases day book, as shown below.

(a) Complete the entries in the purchases day book by inserting the appropriate figures for each invoice

(b) Total the last five columns of the purchases day book

Purchases day book

Date 20XX	Details	Invoice number	Total £	VAT £	Net £	Purchases type 1 £	Purchases type 2 £
30 June	Canoy Ltd	C350	1,608		1,340	1,340	
30 June	McVeigh & Co	5148		390			1,950
30 June	Robinsons	R/862	2,952			2,460	
	Totals						

8 Prepare payments to suppliers

this chapter covers...

In Chapter 6 'Process documents from suppliers' we described the financial documents dealt with by a purchaser of goods and services on credit. These documents included the purchase invoice, credit note, delivery note and goods received note.

In this chapter we describe the next stage in the process – the preparation of the documentation needed when payment is to be made for the goods or services purchased.

The chapter covers the following areas:

■ a brief review of the purchasing process

■ checking a statement of account received from a supplier against the transactions in the account of the supplier in the purchases ledger

■ identifying any discrepancies between a statement of account and transactions in the account of the supplier in the purchases ledger

■ calculating the amount due to each supplier on the correct payment date

■ preparing remittance advices for making payment by cheque or through BACS, the bank computer direct payment system

This chapter will not go into detail about the various bank payment systems. These are fully explained in the Osborne Books text 'Bookkeeping 2 Tutorial'.

A REVIEW OF THE PURCHASING PROCESS

When a business makes a purchase of goods on credit it deals with a number of financial documents. These were covered in Chapter 5 and include:

- **purchase order** – issued by the buyer ordering the goods
- **delivery note** – sent with the goods by the supplier
- **goods received note** – details of goods received and any discrepancies
- **purchase invoice** – received from the supplier, setting out what is owed
- **purchase credit note** – any refund to the buyer's account for missing, damaged or incorrect goods or any mistakes on the invoice

The next stage – dealt with in this chapter – is:

- the receipt of the supplier's **statement of account** setting out what is owed – the transactions on the statement should be checked with the supplier's account in the purchases ledger of the buyer
- the preparation of a **remittance advice** by the buyer, advising the supplier that payment is being made

This stage, and its place in the process, is shown at the bottom of the diagram below.

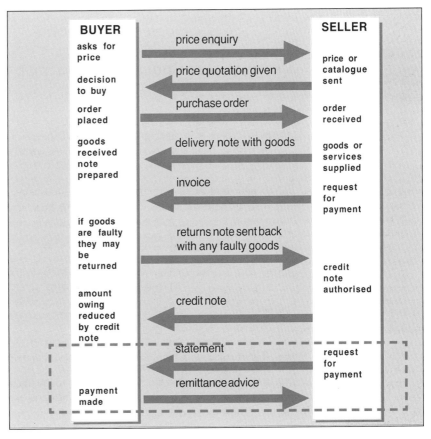

RECONCILING THE SUPPLIER STATEMENT OF ACCOUNT

Chapter 6 described the processes of checking all the purchases documentation to identify and deal with any discrepancies. The documents involved are:

- the delivery note and the actual goods received (possibly using a goods received note)
- the supplier invoices and credit notes for calculation errors
- the supplier invoices and credit notes against the purchase order

By the time that all these checks have been made and the invoices and credit notes have been authorised, the buyer should settle up and pay the **supplier's account in the purchases ledger**. This account should contain details of all the transactions such as payments, purchases and purchases returns. The account should in fact mirror all the items which will appear in the supplier's **statement of account**. See the next page for an example of a statement of account and the supplier account in the purchases ledger. Compare the two. This process is known as **reconciliation**, which basically means 'tying up' the transactions.

This is all illustrated in the Case Study which follows.

Case Study

KNITWICK – SUPPLIER STATEMENT RECONCILIATION

situation

Knitwick Traders is a clothing company which specialises in fashion wear. It has a regular trading relationship with Medici Importers which supplies it with high quality Italian clothes.

Medici Importers sends statements of account to Knitwick at the end of each month and Knitwick normally settles the account at the beginning of the next month. During the month of November 20-5 the following documents were sent to Knitwick by Medici Importers. They were checked by Knitwick and were found to be correct.

2 invoices:	8 November	Ref 4312	£850.00
	14 November	Ref 4367	£120.00
1 credit note:	20 November	Ref 534	£85.00

In addition, Knitwick sent £674.50 in settlement of October's account to Medici Importer's bank account through the BACS system in the first week of November.

In the first week of December, Knitwick received the statement of account shown on the next page. You have been asked to reconcile the statement with the purchases ledger account for Medici Importers also shown on the next page.

STATEMENT OF ACCOUNT

MEDICI IMPORTERS

8 San Marco Avenue, Broadfield, BR2 8DC
Tel 01908 765101 Fax 01908 765109 Email info@medicimporters.co.uk
VAT REG GB 0532 4672 21

TO

Knitwick Traders
Unit 14 Landseer Estate
Hull
HU9 6CV

account   2894

date   30 11 20-5

date	details	debit £		credit £		balance £
01 11 20-5	Balance b/f	674.50	✓			674.50
05 11 20-5	BACS payment			674.50	✓	00.00
08 11 20-5	Invoice 4312	850.00	✓			850.00
14 11 20-5	Invoice 4367	120.00	✓			970.00
20 11 20-5	Credit note 534			85.00	✓	885.00

Electronic payments: pay Medici Importers at National
Bank, Account 76528607, Sort code 54 12 33

TOTAL   885.00

Debit				Purchases Ledger Medici Importers Account		Credit		
20-5	**Details**	**£**	**p**	**20-5**	**Details**		**£**	**p**
5 Nov	Bank	674	50	1 Nov	Balance b/d	✓	674	50
20 Nov	Purchases returns	85	00	8 Nov	Purchases	✓	850	00
				14 Nov	Purchases	✓	120	00

solution

Knitwick will compare the two documents and tick off the items which appear in both documents. These are shown here in the two different grey boxes for purposes of illustration only.

All the transactions are accounted for – there are no unticked amounts which might indicate some form of discrepancy.

This means that the two documents have now been 'reconciled' – ie they both tie up with each other and payment of the account – the £885.00 owing – will be authorised and made on the due date.

DEALING WITH DISCREPANCIES

The Case Study on the previous two pages has shown a situation where all the documentation is correct and has been reconciled; all is well and payment can then be authorised and paid on the due date.

It is assumed here that the relevant financial documents – eg invoices and credit notes – have already been checked for accuracy and are free from any discrepancies.

But there may sometimes be discrepancies between the **supplier's statement of account** and the supplier's account kept in the buyer's **purchases ledger**. These will need to be sorted out before payment can be made.

These problems may be sorted out at accounts assistant level, or if the problem is more serious, by a line manager. Examples include:

■ **an invoice or credit note which appears on the supplier's statement, but for the wrong amount**

– the document will be held by the buyer and the amount can be verified, so this is likely to be an error made by the supplier when entering the amount in the accounts; it will need to be queried by the buyer and investigated and put right by the supplier

■ **an invoice or credit note is on the supplier's statement and not in the buyer's purchases ledger**

– this could be an invoice or credit note not posted to the buyer's purchases ledger, or to the wrong supplier's account, by the buyer; this should be investigated and if there is an error by the buyer, included in the payment of account

■ **an invoice or credit note is in the buyer's purchases ledger and not on the supplier's statement**

– this could be an invoice or credit note not posted to the supplier's accounts, or posted to the wrong customer account by the supplier; this item should be queried by the buyer and, if there is an error made by the supplier, included in the payment of account

■ **an invoice or credit note which appears twice on the supplier's statement**

– this is an obvious duplication of an invoice or credit note by the supplier (it does happen!); the supplier should be notified of the error and the amount not included in the payment of account

The lesson here is that accurate reconciliation of the supplier statement and purchases ledger account is very important: if a payment is made and there is an undetected discrepancy, it can be very difficult to put things right.

INVOICE AUTHORISATION AND DISPUTED INVOICES

statement or no statement?

It has been assumed in this chapter so far that suppliers will send out statements as a matter of course.

If statements are issued, businesses generally pay regularly on receipt of the statement, as this is an easier way of calculating payment. This is the situation set out in the Case Study earlier in this chapter (see pages 168-169).

In commercial practice, however, **statements are not always sent out by suppliers**. Some suppliers rely instead on each customer making payment of invoices when they are due, adjusting for any credit notes issued.

Whatever method is used by a buyer for sorting out the payment of the account, certain principles remain the same:

- invoices should be paid by the due date, which can be calculated from the terms of the invoice
- invoices should be **checked** and **authorised** before the payment date

invoice authorisation

In most organisations invoices that have been checked are passed to the person in the Accounts Department who deals with making payments to suppliers. These invoices will then have to be **authorised** for payment.

When an invoice is checked and found to be correct, the person carrying out the check will usually mark the document and authorise it for payment. This authorisation can take a number of forms:

- the checker can initial and date the invoice, and tick it or write 'pay' as an authorisation
- the organisation may have a special rubber stamp which can be used in the authorisation process – this stamp may also provide space for **coding**, eg the cost code (the account number for the type of expense) and the purchase order reference number which can be entered in the purchases day book and also used for internal filing purposes; it may also contain the signature or initials of the person who has authority to authorise the invoice for payment

This procedure of authorisation helps the efficiency of the organisation:

- the checker's initials will be there in case of any future query on the invoice, eg an undetected error
- the invoice will be in the system for payment on the due date

disputed invoices

In this chapter so far we have assumed that a business

■ will pay the total amount shown on the statement

■ will pay all the invoices that are due and authorised for payment

There are times, however, when a business might decide that an invoice on a statement should not be paid. Normally in an accounts office you will be able to see this on the statement because the invoice will not be ticked, or you may get a note from your line manager telling you not to pay certain items. The invoice may be **disputed** with the supplier: for example, your business may claim that the goods supplied are incorrect.

Now read the following Case Study which explains how to calculate a payment which involves a disputed invoice.

Case Study

ALDERSGATE SUPPLIES – PAYMENT OF ACCOUNT

situation

You work in the Accounts Department of Krumm & Co which is supplied with electrical equipment by Aldersgate Supplies.

It is your job to prepare the payments for all suppliers at the beginning of each month. The latest statement from Aldersgate Supplies is shown on the next page and an email dated 4 December from your supervisor is set out below.

The ticks on the statement indicate the items that are recorded in the purchases ledger and will have to be taken into account when payment is made.

---

email

from   henry@krumm.co.uk
subject   Aldersgate Supplies account - disputed invoice
date   4 December 20-5 12:01:11 GMT
to   a.student@krumm.co.uk

Hi Aslam
Please note that Invoice 16700 for £450 is in dispute. Aldersgate clearly misread our purchase order and sent the wrong equipment, but still claim that they sent us the right stuff. On no account should this invoice be paid until the dispute is settled. Thanks.

Regards
Henry

STATEMENT OF ACCOUNT
ALDERSGATE SUPPLIES
10 Aldersgate Street, London EC1A 7GH
Tel 0207 7051017 Fax 0207 7051231 Email sales@aldersgatesupplies.co.uk
VAT REG GB 6733 8372 99

TO

Krumm & Co 56 Eccles Road Bolton BL7 4DF		account	26742
		date	30 11 20-5

date	details	debit £	credit £	balance £
01 11 20-5	Balance b/f	1250.70 ✓		1250.70
04 11 20-5	BACS payment		1250.70 ✓	00.00
08 11 20-5	Invoice 16700	450.00		450.00
14 11 20-5	Invoice 16810	790.00 ✓		1240.00
20 11 20-5	Credit note 534		79.00 ✓	1161.00
27 11 20-5	Invoice 16985	800.00 ✓		1961.00

Electronic payments: pay Aldersgate Supplies at HRBC Bank, Account 79001875, Sort code 41 22 01	**TOTAL**	1961.00

solution

The payment amount is worked out as follows:

calculation (£)

1 The first two items represent the balance outstanding at the beginning of November and then the payment made by Krumm & Co. They are the same amount (a debit and a credit) and therefore cancel each other out.

0

2 Invoice 16700 for £450 is in dispute and so is not included

0

3 Invoice 16810 for £790 is added on

+ 790.00

4 Credit note 534 for £79 is deducted

– 79.00

5 Invoice 16985 for £800 is added on

+ 800.00

The total payment to be made to Aldersgate Supplies is £1511

= £1511.00

The next step is to prepare a remittance advice note to advise Aldersgate Supplies of the payment being made through the banking system.

PREPARING REMITTANCE ADVICES

definition

As we saw in Chapter 6, a **remittance advice** is a note which can be posted, faxed or emailed, stating that a certain amount of money has been sent by a credit customer to a supplier in settlement of an account. A remittance advice is used:

- **to accompany a cheque** – a practice which is decreasing in use as fewer cheques are now used to make payment
- to advise the sending of a payment **direct to the seller's bank account** through **BACS** or **Faster Payments** electronic payment systems

completing the remittance advice

A remittance advice normally takes one of two forms:

- **a list of all the items which make up the payment**

    This is very useful for the supplier as it will enable the supplier's accounts department to reconcile the incoming payment with the customer's account in the sales ledger by ticking off all the items. Sometimes, if the account is very active and a computer accounting system is used, the remittance advice may contain hundreds of items and take up a number of pages. To make things simple in this text and in your studies, remittance advices are normally restricted to just a few items.

- **notification of the total amount**

    This is the simplest form of remittance advice: it just sets out the fact that a payment for a certain amount is being made by cheque or by BACS.

A cheque remittance advice listing individual transactions is shown below.

An explanation of the details that have to be completed on a BACS remittance advice is given on the next page, continuing the Case Study.

TO	REMITTANCE ADVICE	FROM
Cool Socks Limited Unit 45 Elgar Estate, Broadfield, BR7 4ER	31 October 20-3	**Trends** 4 Friar Street Broadfield BR1 3RF

date	your reference	our reference	payment amount
01 10 20-3	INVOICE 787923	47609	283.20
10 10 20-3	CREDIT NOTE 12157	47609	(28.32)
		CHEQUE TOTAL	254.88

Case Study

ALDERSGATE SUPPLIES – REMITTANCE ADVICE

situation – continued

You work in the Accounts Department of Krumm & Co which has a supplier, Aldersgate Supplies. You are asked to complete the remittance advice advising that a BACS payment is being sent direct to the bank account of Aldersgate Supplies.

solution

The completed document is shown below.

REMITTANCE ADVICE

FROM:
Krumm & Co
56 Eccles Road
Bolton BL7 4DF

TO
Aldersgate Supplies **1**
10 Aldersgate Street, London EC1A 7GH

03 12 20-5 **2**

date **3**	your reference **4**	our reference **5**	payment amount £ **6**
17 11 20-5	Invoice 16810	PO98756	790.00
24 11 20-5	Credit note 534	PO98756	(79.00)
30 11 20-5	Invoice 16985	PO98792	800.00
		TOTAL	1511.00 **7**

8
THIS AMOUNT HAS BEEN PAID BY BACS CREDIT TRANSFER DIRECTLY INTO YOUR BANK ACCOUNT AT HRBC BANK ACCOUNT NO 79001875 SORT CODE 41 22 01

The following details have been completed by Krumm & Co:

1   at the top left, the name and address of the supplier – Aldersgate Supplies

2   at the top right, the date of the transfer of the money – 3 December 20-5

3   'date' – the dates of each of the documents listed

4   'your reference' – the description and supplier reference numbers of the invoices and credit note listed

5   'our reference' – Krumm & Co's purchase order numbers relating to the listed documents

6   'payment amount' – the amounts of the invoices and the credit note; note that the credit note amount is in brackets because it is deducted and not added

7   'total' – the amount being transferred to Aldersgate Supplies' bank account

8   at the bottom – details of the bank account number and sort code number of Aldersgate Supplies' bank (HRBC)

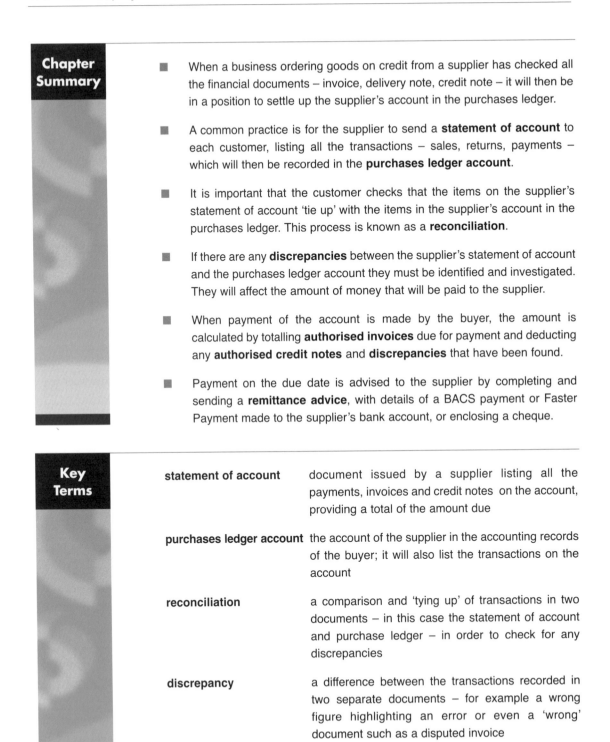

Chapter Summary

- When a business ordering goods on credit from a supplier has checked all the financial documents – invoice, delivery note, credit note – it will then be in a position to settle up the supplier's account in the purchases ledger.

- A common practice is for the supplier to send a **statement of account** to each customer, listing all the transactions – sales, returns, payments – which will then be recorded in the **purchases ledger account**.

- It is important that the customer checks that the items on the supplier's statement of account 'tie up' with the items in the supplier's account in the purchases ledger. This process is known as a **reconciliation**.

- If there are any **discrepancies** between the supplier's statement of account and the purchases ledger account they must be identified and investigated. They will affect the amount of money that will be paid to the supplier.

- When payment of the account is made by the buyer, the amount is calculated by totalling **authorised invoices** due for payment and deducting any **authorised credit notes** and **discrepancies** that have been found.

- Payment on the due date is advised to the supplier by completing and sending a **remittance advice**, with details of a BACS payment or Faster Payment made to the supplier's bank account, or enclosing a cheque.

Key Terms

statement of account	document issued by a supplier listing all the payments, invoices and credit notes on the account, providing a total of the amount due
purchases ledger account	the account of the supplier in the accounting records of the buyer; it will also list the transactions on the account
reconciliation	a comparison and 'tying up' of transactions in two documents – in this case the statement of account and purchase ledger – in order to check for any discrepancies
discrepancy	a difference between the transactions recorded in two separate documents – for example a wrong figure highlighting an error or even a 'wrong' document such as a disputed invoice
remittance advice	an advice sent to a supplier advising the sending of an amount of money, either by cheque or direct to the supplier's account through the banking system

Activities

8.1   The two documents that have to be reconciled to work out the amount owing to a supplier are:

(a)   the invoice and the remittance advice

(b)   the supplier statement and the remittance advice

(c)   the supplier statement and the supplier's purchases ledger account in the books of the buyer

(d)   the remittance advice and the supplier's purchases ledger account in the books of the buyer

State which one of these four options is the correct answer.

8.2   The following must be checked and authorised for payment before a supplier payment can be prepared by a business that has received goods on credit terms:

(a)   supplier invoice

(b)   delivery note

(c)   remittance advice

(d)   supplier account in the purchases ledger

State which one of these four options is the correct answer.

8.3   If you found two purchases invoices for £250 with the same date and invoice number listed in a supplier statement you would need to query it and:

(a)   add £250 to the amount owing to the supplier as shown on the statement

(b)   deduct £250 from the amount owing to the supplier as shown on the statement

(c)   enter the invoice amount in the supplier's account in the purchases ledger

(d)   pay the total amount owing as shown on the supplier statement

State which one of these four options is the correct answer.

8.4   A remittance advice is used:

(a)   instead of a cheque when paying a supplier

(b)   instead of a BACS payment or Faster Payment when paying a supplier

(c)   to accompany a cheque when paying a supplier

(d)   to request payment when returning goods

State which one of these four options is the correct answer.

8.5 You work in the Accounts Department of Hemsley Ltd. One of your routine tasks is to reconcile the supplier statements of account with the supplier accounts in the purchases ledger.

You are to reconcile the statement of account and purchases ledger account of your supplier Luxon Traders shown below. If you find any discrepancies:

- explain what the error could be

- suggest what you would do to resolve the problem

- state the amount you think the payment should be

STATEMENT OF ACCOUNT

LUXON TRADERS
56 High Street, Fowey, Cornwall, TR4 9DS
info@luxontraders.co.uk

TO

Hemsley Limited
6 Enterprise Park
Luton
LU7 3BN

account   9133

date   31 03 20-1

date	details	debit £	credit £	balance £
01 03 20-1	Balance b/f	156.00		156.00
05 03 20-1	BACS payment		156.00	00.00
08 03 20-1	Invoice 76333	150.00		150.00
08 03 20-1	Invoice 76333	150.00		300.00
20 03 20-1	Credit note 923		50.00	250.00
	TOTAL			**250.00**

Debit	Purchases Ledger: Luxon Traders Account					Credit	
20-1	Details	£	p	20-1	Details	£	p
5 Mar	Bank	156	00	1 Mar	Balance b/d	156	00
20 Mar	Purchases returns	50	00	8 Mar	Purchases	150	00

8.6 You work in the Accounts Department of R J Powell Ltd. One of your routine tasks is to reconcile the supplier statements of account with the supplier accounts in the purchases ledger.

You are to reconcile the statement of account and purchases ledger account of your supplier A Krauss Limited shown below. If you find any discrepancies:

- explain what the error could be

- suggest what you would do to resolve the problem

- state the amount you think the payment should be

STATEMENT OF ACCOUNT

A Krauss Limited

213 Farringdon Road, Latcham, LA4 5FG
sales@akrausstrading.co.uk

TO
R J Powell Limited
48,Heathside Street
Broadheath
WR2 8NB

account   32123

date   30 04 20-1

date	details	debit £	credit £	balance £
01 04 20-1	Balance b/f	990.00		990.00
07 04 20-1	BACS payment		990.00	00.00
09 04 20-1	Invoice 12856	233.25		233.25
19 04 20-1	Invoice 12932	109.50		342.75
	TOTAL			342.75

Debit	Purchases Ledger: A Krauss Limited Account					Credit		
20-1	**Details**	**£**	**p**	**20-1**	**Details**		**£**	**p**
7 Apr	Bank	990	00	1 Apr	Balance b/d		990	00
22 Apr	Purchases returns	72	90	9 Apr	Purchases		233	25
				19 Apr	Purchases		109	50

8.7   Complete the remittance advice on the bottom of the page, using the details and the ticked items on the statement shown below. The purchase order number for the invoices are PO85262 and PO85271 and for credit note PO85248. The bank details are on the advice. The date is 3 October.

STATEMENT OF ACCOUNT
ALDERSGATE SUPPLIES

10 Aldersgate Street, London EC1A 7GH
Tel 0207 7051017 Fax 0207 7051231 Email sales@aldersgatesupplies.co.uk
VAT REG GB 6733 8372 99

TO

Hetherington Limited
Unit 23 Wessex Estate
Langborne Road
Seatown SE8 5VZ

account   26742

date   30 09 20–5

date	details	debit £	credit £	balance £
01 09 20-5	Balance b/f	550.00 ✓		550.00
04 09 20-5	BACS payment		550.00 ✓	00.00
08 09 20-5	Invoice 10945	120.75 ✓		120.75
14 09 20-5	Invoice 10963	380.25 ✓		501.00
20 09 20-5	Credit note 109		46.00 ✓	455.00

Electronic payments: pay Aldersgate Supplies at
HRBC Bank, Account 79001875, Sort code 41 22 01

TOTAL	455.00

BACS REMITTANCE ADVICE

FROM:
Hetherington Limited
Unit 23 Wessex Estate
Langborne Road
Seatown SE8 5VZ

TO

date:

date	your reference	our reference	payment amount £
			TOTAL

THIS AMOUNT HAS BEEN PAID BY BACS CREDIT TRANSFER DIRECTLY INTO YOUR BANK ACCOUNT
AT HRBC BANK ACCOUNT NO 79001875, SORT CODE 41 22 01

8.8 Hetherington Limited also sends out cheques with some remittance advices.

Complete the cheque remittance advice and cheque set out below. You should not sign the cheque as only a director has authority to do so. The settlement details are as follows:

Date: 5 June 20-5

Supplier: Sutherland & Co, 67 Great March Street, Eastwick, EA3 9JN

Invoice 7856 for £345.90 dated 23 May 20-5, purchase order 472984

Credit note 4562 for £87.50 dated 29 May 20-5, purchase order 472975

REMITTANCE ADVICE

FROM:
Hetherington Limited
Unit 23 Wessex Estate
Langborne Road
Seatown SE8 5VZ

TO

date:

date	your reference	our reference	payment amount £

CHEQUE TOTAL

Southern Bank PLC
Mereford Branch
16 Broad Street, Mereford MR1 7TR

date

97-76-54

Pay

only

Account payee only

£

HETHERINGTON LTD

123456   97 76 54   68384939

Director

9 Three column cash book

this chapter covers...

The cash book records the money transactions of the business, such as receiving payments from customers, and making payments to suppliers and for other expenses. Such money transactions are received and paid either in cash, by cheque, BACS (the bank computer payment transfer system), debit or credit card, and Faster Payments.

This is the first of two chapters dealing with the cash book:

- in this chapter we look at how financial transactions are recorded in a three column cash book with money columns for bank, cash and settlement discount
- in the next chapter we extend the money columns of the cash book to include analysis between VAT, trade receivables, trade payables, cash sales, cash purchases, income and expenses

In both chapters we see how cash is written up from financial transactions, is totalled and balanced.

The cash book of a business is usually controlled by the cashier. Entries made in cash book must be transferred to the general ledger, business's ledger and purchases ledger, for example transfers in respect of:

- cash sales
- cash purchases
- receipts from credit customers
- payments to credit suppliers
- settlement discounts allowed
- settlement discounts received
- other payments and receipts, eg non-current assets, expenses paid, loans received and repaid

There are two Case Studies in this chapter. The first is for a business that is just setting up; the second is for an established business receiving money from customers and making payments to suppliers. In both Case Studies we examine how the financial transactions are transferred from cash book to the ledgers.

THE CASH BOOK IN THE ACCOUNTING SYSTEM

The cash book is used to record the money transactions of the business. It is the book of prime entry for bank receipts and payments. There are two ways in which the cash book is used in the accounting system:

■ either the cash book combines the roles of the book of prime entry and double-entry bookkeeping

■ or the cash book is the book of prime entry only and a separate bank control account is kept in general ledger in order to complete double-entry bookkeeping

These two methods will be examined in detail in Chapter 10.

Note that, as well as the cash book, businesses often have a petty cash book which is used for low-value cash payments for purchases and expenses. We will study petty cash book in Chapter 11.

USES OF THE CASH BOOK

The cash book records the money transactions of the business, such as:

receipts

- – from cash sales
- – from trade receivables
- – loans from the bank
- – VAT refunds
- – capital introduced by the owner

payments

- – for cash purchases
- – to trade payables
- – for expenses
- – for bank loan repayments
- – for VAT payments
- – for the purchase of non-current assets, eg vehicles, office equipment
- – for drawings (money taken by the owner of the business for personal use)

Note that the cash book is the record kept by the business of its bank transactions – the bank will keep its own records, and bank statements will either be sent regularly or will be available online through internet banking.

The cash book is controlled by the cashier who:

■ records receipts and payments through the bank

■ makes payments, and prepares cheques and bank transfers for signature by those authorised to sign

■ pays cash and cheques received into the bank

■ has control over the business cash – in a cash till, cash box or safe

■ issues cash to the petty cashier who operates the petty cash book (see Chapter 11)

■ checks the accuracy of the cash and bank balances at regular intervals

It is important to note that transactions passing through the cash book must be supported by documentary evidence. In this way a link is established that can be followed through the accounting system to ensure that it is complete. This link runs through:

■ financial document

■ book of prime entry

■ double-entry accounts

This linking of the transactions is required both as a security feature within the business (to help to ensure that false and fraudulent transactions cannot be made), and also for taxation purposes.

The cashier has an important role to play within the accounting function of a business – most business activities will, at some point, involve a money transaction of either a receipt or a payment. The cash book and the cashier are therefore at the hub of the accounting system. In particular, the cashier is responsible for:

■ issuing receipts for cash (and sometimes bank transfers) received

■ making authorised payments in cash and by cheque/bank transfer against documents received (such as invoices and statements) showing the amounts due

At all times, payments can only be made by the cashier when authorised to do so by the appropriate person within the business, eg the accounts supervisor or the purchasing manager.

With so many transactions passing through the cash book, accounting procedures must include:

■ security – of cash, cheque books and internet banking, the correct authorisation of payments

■ confidentiality – that all cash/bank transactions, including cash and bank balances, are kept confidential

If the cashier has any queries about any transactions, he or she should refer them to the accounts supervisor.

LAYOUT OF THE THREE COLUMN CASH BOOK

Although a cash book can be set out in many formats to suit the requirements of a particular business, a common format is the three column cash book – so called because it has three money columns on each side. This is set out in the same way as a double-entry account, with debit and credit sides, but with several money columns on each side, as shown below:

Dr					Cash Book						Cr
Date	Details	Acc code	Discount allowed	Cash	Bank	Date	Details	Acc code	Discount received	Cash	Bank
			£	£	£				£	£	£
			money in						money out		

Note the following points:

- This layout includes both the bank account and the cash account (used for cash kept on the business premises).
- The cash and bank columns on the debit side are used for money in, ie receipts.
- The cash and bank columns on the credit side are used for money out, ie payments.
- A third money column on each side is used to record settlement discount (that is, an allowance offered for quick settlement of the amount due, eg 2% cash discount for settlement within seven days).
- The discount column on the debit side is for settlement discount allowed to customers.
- The discount received column on the credit side is for settlement discount received from suppliers.
- The discount columns are not part of the double-entry system – they are used in the cash book as a listing device or memorandum column. As we will see – later in the chapter – they are totalled and transferred into the double-entry system.
- The account code column is used to code or cross-reference to the other entry in the ledger system.

Two Case Studies now follow. The first, below, uses the cash and bank columns of the three column cash book; the second, on page 190, includes use of the discount columns. In both Case Studies we see how the cash books are written up and the data is transferred from cash book into the double-entry bookkeeping system.

Case Study

CASH BOOK FOR A NEW BUSINESS

situation

Jayne Hampson sets up a new business on 1 June 20-8. The following transactions of her business take place during the first month and are to be entered in her cash book:

1 June	Started in business with capital of £10,000 paid into the bank
4 June	Bought a delivery van for £7,500 paying by cheque
7 June	Paid rent for the month of £500 by cheque
12 June	Transferred £1,000 from bank to cash
18 June	Paid wages £500 in cash
20 June	Received a loan from the bank of £2,000
26 June	Jayne Hampson took drawings of £200 in cash

Note that Jayne Hampson's business is not registered for Value Added Tax.

solution

The cash book is written up as follows.

Dr						**Cash Book**				**CB52**		Cr
Date	Details	Acc code	Discount allowed	Cash	Bank	Date	Details	Acc code	Discount received	Cash	Bank	
			£	£	£				£	£	£	
20-8						20-8						
1 Jun	Capital	GL3100			10,000	4 Jun	Delivery van	GL0750			7,500	
12 Jun	Bank	C		1,000		7 Jun	Rent	GL6350			500	
20 Jun	Bank loan	GL2140			2,000	12 Jun	Cash	C			1,000	
						18 Jun	Wages	GL6380		500		
						26 Jun	Drawings	GL3200		200		
						30 Jun	Balances c/d			300	3,000	
				1,000	12,000					1,000	12,000	
1 Jul	Balances b/d			300	3,000							

Notes:

- Money in – eg capital introduced – has been recorded on the debit side, ie the business has gained value
- Money out – eg rent and wages paid – has been recorded on the credit side, ie the business has given value
- The balance of the cash and bank columns has been calculated as the difference between money in and money out (receipts minus payments equals the balance). Balancing of accounts is usually carried out at the end of each month where the balances are *carried down (c/d)* to the first day of the next month where they are *brought down (b/d)*. We will look in more detail at balancing the cash book later in this chapter.

From the completed cash book, we need to transfer the data into the double-entry system. To do this we need to:

- identify on which side of the cash book the transaction has been recorded – debit (money in), or credit (money out)
- record the other double-entry transaction on the opposite side of the appropriate account

The other accounts from this cash book can now be recorded and, over the next few pages, we will look at each transaction and see how each is recorded in the double-entry bookkeeping system. Note that the transaction on 12 June (transferred £1,000 from bank to cash) involves both a receipt and a payment within the cash book; it is usual to indicate both of them in the account code column with a 'C' – this stands for 'contra' and shows that both parts of the transaction are in the same book, ie no further accounting transactions are needed.

The page of the cash book is coded CB52 and this will be the cross-reference for the other ledger accounts.

Note that in this Case Study there are no entries in the discount columns. These columns will be illustrated and explained in the second Case Study on page 190.

TRANSFERS TO THE DOUBLE-ENTRY SYSTEM

capital

Capital is the amount of money invested in the business by the owner. A capital account records the amount paid into the business; the accounting entries are:

- debit cash book bank or cash column
- credit capital account

The capital transaction from Jayne Hampson's cash book is entered in capital account as follows:

GENERAL LEDGER

Dr		**Capital Account** (GL3100)			Cr
20-8		£	20-8		£
			1 Jun Bank	CB52	10,000

Note: the introduction of capital into a business is often the very first business transaction entered into the double-entry system.

non-current assets

Non-current assets are items purchased by a business for use on a long-term basis. Examples are premises, vehicles, machinery and office equipment.

When non-current assets are purchased, a separate account for each type of non-current asset is used in general ledger, eg premises account, vehicles account, machinery account, etc. The bookkeeping entries are:

– debit non-current asset account (using the appropriate account)

– credit cash book bank or cash column

The non-current asset transaction in Jayne Hampson's cash book is entered in vehicles account as follows:

GENERAL LEDGER

Dr		**Vehicles Account** (GL0750)			Cr
20-8		£	20-8		£
4 Jun Bank	CB52	7,500			

payments for expenses

Businesses pay various day-to-day expenses – revenue expenditure – such as rent, wages, electricity, telephone, vehicle running expenses, etc. A separate account is used in general ledger for each main class of revenue expenditure, eg rent account, wages account, etc.

The accounting entries are:

– debit expense account (using the appropriate account)

– credit cash book bank or cash column

The two expenses transactions in Jayne Hampson's cash book are entered in the expenses accounts as follows:

GENERAL LEDGER

Dr			Rent Account (GL6350)		Cr
20-8		£	20-8		£
7 Jun Bank	CB52	500			

Dr			Wages Account (GL6380)		Cr
20-8		£	20-8		£
18 Jun Cash	CB52	500			

loans

loan received

When a business receives a loan, eg from the bank, it is the bank column of cash book which is debited, while a loan account (in the name of the lender) is credited:

- debit cash book bank column
- credit loan account (in the name of the lender)

The loan transaction from Jayne Hampson's cash book is entered in loan account as follows:

GENERAL LEDGER

Dr			Bank Loan Account (GL2140)		Cr
20-8		£	20-8		£
			20 Jun Bank	CB52	2,000

loans repaid

A loan repayment, on the other hand (not shown in the Case Study), is recorded the opposite way round to a loan received because money is being paid from the bank to repay the lender. Therefore loan account is debited and the bank column of cash book is credited:

- debit loan account
- credit cash book bank column

Note that loans are not usually received or repaid in cash, so it is the cash book bank column that records the transaction.

drawings

Drawings is the term used when the owner takes money from the business for personal use. A drawings account is used to record such amounts; the accounting entries for withdrawal of money are:

- – debit drawings account
- – credit cash book bank or cash column

The transaction in Jayne Hampson's cash book is entered in drawings account as follows:

GENERAL LEDGER

Dr			**Drawings Account** (GL3200)			Cr
20-8		£	20-8			£
26 Jun	Cash	CB52	200			

CASH BOOK – FURTHER ASPECTS

In the first Case Study we saw how the cash book was written up for a new business. We looked at ledger transfers from the cash book for capital, drawings, non-current assets, expenses and loans.

In the second Case Study of this chapter we see a cash book for a business which receives payments from its trade receivables – including settlement discount - and makes payments to its trade payables – including settlement discount. With settlement discount, we will see how the discount columns of the cash book are used. The cash book also includes transactions for cash purchases and cash sales.

Case Study

THREE COLUMN CASH BOOK

situation

The following transactions are to be recorded in the three column cash book of Zofia Studios for the month of April 20-7:

1 April	Balances at start of month: cash £300, bank £150
4 April	Received a cheque from T Wright, a trade receivable, for £98 – we have allowed her £2 cash discount
10 April	Paid a cheque to J Crane, a trade payable, for £265 – we have received £5 cash discount

15 April	Cash purchases £275, paid in cash
18 April	Paid by cheque the account of T Lewis £120, a trade payable, deducting £3 cash discount
22 April	J Jones, a trade receivable, settles in cash her account of £80, deducting £4 cash discount
26 April	Cash sales £110, cheque received
30 April	The cash book is balanced and the balances carried down to 1 May

All cheques are banked on the day of receipt.

Note that Zofia Studios is not registered for Value Added Tax.

solution

The cash book records these transactions (as shown below) and, after they have been entered, is balanced on 30 April and the balances carried down to 1 May. The other part of each double-entry bookkeeping transaction is explained over the next few pages.

Dr															Cr
						Cash Book					**CB88**				
Date	Details	Acc code	Discount allowed	Cash	Bank		Date	Details	Acc code	Discount received	Cash	Bank			
			£	£	£					£	£	£			
20-7							20-7								
1 Apr	Balances b/d			300	150		10 Apr	J Crane (trade payable)	GL2350 PL360	5		265			
4 Apr	T Wright (trade receivable)	GL1200 SL440	2		98		15 Apr	Cash purchases	GL5100		275				
22 Apr	J Jones (trade receivable)	GL1200 SL245	4	76			18 Apr	T Lewis (trade payable)	GL2350 PL485	3		117			
26 Apr	Cash sales	GL4100			110		30 Apr	Balance c/d			101				
30 Apr	Balance c/d				24										
			6	376	382					8	376	382			
			GL6310							GL4360					
1 May	Balance b/d			101			1 May	Balance b/d				24			

BALANCING THE CASH BOOK

The cash book – like the other accounts in the double-entry system – needs to be balanced in order to show the running total of the account. For cash book, it is the cash and bank columns that are separately balanced in order to show:

■ the amount of cash held by the business

■ the amount of money in the bank or an overdraft

The cash book is balanced in the following way (using the cash book from the Case Study on page 191, as an example):

cash columns

■ add the two cash columns and subtotal in pencil (ie £376 in the debit column, and £275 in the credit column); remember to erase the subtotals afterwards

■ deduct the lower total from the higher (payments from receipts) to give the balance of cash remaining (ie £376 – £275 = £101)

■ the higher total is recorded at the bottom of both cash columns in a totals 'box' (£376)

■ the balance of cash remaining (£101) is entered as a balancing item above the totals box (on the credit side), and is brought down underneath the total on the debit side as the opening balance for next month (£101)

bank columns

■ the bank columns are dealt with in a similar way but note that, in this cash book, the balance b/d of £24 is on the credit side – this means that payments exceed receipts and indicates a bank overdraft

■ add the two bank columns and sub-total in pencil giving £358 on the debit side and £382 on the credit side

■ deducting the lower from the higher total gives £382 – £358 = £24

■ the bank balance of £24 is entered on the side with the lower sub-total – here the debit side – as balance carried down and then brought down on the credit side, below the totals line, to indicate a bank overdraft

Note that a cash balance can be brought down on the debit side only, indicating the amount of cash held. A bank balance can be brought down on either debit or credit side – a debit balance indicates money in the bank, while a credit balance indicates a bank overdraft.

It is very important to appreciate that the bank columns of cash book represent a business' own records of bank transactions and the balance at bank. The bank keeps its own records of the business' bank transactions – as shown by the bank statement.

At the end of the month, each discount column is totalled separately – no attempt should be made to balance them. At this point, amounts recorded in the columns and the totals are not part of the double-entry system. However, the two totals are transferred into the general ledger in the double-entry system as described in the following section.

LEDGER TRANSFERS FROM THE THREE COLUMN CASH BOOK

Over the next few pages we see how the entries from the three column cash book in the Case Study of Zofia Studios are transferred to the double-entry system. These transfers are for:

- receipts from credit customers
- payments to credit suppliers
- settlement discounts allowed
- settlement discounts received
- cash sales
- cash purchases

settlement discount allowed

From cash book the total of the debit side discount column (£6 in the Case Study) is:

- debited to **discount allowed account**
- credited to **sales ledger control account**

The entries for these two general ledger accounts are shown on the next two pages.

GENERAL LEDGER

Dr			Discount Allowed Account (GL6310)			Cr
20-7			£	20-7		£
30 Apr	Sales ledger control	GL1200	6			

Dr			Sales Ledger Control Account (GL1200)*			Cr
20-7		£	20-7			£
			30 Apr	Cash/Bank	CB88*	174
			30 Apr	Discount allowed	GL6310	6

* Entry in respect of receipts from trade receivables: £98 + £76.

This completes the double-entry for discount allowed in general ledger. However, the discount allowed amounts must be recorded in the subsidiary accounts of trade receivables in sales ledger.

receipts from credit customers

Discount allowed and cash or bank amounts received from trade receivables are recorded in the sales ledger accounts as follows:

SALES LEDGER

Dr		T Wright (SL440)			Cr
20-7		£	20-7		£
			4 Apr	Bank	CB88	98
			4 Apr	Discount allowed	GL6310	2

Dr		J Jones (SL245)			Cr
20-7		£	20-7		£
			22 Apr	Cash	CB88	76
			22 Apr	Discount allowed	GL6310	4

settlement discount received

From cash book the total of the credit side discount column (£8 in the Case Study) is:

- credited to **discount received account**
- debited to **purchases ledger control account**

The entries for these two general ledger accounts are:

GENERAL LEDGER

Dr				Discount Received Account (GL4360)		Cr
20-7			£	20-7		£
				30 Apr	Purchases ledger GL2350 control	8

Dr				Purchases Ledger Control Account (GL2350)		Cr
20-7			£	20-7		£
30 Apr	Bank	CB88*	382			
30 Apr	Discount received	GL4360	8			

* Entry in respect of payments to trade payables: £265 + £117.

This completes the double-entry for discount received in general ledger. However, the discount received amounts must be recorded in the subsidiary accounts of trade payables in purchases ledger.

payments to credit suppliers

Discount received and cash or bank amounts paid to trade payables are recorded in the purchases ledger accounts as follows:

PURCHASES LEDGER

Dr				J Crane (PL360)		Cr
20-7			£	20-7		£
10 Apr	Bank	CB88	265			
10 Apr	Discount received	GL4360	5			

Dr				T Lewis (PL485)		Cr
20-7			£	20-7		£
18 Apr	Bank	CB88	117			
18 Apr	Discount received	GL4360	3			

cash sales

Cash sales are where a customer of the business buys goods or services and pays in full immediately – either in cash, by cheque, BACS, debit or credit card, Faster Payments. The receipt of money is recorded on the debit side of cash book – using either the cash column or the bank column, as appropriate. The corresponding credits in the double-entry system are to sales account in the general ledger, as follows (using the cash sales transaction from Zofia Studios' cash book as an example):

GENERAL LEDGER

Dr			**Sales Account** (GL4100)			Cr
20-7		£	20-7			£
			26 Apr Bank		CB88	110

Note that, as Zofia Studios (from the Case Study) is not registered for Value Added Tax, there is no VAT to record. We will see – in the next chapter – how VAT from cash sales is handled in the analysed cash book.

cash purchases

Cash purchases are where a business buys goods or services from a supplier and pays in full immediately – either in cash, by cheque, BACS, debit or credit card or Faster Payments service. The payment of money is recorded on the credit side of cash book – using either the cash column or the bank column, as appropriate. The corresponding debit in the double-entry system is to purchases account in the general ledger, as follows (using the cash purchases transaction from Zofia Studios' cash book as an example):

GENERAL LEDGER

Dr			**Purchases Account** (GL5100)		Cr
20-7		£	20-7		£
15 Apr Cash	CB88	275			

Note that, as with cash sales, no VAT is recorded for this business as it is not VAT-registered. The analysed cash book in the next chapter will include VAT on cash purchases.

Chapter Summary

- The cash book records the money transactions of the business in the form of cash and bank receipts and payments.

- Receipts are recorded on the debit side; payments are recorded on the credit side.

- A common form of cash book is the three column cash book with columns for settlement discount, cash and bank.

- Transactions recorded in the cash book include:
  - cash sales
  - cash purchases
  - receipts from credit customers
  - payments to credit suppliers
  - settlement discount allowed
  - settlement discount received
  - other payments and receipts, eg non-current assets, expenses paid, loans received and repaid

- The total of the discount allowed column in cash book is transferred to the double-entry system as:
  - debit discount allowed account
  - credit sales ledger control account

- The total of the discount received column in cash book is transferred to the double-entry system as:
  - debit purchases ledger control account
  - credit discount received account

Key
Terms

cash book	records cash and bank receipts and payments; can combine the roles of the book of prime entry for bank receipts and payments and the double-entry account for cash and bank, or can be a book of prime entry only
three column cash book	cash book with columns for settlement discount, cash and bank
capital	the amount of money invested in the business by the owner
non-current assets	items purchased by a business for use on a long-term basis
drawings	when the owner takes money from the business for personal use
cash sales	where a customer buys goods or services and pays in full immediately
cash purchases	where a business buys goods or services from a supplier and pays in full immediately
discount allowed	amount allowed by a business to its trade receivables who settle amounts due within the period for cash discount stated on the sales invoice
discount received	amount received by a business from its trade payables for quick settlement within the period for cash discount stated on the supplier's invoice

Activities

9.1 The cash book is:

(a) a financial document

(b) the account kept by the bank of its customer's bank receipts and payments

(c) a part of double-entry bookkeeping only

(d) the book of prime entry for bank receipts and payments

Answer (a) or (b) or (c) or (d)

9.2 The following cash book shows a number of transactions of a new business set up by Hannah Wyrembak on 30 April 20-7:

Dr							Cash Book				CB70	Cr
Date	Details	Acc code	Discount allowed	Cash	Bank	Date	Details	Acc code	Discount received	Cash	Bank	
			£	£	£	20-7			£	£	£	
20-7				2,000	8,000	30 Apr	Rent				1,000	
30 Apr	Capital					30 Apr	Wages			800		
30 Apr	Loan from bank				5,000	30 Apr	Drawings				500	
						30 Apr	Vehicle				10,000	
						30 Apr	Balances c/d			1,200	1,500	
				2,000	13,000					2,000	13,000	
1 May	Balances b/d			1,200	1,500							

Note that Hannah Wyrembak's business is not registered for Value Added Tax.

You are to transfer the data from the cash book into the double-entry system of Hannah Wyrembak. Note: full account codes are not required.

9.3 The following cash book shows a number of transactions of Teme Traders which all took place on 30 April 20-5:

Dr						**Cash Book**					CB32	Cr
Date	Details	Acc code	Discount allowed	Cash	Bank	Date	Details	Acc code	Discount received	Cash	Bank
20-5			£	£	£	20-5			£	£	£
30 Apr	Balances b/d			275	2,080	30 Apr	Mereford Mills				
30 Apr	Cash sales			40			(trade payable)		50		3,200
30 Apr	Commission					30 Apr	Cash purchases				96
	received				48	30 Apr	Office equipment				2,600
30 Apr	Lindum Ltd					30 Apr	Wages				1,550
	(trade receivable)			40	2,400	30 Apr	General expenses			80	
30 Apr	Loan from bank				2,000	30 Apr	Balance c/d			235	
30 Apr	Balance c/d				918						
				40	315	7,446				50	315	7,446
1 May	Balance b/d				235		1 May	Balance b/d				918

Note that Teme Traders' business is not registered for Value Added Tax.

(a) The balance brought down of £2,080 on 30 April shows that, according to the cash book, the business has money in the bank. True or false?

(b) The balance brought down of £918 on 1 May shows that, according to the cash book, the business has money in the bank. True or false?

(c) You are to transfer the data from the cash book into the general ledger of Teme Traders.

(d) Show the entries in the sales ledger and purchases ledger of Teme Traders.
   Note: full account codes are not required.

9.4 At the end of the month, the cash book of a business has a total of £80 for discount received and a total of £120 for discount allowed. Which one of the following is correct double-entry to record the settlement discount in the discount accounts?

(a) debit discount allowed £120, credit discount received £80

(b) debit discount allowed £40

(c) debit discount received £80, credit discount allowed £120

(d) debit discount received £40

Answer (a) or (b) or (c) or (d)

9.5 Walter Harrison, a trader, records his cash and bank transactions in a three column cash book. The following are the transactions for June 20-2:

1 June	Balances: cash £280; bank overdraft £1,240
3 June	Received a cheque from G Wheaton, a trade receivable, for £195, in full settlement of a debt of £200
5 June	Received cash of £92 from T Francis, a trade receivable, in full settlement of a debt of £94
10 June	Paid wages in cash £165
12 June	Paid A Morris, a trade payable, in cash, £100 less £3 cash discount
18 June	Received a cheque for £640 from H Watson, a trade receivable, in full settlement of a debt of £670
24 June	Paid D Farr £65, a trade payable, by cheque, in full settlement of a debt of £67
26 June	Paid telephone account £105 by cheque

All cheques are banked on the day of receipt.

Note that Walter Harrison's business is not registered for Value Added Tax.

You are to:

(a) enter the above transactions in Walter Harrison's three column cash book, balance the cash and bank columns, and carry the balances down to 1 July

(b) total the two discount columns and transfer them to the appropriate accounts

10 Analysed cash book

this chapter covers...

In the previous chapter we saw the role of the cash book and how a business uses a cash book with three money columns – for bank, cash and settlement discount. We also saw how financial transactions from the cash book are transferred into the ledgers.

In this chapter we extend the use of the cash book to look at an analysed cash book, which divides receipts and payments between a number of categories – including VAT – and so provides more information to a business.

Towards the end of the chapter we see how the cash book fits into the accounting system

– either as a book of prime entry and a double-entry account

– or as a book of prime entry

In the latter case a separate control account for cash and bank is kept in the general ledger in order to complete double-entry bookkeeping.

ANALYSED CASH BOOK

Many businesses use an analysed cash book to provide more information. As well as the columns for settlement discount, cash and bank which we have seen in the previous chapter, an analysed cash book divides receipts and payments between a number of analysis columns, such as:

- receipts
  - cash sales
  - VAT on cash sales and other income
  - receipts from trade receivables in the sales ledger
  - other income
- payments
  - cash purchases
  - VAT on cash purchases and other expenses
  - payments to trade payables in the purchases ledger
  - other expenses, including dealing with dishonoured ('bounced') cheques (see page 208)

A business will use whatever analysis columns suit it best: the cash book should be adapted to meet the needs of the business in the best possible way.

ANALYSED CASH BOOK

situation

Wyvern Auto Spares buys car parts from manufacturers, and sells to local garages and to members of the public. The business is registered for VAT.

The business uses a cash book which analyses receipts and payments as follows:

RECEIPTS	PAYMENTS
bank	bank
cash	cash
discount allowed	discount received
VAT	VAT
cash sales	cash purchases
trade receivables	trade payables
other income	other expenses

The following transactions are to be entered for the first week of December 20-7:

1 Dec	Balances from previous week: cash £255, bank £875
1 Dec	Sales for cash £240 + VAT
1 Dec	Commission received by cheque, £40 + VAT
1 Dec	A customer, Main Street Garage, settles an invoice for £195, paying by bank transfer
2 Dec	Paid rent on premises £325 (no VAT) by cheque
2 Dec	Sales for cash £160 + VAT
2 Dec	Paid an invoice for £250 from Boxhall Supplies Ltd (a supplier) by bank transfer for £240, £10 being deducted for prompt settlement
3 Dec	Transferred £500 of cash into the bank
3 Dec	Paid for office stationery in cash, £40 + VAT
3 Dec	A45 Service Station, settles an invoice for £143, paying £140 by cheque and is allowed £3 discount for prompt settlement
4 Dec	Sales £320 + VAT, received half in cash, and half by cheque
4 Dec	Paid for urgently needed spares in cash, £80 + VAT
5 Dec	Paid an invoice for £155 from Vord Supplies (a supplier) by bank transfer for £150, £5 being deducted for prompt settlement
5 Dec	Sales for cash £200 + VAT
5 Dec	Paid wages £385 in cash
5 Dec	Balanced the cash book at the end of the week

As cashier to Wyvern Auto Spares Limited, you are to:

• write up the analysed cash book for the week commencing 1 December 20-7

• balance the cash book at 5 December 20-7

The rate of Value Added Tax is 20%. All cheques are banked on the day of receipt.

solution

Dr (Receipts)

Date	Details	Acc code	Discount allowed	Cash	Bank	VAT	Cash sales	Trade receivables	Other income
20-7			£	£	£	£	£	£	£
1 Dec	Balances b/d			255	875				
1 Dec	Sales	GL		288		48	240		
1 Dec	Commission	GL			48	8			40
1 Dec	Main Street Garage	SL			195			195	
2 Dec	Sales	GL		192		32	160		
3 Dec	Cash	C			500				
3 Dec	A45 Service Station	SL	3		140			140	
4 Dec	Sales	GL		192	192	64	320		
5 Dec	Sales	GL		240		40	200		
			3	1,167	1,950	192	920	335	40
6 Dec	Balances b/d			138	1,235				

Cr (Payments)

Date	Details	Acc code	Discount received	Cash	Bank	VAT	Cash purchases	Trade payables	Other expenses
20-7			£	£	£	£	£	£	£
2 Dec	Rent	GL			325				325
2 Dec	Boxhall Supplies Ltd	PL	10		240			240	
3 Dec	Bank	C		500					
3 Dec	Office stationery	GL		48		8			40
4 Dec	Purchases	GL		96		16	80		
5 Dec	Vord Supplies	PL	5		150			150	
5 Dec	Wages	GL		385					385
5 Dec	Balances c/d			138	1,235				
			15	1,167	1,950	24	80	390	750

Note the following points:

- The analysed cash book analyses each receipt and payment between a number of headings. A business will adapt the cash book and use whatever analysis columns suit it best.

- For transactions involving receipts from trade receivables and payments to trade payables, no amount for VAT is shown in the VAT columns. This is because VAT has been charged on invoices issued and received and was recorded in the VAT account (via the day books) when the sale or purchase was made.

- The cash and bank columns are balanced in the way described in the previous chapter (pages 192-193).

- The discount columns are totalled at the end of the week ready to be transferred to the double-entry system.

The column for account codes indicates the ledger section for completing double-entry. The transaction on 3 December of the transfer of cash to bank is coded 'C' and is shown on both sides of the cash book – no further entries need to be made.

LEDGER TRANSFERS FROM THE ANALYSED CASH BOOK

Set out over the next few pages are the entries from the analysed cash book in the Case Study of Wyvern Auto Spares as they are transferred to the double-entry system. These transfers are for:

■ settlement discounts allowed

■ settlement discounts received

■ VAT

■ cash sales

- cash purchases
- receipts from trade receivables
- payments to trade payables
- other income
- other expenses

The entries for general ledger, sales ledger and purchases ledger are as follows (note that these transfers are described in more detail in the previous chapter):

GENERAL LEDGER

Dr		Discount Allowed Account		Cr
20-7		£	20-7	£
5 Dec	Sales ledger control	3		

Dr		Discount Received Account		Cr
20-7		£	20-7	£
			5 Dec Purchases ledger control	15

Dr		Sales Ledger Control Account		Cr
20-7		£	20-7	£
			5 Dec Cash Book	*335
			5 Dec Discount allowed	3

Dr		Purchases Ledger Control Account		Cr
20-7		£	20-7	£
5 Dec Cash Book		*390		
5 Dec Discount received		15		

*Note how only the total of the analysis column for trade receivables and trade payables from the cash book is entered in the appropriate control account.

Dr		Sales Account		Cr
20-7		£	20-7	£
			5 Dec Cash Book	**920

Dr		Purchases Account		Cr
20-7		£	20-7	£
5 Dec Cash Book		**80		

** Total of the analysis column from the analysed cash book.

Dr		Value Added Tax Account		Cr
20-7		£	20-7	£
5 Dec Cash Book		***24	5 Dec Cash Book	***192

*** Total of the analysis column from the analysed cash book.

Dr		Commission Received Account		Cr
20-7		£	20-7	£
			1 Dec Bank	40

Dr		Rent Paid Account		Cr
20-7		£	20-7	£
2 Dec Bank		325		

Dr		Office Stationery Account		Cr
20-7		£	20-7	£
3 Dec Cash		40		

Dr		Wages Account		Cr
20-7		£	20-7	£
5 Dec Cash		385		

Note that, in the above accounts, the term 'Cash Book' is used as the cross-reference when the total of an analysis column is recorded. This is because transactions will often be a mix of cash and bank items. Where the receipt or payment can be identified to 'Cash' of 'Bank' – as with the income and expenses here – then the cross-reference is to the appropriate word.

SALES LEDGER

Dr	Main Street Garage		Cr
20-7	£	20-7	£
		1 Dec Bank	195

Dr	A45 Service Station		Cr
20-7	£	20-7	£
		3 Dec Bank	140
		3 Dec Discount allowed	3

PURCHASES LEDGER

Dr	Boxhall Supplies Ltd		Cr
20-7	£	20-7	£
2 Dec Bank	240		
2 Dec Discount received	10		

Dr	Vord Supplies		Cr
20-7	£	20-7	£
5 Dec Bank	150		
5 Dec Discount received	5		

Note that the transactions recorded in sales ledger and purchases ledger are – as totals – recorded in sales ledger control account and purchases ledger control account.

DEALING WITH DISHONOURED CHEQUES

Sometimes a business pays into its bank account a cheque received from one of its customers and that cheque is **dishonoured** ('bounces'). In other words, the customer's bank – for one of a number of reasons – decides that it will not pay the cheque, which will then become an unpaid cheque.

The practical consequence of this is that the cheque is then deducted from the business bank account and sent back to bank of the business which paid it in. It will be shown on the business bank statement as an unpaid cheque in the payments column.

The reason for a bank returning a cheque in this way can vary:

- the cheque may be 'stopped' by the customer
- there may be something technically wrong with it (it may not have been signed)
- the person issuing the cheque may not have enough money in their bank account; in this case the cheque will be returned marked 'refer to drawer' – which often means that the issuer of the cheque (the customer of the business) is in financial difficulty; this is bad news for the business which should have received the money

An unpaid cheque – like any payment – must be recorded in the cash book bank column (credit side) when it is received back from the bank. A debit entry will be recorded in the ledgers so as to reverse the original financial transaction. For example, if the bounced cheque is from a trade receivable, the debit entry is to sales ledger control account, with a debit entry also in the subsidiary account of the trade receivable.

HOW THE CASH BOOK FITS INTO THE ACCOUNTING SYSTEM

Over this chapter and the previous chapter we have looked at a number of bank and cash receipts and payments which are recorded firstly in the cash book and secondly in the ledger system of the general ledger, sales ledger and purchases ledger. As the cash book is the first place in the accounting system to record bank transactions, it is the **book of prime entry** for bank and cash receipts and payments.

There are two ways in which the cash book can fit into the accounting system:

- as well as being a book of prime entry the cash book can perform the function of being a double-entry account, ie a debit entry made in cash book is recorded on the credit side of another double-entry account
- the cash book is treated solely as a book of prime entry, in which case separate double-entry accounts – called **cash control account** and **bank control account** – are used in the general ledger

The diagram on the next page shows how the cash book performs the functions of a book of prime entry and a double-entry account. The diagram shows the flow involving:

- financial documents – primary records for bank receipts and payments
- the cash book as a book of prime entry
- double-entry bookkeeping, involving the cash book and other ledgers

In accounting systems where the cash book is used as a book of prime entry only, separate control accounts for cash and bank are used in the general ledger. The use of these is explained on page 211.

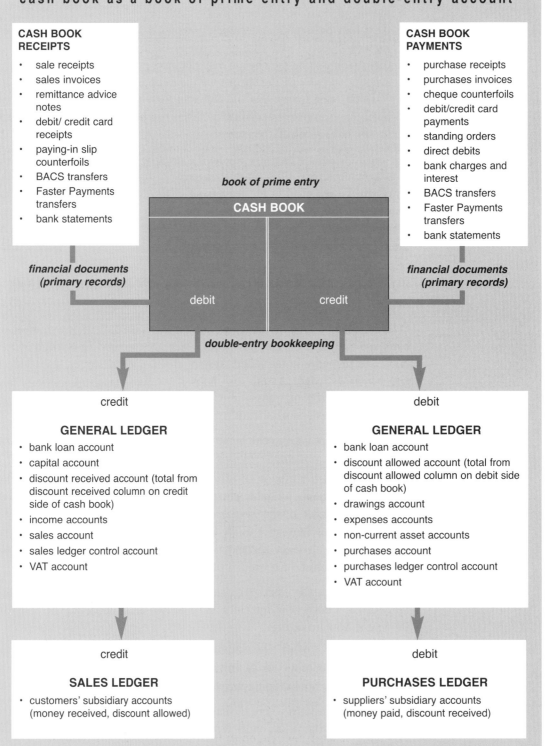

cash book as a book of prime entry and double-entry account

CASH BOOK RECEIPTS

- sale receipts
- sales invoices
- remittance advice notes
- debit/ credit card receipts
- paying-in slip counterfoils
- BACS transfers
- Faster Payments transfers
- bank statements

CASH BOOK PAYMENTS

- purchase receipts
- purchases invoices
- cheque counterfoils
- debit/credit card payments
- standing orders
- direct debits
- bank charges and interest
- BACS transfers
- Faster Payments transfers
- bank statements

book of prime entry

CASH BOOK

debit   credit

financial documents (primary records)

financial documents (primary records)

double-entry bookkeeping

credit

GENERAL LEDGER

- bank loan account
- capital account
- discount received account (total from discount received column on credit side of cash book)
- income accounts
- sales account
- sales ledger control account
- VAT account

debit

GENERAL LEDGER

- bank loan account
- discount allowed account (total from discount allowed column on debit side of cash book)
- drawings account
- expenses accounts
- non-current asset accounts
- purchases account
- purchases ledger control account
- VAT account

credit

SALES LEDGER

- customers' subsidiary accounts (money received, discount allowed)

debit

PURCHASES LEDGER

- suppliers' subsidiary accounts (money paid, discount received)

CASH AND BANK CONTROL ACCOUNT

As noted above, where an accounting system treats the cash book solely as a book of prime entry, a cash control account and a bank control account are used in the general ledger to complete double-entry. These accounts show the total receipts and payments made in cash or through the bank during the period, together with opening and closing balances.

From the cash book of Wyvern Auto Spares, in the Case Study on page 203, the totals of the receipts and payments from the cash and bank columns are entered in cash control account and bank control account as shown below.

GENERAL LEDGER

Dr			Cash Control Account			Cr
20-7		£	20-7			£
1 Dec	Balance b/d	255	5 Dec	Cash Book		**1,029
5 Dec	Cash Book	*912	5 Dec	Balance c/d		138
		1,167				1,167
6 Dec	Balance b/d	138				

* £288 + £192 + £192 + £240   see cash book on pages 204-205

** £500 + £48 + £96 + £385

Dr			Bank Control Account			Cr
20-7		£	20-7			£
1 Dec	Balance b/d	875	30 Apr	Cash Book		**715
5 Dec	Cash Book	*1,075	5 Dec	Balance c/d		1,235
		1,950				1,950
6 Dec	Balance b/d	1,235				

* £48 + £195 + £500 + £140 + £192   see cash book on pages 204-205

** £325 + £240 + £150

Note that the amounts shown as Cash Book on the debit sides of the two control accounts are the total receipts from the cash book, excluding balances brought down (and, if applicable, carried down). Likewise, the amounts shown on the credit sides are the total payments from the cash book, excluding balances brought down (if applicable) and carried down.

CHECKING THE CASH BOOK

As the cash book forms such an integral part of a business double-entry system, it is essential that transactions are recorded accurately and that balances are calculated correctly at regular intervals, eg weekly or monthly – depending on the needs of the business. How can the cash book be checked for accuracy?

cash columns

To check the cash columns is easy. It is simply a matter of counting the cash in the cash till, cash box, or safe, and agreeing it with the balance shown by the cash book. In the example from the cash book of Wyvern Auto Spares, in the Case Study on page 203, there should be £138 in the cash till at 6 December 20-7. If the cash cannot be agreed in this way, the discrepancy needs to be investigated urgently.

bank columns

How are these to be checked? We could, perhaps, enquire at the bank and ask for the balance at the month-end, or we could arrange for a bank statement to be sent to us, or we could use internet banking to print off a statement. However, the balance of the account at the bank may well not agree with that shown by the bank columns of the cash book. There are several reasons why there may be a difference: for example, a cheque that has been written out recently to pay a bill may not yet have been recorded on the bank statement, ie it has been entered in the cash book, but is not yet on the bank statement. To agree the bank statement and the bank columns of the cash book, it is usually necessary to prepare a bank reconciliation statement, and this topic is dealt with fully in Chapter 5 of *Bookkeeping 2 Tutorial*.

Chapter Summary

■ An analysed cash book provides more information and divides receipts and payments between a number of analysis columns.

■ Analysis columns for receipts include:
- cash sales
- VAT on cash sales and other income
- receipts from trade receivables
- other income

■ Analysis columns for payments include:
- cash purchases
- VAT on cash purchases and other expenses
- payments to trade payables
- other expenses

■ A dishonoured cheque is recorded in the cash book bank column (credit side) when it is received back from the bank. The debit entry will be recorded in the ledgers so as to reverse the original financial transaction.

■ In the accounting system cash book can combine the roles of:
- the book of prime entry for bank and cash receipts and payments
- the double-entry account for cash and bank

■ When the cash book is used solely as the book of prime entry, a cash control account and a bank control account are used in general ledger to complete double-entry bookkeeping.

analysed cash book	a cash book which divides receipts and payments between a number of analysis columns
receipts analysis columns	for example: – cash sales – VAT on cash sales and other income – receipts from trade receivables – other income
payments analysis columns	for example: – cash purchases – VAT on cash purchases and other expenses – payments to trade payables – other expenses
dishonoured cheque	a cheque which is paid into a bank account, but is returned unpaid by the bank; it is credited in the cash book bank columns and debited to the account of the business or person that paid it in and to the sales ledger control account
cash control account and bank control account	double-entry accounts in the general ledger used when the cash book is treated solely as the book of prime entry; they show the total receipts and payments made in cash or through the bank during the period, together with the opening and closing balances

Activities

10.1 Which one of the following transactions will not be recorded on the payments side of cash book?

(a)   purchase of a vehicle for £10,000 paid for by cheque

(b)   cash purchase for £150

(c)   cheque received from a trade receivable for £1,350

(d)   BACS transfer to a supplier for £2,200

Answer (a) or (b) or (c) or (d)

10.2 Which one of the following transactions will not be recorded on the receipts side of cash book?

(a)   cheque paid to a trade payable for £870

(b)   Faster Payment transfer from a trade receivable for £3,250

(c)   debit card payment by a customer for £580

(d)   cash sales of £195

Answer (a) or (b) or (c) or (d)

10.3 Indicate whether the following statements are true by putting a tick in the relevant column of the table below.

		True	False
(a)	Cash book is the book of prime entry for bank and cash receipts and payments		
(b)	Cash book can be the double-entry account for bank and cash		
(c)	The discount received column total from cash book is debited to discount received account in general ledger		
(d)	The VAT column total on the receipts side of an analysed cash book is debited to VAT account in general ledger		
(e)	The trade receivables column total from an analysed cash book is credited to sales ledger control account in general ledger		

10.4 David Lewis runs a shop selling carpets to the public on cash terms and to trade customers on credit terms. He buys his carpets direct from manufacturers, who allow him credit terms.

David Lewis' business is registered for VAT. The VAT rate is 20%. He uses an analysed cash book, which is a book of prime entry and a double-entry account.

The following transactions take place during the week commencing 12 May 20-7 (all cheques are banked on the day of receipt):

12 May	Debit balances from previous week: cash £205, bank £825
12 May	Cash sales £600 (including VAT), cheque received
12 May	Paid shop rent by bank transfer £255 (no VAT)
13 May	Cash sales £180 (including VAT), cash received
13 May	A trade receivable, T Jarvis, settles an invoice for £158, paying £155 by bank transfer, £3 settlement discount being allowed
13 May	Paid an invoice for £368 from Terry Carpets (a trade payable) by cheque for £363 and receiving £5 settlement discount
14 May	Cash sales £720 (including VAT), cheque received
14 May	Paid an invoice for £149 from Trade Supplies (a trade payable) for £145, paying by cheque and receiving £4 settlement discount
14 May	Purchases paid for in cash, £36 (including VAT)
15 May	Transferred £250 of cash into the bank
15 May	Cash sales £288 (including VAT), cash received
15 May	Paid an invoice for £295 from Longlife Carpets (a trade payable), by bank transfer for £291 and receiving £4 settlement discount
16 May	Cash purchases of £240 (including VAT) paid by BACS
16 May	A trade receivable, Wyvern Council, settles an invoice for £564, paying £560 by BACS and is allowed £4 discount for prompt settlement

You are to:

(a) Enter the above transactions in the analysed cash book of David Lewis shown on the next page.

(b) Balance the cash book at 16 May 20-7, bringing down the balances at 17 May 20-7.

(c) Explain how the totals for the discount columns will be entered in the accounts in the general ledger (the general ledger accounts do not need to be shown).

(d)   Show the cash book transactions in the following accounts:

      sales ledger   –   T Jarvis

                             –   Wyvern Council

      purchases ledger   –   Terry Carpets

                             –   Trade Supplies

                             –   Longlife Carpets

Note: full account codes are not required.

Dr (Receipts)

Date	Details	Acc code	Discount allowed £	Cash £	Bank £	VAT £	Cash sales £	Trade receivables £	Other income £

Cr (Payments)

Date	Details	Acc code	Discount received £	Cash £	Bank £	VAT £	Cash purchases £	Trade payables £	Other expenses

10.5 You are an accounts assistant at Trafalgar Limited. One of your duties is to write-up the cash book.

There are five payments to be entered in Trafalgar Limited's cash book.

Receipts for cash payments

Received cash with thanks for goods bought.	Received cash with thanks for goods bought.
From Trafalgar Ltd, a customer without a credit account.	From Trafalgar Ltd, a customer without a credit account.
Net £25	Net £80
VAT £5	VAT £16
Total £30	Total £96
Knowles & Co	*S Goulding*

Bank payments

Liyan Ltd	Nelson Street Garage	Sandhu & Co
(Purchases ledger account PL320)	(No credit account with this supplier)	(Purchases ledger account PL540)
£920	£132 including VAT	£645
Note: £10 settlement (cash) discount taken		Note: no settlement (cash) discount taken

(a) Enter the details from the two receipts for cash payments and the three bank payments into the credit side of the cash book shown below and total each column.

Cash book – credit side

Details	Discount	Cash	Bank	VAT	Trade payables	Cash purchases	Vehicle expenses
Balance b/f							
Knowles & Co							
S Goulding							
Liyan Ltd							
Nelson Street Garage							
Sandhu & Co							
Totals							

There are three amounts received to be entered in Trafalgar Limited's cash book.

Cheques received from credit customers:

Watkin Ltd   £429

P Pandya   £1,522 Note: £12 settlement (cash) discount taken

Cash received:

£235 received from Matt Martin for rent of parking spaces (No VAT)

(b)   Enter the above details into the debit side of the cash book and total each column.

Cash book – debit side

Details	Discount	Cash	Bank	Trade receivables	Other income
Balance b/f		254	1,598		
Watkin Ltd					
P Pandya					
Matt Martin					
Totals					

(c)   Using your answers to (a) and (b) above, calculate the cash balance.

£

(d)   Using your answers to (a) and (b) above, calculate the bank balance.

£

(e)   Will the bank balance calculated in (d) above be a debit or credit balance?

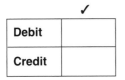

	✓
Debit	
Credit	

11 Petty cash book

this chapter covers...

In this chapter we look at the petty cash book, which is used to record low-value cash payments for small purchases and expenses incurred by a business. Examples of these payments include the purchase of office stationery items, and the payment of travel expenses.

The way that the petty cash book works is that an amount of cash is handed by the cashier to a member of staff, the petty cashier, who:

■ *is responsible for security of the petty cash money*

■ *makes cash payments against authorised petty cash vouchers*

■ *records the payments made, and analyses them, in a petty cash book*

■ *reconciles the petty cash book with the amount of cash held*

We look at the layout of the petty cash book, with analysis columns for expenses and see how it is written up by the petty cashier from authorised petty cash vouchers.

We see how a petty cash book is balanced and how the petty cashier claims reimbursement from the cashier of amounts of money paid out.

Towards the end of the chapter we will see how a petty cash book fits into the accounting system as the book of prime entry for low-value cash payments and as part of the double-entry system.

THE PETTY CASH BOOK IN THE ACCOUNTING SYSTEM

The petty cash book is used to record low-value cash payments for purchases and expenses – such as small items of stationery, postages, etc. Items like these are not appropriate to enter in the cash book because they would 'clutter' it up with lots of small amounts. Instead a member of staff is given the responsibility of being the petty cashier.

Petty cash book is the book of prime entry for low-value cash payments.

USES OF THE PETTY CASH BOOK

The petty cash book records the low-value cash payments for purchases and expenses of the business, such as:
– stationery items
– small items of office supplies
– casual wages
– window cleaning
– bus, rail and taxi fares incurred on behalf of the business
– meals and drinks incurred on behalf of the business
– postages
– tips and donations

Petty cash payments are usually for amounts up to a maximum value, for example, up to £25 for any one expense item. The petty cashier of a business will be told the maximum amount that can be paid out on any one voucher.

As well as payments there may, from time-to-time, be small receipts of cash to be recorded. For example, if a member of staff purchases items such as postage stamps or stationery, they will pay the petty cashier who issues a receipt to record the details and the amount of money received.

The petty cash book is the responsibility of the petty cashier who:

■ receives an amount of money (known as the petty cash float) from the cashier to be used for petty cash payments

■ is responsible for security of the petty cash money

■ makes cash payments against authorised petty cash vouchers

■ records the payments made, and analyses them in a petty cash book

■ receives and records any small amounts of income, eg postage stamps sold to staff for their private use

- balances the petty cash book at regular intervals, usually weekly or monthly

- tops up the petty cash float by claiming reimbursement from the cashier of amounts paid out

- passes the completed petty cash book to the bookkeeper so that data can be transferred into the ledger system

THE IMPREST SYSTEM

Petty cash books usually operate using the imprest system. With this system, the petty cashier starts each week (or month) with a certain amount of money – the imprest amount. As payments are made during the week (or month) the amount of money will reduce and, at the end of the period, the cash will be made up by a payment from bank account to restore the imprest amount. For example:

Started week with imprest amount	£100.00
Total of petty cash amounts paid out during week	£80.00
Cash held at end of week	£20.00
Amount drawn from bank to restore imprest amount	£80.00
Cash at start of next week, ie imprest amount	£100.00

If, at any time, the imprest amount proves to be insufficient, further amounts of cash can be drawn from the cashier. Also, from time-to-time, it may be necessary to increase the imprest amount so that regular shortfalls of petty cash are avoided.

PETTY CASH VOUCHERS – PURPOSE AND CONTENT

The purpose of petty cash vouchers is to enable payments to be made out of petty cash. They are the financial documents used by the petty cashier to write up the petty cash book.

Petty cash vouchers contain the following:

- the date, details and amount of expenditure

- the signature of the person making the claim and receiving the money

- the signature of the person authorising the payment to be made – usually the manager of the person making the claim

- additionally, most petty cash vouchers are numbered, so that they can be controlled, the number being entered in the petty cash book
- with the relevant documentation, such as a receipt from a shop or post office etc, attached to the petty cash voucher

An example petty cash voucher is as follows:

petty cash voucher			Number *47*
		date	*5 April 20-4*
description		amount	
		£	p
Photocopier paper		*3*	*20*
VAT at 20%		*0*	*64*
Total		*3*	*84*
signature	*T Harris*		
authorised	*R Singh*		

LAYOUT OF THE PETTY CASH BOOK

Petty cash book is usually set out as follows:

The layout shows that:

Receipts	Date	Details	Voucher number	Total payment	Analysis columns				
					VAT	Postages	Stationery	Travel	Ledger
£				£	£	£	£	£	£
money in: debit side				money out: credit side					

- there are columns showing the date and details of all receipts and payments
- receipts are shown in the debit column on the extreme left
- there is a column for the petty cash voucher number
- the total payment (ie the amount paid out on each petty cash voucher) is in the next column, which is the credit side of the petty cash book
- then follow the analysis columns which analyse each transaction entered in the 'total payment' column

A business will use whatever analysis columns are most suitable for it and, indeed, there may be more columns than shown in the example. It is important that expenses are recorded in the correct analysis columns so that petty cash book shows a true picture of petty cash expenditure.

PETTY CASH AND VAT

Value Added Tax is charged by VAT-registered businesses on their taxable supplies. Therefore, there will often be VAT included as part of the expense paid out of petty cash. Often the indication of the supplier's VAT registration number on a receipt or invoice will tell you that VAT has been charged on the items purchased.

Where VAT has been charged, the amount of tax might be indicated separately on the receipt or invoice. However, for small money amounts it is quite usual for a total to be shown without indicating the amount of VAT. An example of a receipt which does not show the VAT content is illustrated below. The receipt is for a box of envelopes purchased from Wyvern Stationers. It shows:

- the name and address of the retailer

- the date and time of the transaction

- the VAT registration number of the retailer

- the price of the item, £4.80

- the amount of money given, a £10 note

- the amount of change given, £5.20

```
            Wyvern Stationers
            25 High St Mereford
              08 10 -4  16.07
            VAT Reg 454 7106 34

Salesperson Rashid

Stationery          4.80

TOTAL               4.80
CASH               10.00
CHANGE              5.20
```

What the receipt does not show, however, is the VAT content of the purchase price – it only shows the price after the VAT has been added on.

How do we calculate the purchase price before the VAT is added on?

The formula is:

$$\frac{\textbf{amount paid x 100}}{\textbf{100 + VAT rate}} = \textbf{price before VAT is added on}$$

If we assume that the VAT rate is 20%, the calculation is

$$\frac{£4.80 \times 100}{100 + 20} = \frac{£480}{120} = £4.00$$

The VAT content is therefore

£4.80 minus £4.00 = 80p

In this case £0.80 will be entered in the VAT column in the petty cash book, £4.00 in the appropriate expense column, and the full £4.80 in the total payment column.

Remember when calculating VAT amounts that fractions of a penny are ignored, ie the tax is rounded down to a whole penny.

Case Study

PETTY CASH BOOK

> This Case Study shows how a petty cash book is written up by the petty cashier from authorised petty cash vouchers. The petty cash float is reimbursed at the end of the week and the petty cash book is balanced.

situation

You work in the accounts office of Wyvern Traders. One of your tasks is to keep the petty cash book, which is operated using the imprest system. There are a number of transactions which have been authorised (all transactions, unless otherwise indicated, include VAT at 20%) to be entered for the week in the petty cash book (PCB30):

20-4

5 Apr	Started the week with an imprest amount of £100.00
5 Apr	Paid stationery £3.84 on voucher no 47
5 Apr	Paid taxi fare £5.76 on voucher no 48
6 Apr	Cash received £10 from Fred Dexter for postage stamps purchased (receipt no 122 issued)
6 Apr	Paid postages £2.75 (no VAT) on voucher no 49
7 Apr	Paid taxi fare £9.60 on voucher no 50
7 Apr	Paid J Jones, a trade payable (PL054), £15.00 (no VAT shown in petty cash book – amount will be on VAT account already) on voucher no 51
8 Apr	Paid stationery £7.20 on voucher no 52
8 Apr	Paid postages £5.85 (no VAT) on voucher no 53
9 Apr	Paid taxi fare £12.00 on voucher no 54

The petty cash book is to be balanced on 9 April with reimbursement of the imprest amount from cash book (CB55). The balance is to be brought down on 10 April.

solution

The following petty cash book is written up by the petty cashier of Wyvern Traders for the week ended 9 April 20-4 as follows:

Petty Cash Book										PCB30
Receipts	Date	Details	Voucher number	Total payment	Analysis columns					
					VAT	Postages	Stationery	Travel	Ledger	
£	20-4			£	£	£	£	£	£	
100.00	5 Apr	Balance b/d								
	5 Apr	Stationery	47	3.84	0.64		3.20			
	5 Apr	Taxi fare	48	5.76	0.96			4.80		
10.00	6 Apr	Fred Dexter (postage stamps)	122							
	6 Apr	Postages	49	2.75		2.75				
	7 Apr	Taxi fare	50	9.60	1.60			8.00		
	7 Apr	J Jones (PL054)	51	15.00					15.00	
	8 Apr	Stationery	52	7.20	1.20		6.00			
	8 Apr	Postages	53	5.85		5.85				
	9 Apr	Taxi fare	54	12.00	2.00			10.00		
				62.00	6.40	8.60	9.20	22.80	15.00	
					GL2200	GL6330	GL6360	GL6370	GL2350	
52.00	9 Apr	Bank (CB55)								
	9 Apr	Balance c/d		100.00						
162.00				162.00						
100.00	10 Apr	Balance b/d								

Notes:

- This petty cash book has been written up for the week. It is for a business to decide how often petty cash book is to be totalled and balanced – generally, though, this will be done either weekly or monthly.

- This cash book starts each new week with a cash float of £100 – this is the imprest amount. The amount of the float at the start is for the business to decide based on the level of expenses regularly paid out in petty cash – £100 may be sufficient, but larger floats may be needed. In any case, if the petty cashier runs out of cash during the week or month, a top-up can be made from cash book.

- The analysis columns are for a business to decide what is suitable for their circumstances. The ledger column is used for payments from petty cash to trade payables who have accounts in purchases ledger – these suppliers are more usually paid through the bank but, if the amount is small, they may be paid in cash from petty cash.

We will now see in the main text below how the data is transferred into the double-entry bookkeeping system.

Note that the page of the petty cash book is coded PCB30 and this will be the cross-reference for the other ledger accounts.

BALANCES

5 Apr Balance b/d

The week commences with a petty cash book float of £100, described as 'balance b/d', ie brought down from the previous page of the petty cash book. (Note that this can also be written as 'balance b/f', ie brought forward from the previous page.) The imprest amount for this petty cash book is £100.

9 Apr Balance c/d

The petty cashier has claimed reimbursement from the cashier of £52.00, ie petty cash paid out £62.00 less £10 received from Fred Dexter for postage stamps. This restores the cash float to £100 which is now recorded as the balance c/d on the credit (payments) side. The receipts and payments columns are then both totalled to £162.00.

10 Apr Balance b/d

To complete double-entry bookkeeping the balance of £100 is brought down on the debit side. Note that, here, the date used in the day following the balance carried down – this shows that the cash float of £100 is ready for the next week's transactions.

TRANSFERRING THE ANALYSIS COLUMNS

In order to complete double-entry the totals of the analysis columns are transferred into the double-entry bookkeeping system. The entries are:

■ payment of an expense
  – debit expense account (using the appropriate account)
■ payment to a supplier (from the 'ledger' column)
  – debit purchases ledger control account (in general ledger)
  – debit the trade payables' subsidiary account (in purchases ledger)

From the Case Study the general ledger accounts will be written up as follows at the end of the week (9 April):

GENERAL LEDGER

Dr	Value Added Tax Account (GL2200)		Cr
20-4		£	20-4	£
9 Apr	Petty cash book PCB30	6.40	

Dr	Postages Account (GL6330)		Cr
20-4		£	20-4	£
9 Apr	Petty cash book PCB30	8.60	6 Apr	Petty cash book PCB30 *10.00

* cash received by the petty cashier from Fred Dexter for postage stamps purchased

Dr	Stationery Account (GL6360)		Cr
20-4		£	20-4	£
9 Apr	Petty cash book PCB30	9.20	

Dr	Travel Expenses Account (GL6370)		Cr
20-4		£	20-4	£
9 Apr	Petty cash book PCB30	22.80	

Dr	Purchases Ledger Control Account (GL2350)		Cr
20-4		£	20-4	£
9 Apr	Petty cash book PCB30	15.00	

The above £15 payment ledger transaction will also be debited to the account of the trade payable – here J Jones – in the purchases ledger, as follows:

PURCHASES LEDGER

Dr	J Jones (PL054)		Cr
20-4		£	20-4	£
7 Apr	Petty cash book PCB30	15.00	

RESTORING THE CASH FLOAT

To restore the petty cash float to the imprest amount, the petty cashier completes a cheque requisition form for a cheque made payable to cash. The petty cashier takes the cheque to the bank and obtains the cash. An example of a cheque requisition is shown below:

CHEQUE REQUISITION	
Amount	*£52.00*
Payee	*Cash*
Date	*9 April 20-4*
Details	*Reimbursement of petty cash*
Signature	*Jane Watkins, petty cashier*
Authorised by	*Natalie Wilson, supervisor*
Cheque no	*017234*

cheque requisition form

The double-entry bookkeeping entries to record this reimbursement are:

— *debit* petty cash book

— *credit* cash book, ie the payments side

The amount of £52.00 cash paid from the bank to the petty cashier is recorded in the cash book as follows:

Dr						Cash Book			CB55		Cr
Date	Details	Acc code	Discount allowed	Cash	Bank	Date	Details	Acc code	Discount received	Cash	Bank
20-4			£	£	£	20-4 9 Apr	Petty cash	PCB30	£	£	£ 52.00

After this reimbursement, the petty cash float is restored and the petty cash book has a balance brought down of £100.00 on 9 April. The petty cash book is now ready for next week's transactions.

CONTROL OF PETTY CASH

The petty cashier is usually responsible to the accounts supervisor for control of the petty cash and for correct recording of authorised petty cash transactions.

Most businesses set out in writing the procedures to be followed by the petty cashier. This is of benefit not only for the petty cashier to know the extent of his or her duties, but also to help the person who takes over at holiday or other times. The main procedures for the operation and control of petty cash are as follows:

1   On taking over, the petty cashier should check that the petty cash book has been balanced and that the amount of cash held agrees with the balance shown in the book. If there is any discrepancy, this should be referred to the accounts supervisor immediately.

2   The petty cashier should ensure that each week or month is started with the imprest amount of cash which has been agreed with the accounts supervisor.

3   The petty cash is to be kept securely in a locked cash box, and control kept of the keys.

4   Petty cash vouchers (in number order) are to be provided on request.

5   Petty cash is paid out against correctly completed petty cash vouchers after checking that:

– the voucher is signed by the person receiving the money

– the voucher is signed by the person authorising payment (a list of authorised signatories will be provided)

– a receipt (or other supporting evidence) is attached to the petty cash voucher, and that receipt and petty cash voucher are for the same amount

– the amount being claimed is within the authorised limit of the petty cashier

6   The petty cash book is written up (to include calculation of VAT amounts when appropriate); it is important that the petty cash book is accurate.

7   Completed petty cash vouchers are stored safely – filed in numerical order. The vouchers will need to be kept for at least six years. They may

be needed by the auditors or in the event of other queries. Completed petty cash books will also need to be retained.

8   A surprise check of petty cash will be made by the accounts supervisor – at any one time the cash held plus amounts of petty cash vouchers should equal the imprest amount.

9   At the end of each week or month the petty cash book is to be balanced.

10   Details of the totals of each analysis column are given to the person who looks after the double-entry accounts so that the amount of each expense can be entered into the double-entry system.

11   An amount of cash is drawn from the cashier equal to the amount of payments made, in order to restore the imprest amount.

12   The petty cash book and cash in hand are to be presented to the accounts supervisor for checking.

13   Any discrepancies are to be dealt with promptly; these may include:

-   petty cash claims that have not been authorised

-   insufficient supporting evidence (eg missing receipt) attached to the petty cash voucher

-   amounts being claimed which exceed the authorised limit of the petty cashier

-   a receipt and petty cash voucher total differing – the matter should be queried with the person who made the purchase

-   a difference between the totals of the analysis columns and the total payments column in the petty cash book – check the addition of the columns, the figures against the vouchers, the VAT calculations (does the VAT plus the analysis column amount equal the total payment amount?)

-   a difference between the cash in the petty cash box and the balance shown in the petty cash book – if this is not an arithmetic difference it may be a case of theft, and should be reported promptly to the accounts supervisor

-   where discrepancies and queries cannot be resolved, they should be referred to the accounts supervisor

CHECKING THE CASH

An important aspect of petty cash, which has been noted in the previous section, is that the petty cashier must ensure that the amount of cash held is what it should be. This process – known as reconciling the petty cash book with cash in hand – takes place on different occasions, as follows:

■ at the beginning of the weekly or monthly period of the petty cash book, the petty cashier should check that the amount of cash held agrees with the balance shown in the book – this is usually the imprest amount

■ at any one time during the week or month the amount of cash held plus the amounts of petty cash vouchers which have been paid out should be equal to the imprest amount – a surprise check may be made by the accounts supervisor

■ at the end of the week or month, the amount paid out by the petty cashier will be reimbursed from cash book – this should restore the cash in hand to the imprest amount

Any difference in cash – whether a shortfall or a surplus – at any stage during the week or month should be investigated promptly and, if it cannot be resolved, should be referred to the accounts supervisor.

Case Study

CHECKING THE CASH

situation

Jameson Limited keeps an amount of petty cash in a locked box in the office. The imprest amount is £100 which is restored at the beginning of each month.

The following payments were made in April and have been recorded in the petty cash book:

6 April	Stationery	£12.50
10 April	Taxi fare	£10.00
14 April	Postage stamps	£4.55
20 April	Window cleaning	£12.00
25 April	Donation to charity	£10.00

At 30 April the petty cash remaining in the locked box comprised:

1 x £10 note, 7 x £5 notes, 5 x £1 coins, 1 x 50p coin, 1 x 20p coin, 1 x 10p coin, 2 x 5p coins, 1 x 2p coin, 3 x 1p coins

solution

• Total payments for April are £49.05
• Therefore cash remaining should be £100.00 − £49.05 = £50.95

- Actual cash remaining is:

	as at 30 April	
	number held	value (£)
£10 notes	1	10.00
£5 notes	7	35.00
£1 coins	5	5.00
50p coins	1	0.50
20p coins	1	0.20
10p coins	1	0.10
5p coins	2	0.10
2p coins	1	0.02
1p coins	3	0.03
TOTAL		50.95

- Therefore, at 30 April, the petty cash book reconciles (agrees) with cash in hand

Notes on the Case Study:

- If there is a discrepancy, it should be investigated promptly and, if it cannot be resolved should be referred to the accounts supervisor.
- From a practical point of view it is advisable to keep the cash in the form of lower denomination notes and a stock of coins – these will make it easier to pay out the amounts of petty cash claims (with less risk of error) than if larger denomination notes, such as £50 and £20, are used.

HOW PETTY CASH BOOK FITS INTO THE ACCOUNTING SYSTEM

Over the last few pages we have seen how low-value cash payments for small purchases and expenses are recorded firstly in the petty cash book and secondly in the general ledger (and sometimes also in purchases ledger). As the petty cash book is the first place in the accounting system to record these transactions, it is the book of prime entry for low-value cash payments.

In accounting systems the petty cash book is:

- either the book of prime entry for low-value cash payments <u>and</u> the double-entry account for petty cash (kept in general ledger)
- or the book of prime entry only, with a separate petty cash control account (see page 235) kept in general ledger in order to complete double-entry bookkeeping

as a book of prime entry and double-entry account

The diagram below shows the petty cash book performing two functions within the accounting system:

■ as the **book of prime entry** for low-value cash payments

■ as **part of the double-entry** system

This diagram shows the flow involving:

■ financial documents – petty cash vouchers

■ the petty cash book as a book of prime entry

■ double-entry bookkeeping, involving petty cash and the other ledgers

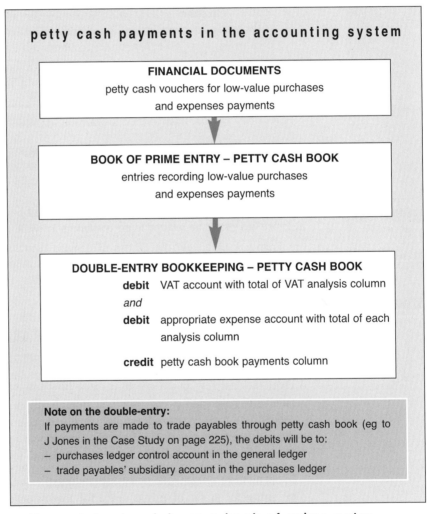

petty cash payments in the accounting system

> **FINANCIAL DOCUMENTS**
> petty cash vouchers for low-value purchases
> and expenses payments

> **BOOK OF PRIME ENTRY – PETTY CASH BOOK**
> entries recording low-value purchases
> and expenses payments

> **DOUBLE-ENTRY BOOKKEEPING – PETTY CASH BOOK**
> **debit** VAT account with total of VAT analysis column
> *and*
> **debit** appropriate expense account with total of each
> analysis column
>
> **credit** petty cash book payments column

> **Note on the double-entry:**
> If payments are made to trade payables through petty cash book (eg to
> J Jones in the Case Study on page 225), the debits will be to:
> – purchases ledger control account in the general ledger
> – trade payables' subsidiary account in the purchases ledger

petty cash book solely as a book of prime entry

The alternative to the above is for the accounting system to treat petty cash book solely as a book of prime entry, in which case a separate double-entry account – called **petty cash control account** – is used in the general ledger.

The use of a petty cash control account, using the petty cash book of Wyvern Traders (from the Case Study), is shown below.

PETTY CASH CONTROL ACCOUNT

As noted above, where an accounting system treats petty cash book solely as a book of prime entry, a **petty cash control account** is used in general ledger to complete double-entry. From Wyvern Traders' petty cash book (on page 225) the totals of receipts and payments are entered in petty cash control account (which has been given the account number GL0180) as follows:

GENERAL LEDGER

Dr			**Petty Cash Control Account** (GL0180)			Cr
20-4		£	20-4			£
5 Apr	Balance b/d	100.00	9 Apr	Petty cash book	PCB30	62.00
9 Apr	Petty cash book		9 Apr	Balance c/d		100.00
	PCB30	10.00				
9 Apr	Bank CB55	52.00				
		162.00				162.00
10 Apr	Balance b/d	100.00				

Notes:

■ The debit 'balance b/d' on 5 April of £100.00 is the same as the opening balance in petty cash book – see page 225. This is the imprest amount for this petty cash book.

■ The credit entry for 'petty cash book PCB30' on 9 April of £62.00 is the total of the analysis columns (VAT and expenses) from petty cash book. These amounts are debited to their respective accounts in general ledger, as already seen on page 228.

■ The debit entry for 'petty cash book PCB30' on 9 April for £10.00 is the receipt of cash from Fred Dexter – payment for the purchase of postage stamps. This amount is credited to the relevant account – here postages account – in general ledger, as already seen on page 228.

■ The debit entry for 'bank CB55' on 9 April for £52.00 is the reimbursement of petty cash in order to restore the imprest amount. The cheque requisition for this is shown on page 229.

- The 'balance c/d' on 9 April (and brought down on 10 April) for £100.00 is the new balance on petty cash book, ready for next week's transactions.

- In petty cash control account, the cross reference to petty cash book enables a transaction to be followed through the accounting system – from book of prime entry to double-entry account – to ensure that it is complete.

Chapter Summary

- The petty cash book records low-value cash payments for small purchases and expenses incurred by a business.

- Petty cash receipts are recorded on the debit side; payments are recorded on the credit side.

- Transactions recorded in the petty cash book include:
  - stationery items
  - small items of office supplies
  - casual wages
  - window cleaning
  - bus, rail and taxi fares incurred on behalf of the business
  - meals and drinks incurred on behalf of the business
  - postages
  - tips and donations

- The petty cash book is controlled by the petty cashier.

- The petty cashier writes up the petty cash book from petty cash vouchers, which are analysed under various expense headings.

- At regular intervals – weekly or monthly – the data from the completed petty cash book is transferred to general ledger where the total of each analysis column is debited to the relevant account.

- The petty cash book is the book of prime entry for low-value cash payments.

- The petty cash book may combine the roles of:
  - the book of prime entry for low-value cash payments
  - the double-entry account for petty cash

- When the petty cash book is used as the book of prime entry only, a petty cash control account in general ledger completes double-entry bookkeeping.

Key Terms	**petty cash book**	records low-value cash payments for small purchases and expenses; is the book of prime entry for low-value cash payments (and may also be the double-entry account for petty cash)
	petty cashier	the person responsible for the petty cash book
	petty cash voucher	financial document against which payments are made out of petty cash
	imprest method	where the money held in the petty cash float is restored to the same amount for the beginning of each week or month
	petty cash float	amount of money held at any one time by the petty cashier
	analysis columns	used in the petty cash book to record expense payments under various headings to suit the circumstances of the business
	petty cash control account	double-entry account in the general ledger used when the petty cash book is treated solely as the book of prime entry; it shows the total payments made by the petty cashier during the week or month, and records receipts from bank account, together with the opening and closing balances

Activities

11.1 The petty cash book:

    (a)   is a financial document

    (b)   is a part of double-entry bookkeeping only

    (c)   is the book of prime entry for low-value cash payments

    (d)   records and analyses expenses payments on the debit side

    Answer (a) or (b) or (c) or (d)

11.2 A petty cash voucher:

    (a)   is a financial document against which payments are made out of petty cash

    (b)   is used to draw cash from bank to top-up the petty cash float

    (c)   is passed to the bookkeeper for posting to the general ledger expenses accounts

    (d)   is used to restore the imprest amount of the cash float

    Answer (a) or (b) or (c) or (d)

11.3 Most petty cash books operate using the imprest system. This means that:

    (a)   the petty cashier draws money from the cashier as and when required

    (b)   the cashier has to authorise each petty cash payment

    (c)   a copy has to be kept of each petty cash voucher

    (d)   the petty cashier starts each week or month with a fixed amount of money

    Which one of these options is correct?

11.4 When the total of a petty cash book's analysis column for VAT is transferred to the VAT account in the general ledger, will it be recorded as a debit or credit entry in general ledger?

	✓
Debit	
Credit	

11.5 The petty cashier of the business where you work tops up the petty cash at the end of the month with £75 withdrawn from the bank. What will be the entries in the general ledger?

General ledger

Account name	Amount £	Debit ✓	Credit ✓

11.6 The business for which you work is registered for VAT. The following petty cash amounts include VAT at 20% and you are required to calculate the amount that will be shown in the VAT column and the appropriate expense column (remember that VAT amounts should be rounded down to the nearest penny):

(a) £9.60

(b) £4.80

(c) £2.40

(d) £2.46

(e) £5.60

(f) £3.48

(g) £8.76

(h) 96p

(i) 99p

(j) £9.43

11.7 The following petty cash book shows a number of transactions of Nelson and Company for March 20-9. The petty cash book is kept solely as a book of prime entry.

Petty Cash Book											PCB20
Receipts	Date	Details	Voucher	Total	Analysis columns						
			number	payment	VAT	Travel	Postages	Stationery	Meals	Ledger	
£	20-9			£	£	£	£	£	£	£	
100.00	1 Mar	Balance b/d									
	4 Mar	Taxi fare	39	6.72	1.12	5.60					
	6 Mar	Postages	40	6.80			6.80				
	9 Mar	Pens	41	4.80	0.80			4.00			
	11 Mar	Travel expenses	42	5.46		5.46					
8.50	12 Mar	J Humphries	317								
		(postage stamps)									
	16 Mar	Envelopes	43	2.88	0.48			2.40			
	18 Mar	P Andrews (PL)	44	13.50						13.50	
	19 Mar	Rail fare/meal allow	45	10.60		5.60			5.00		
	20 Mar	Postage	46	4.75			4.75				
	23 Mar	Tape	47	3.84	0.64			3.20			
	25 Mar	Postage	48	5.10			5.10				
	27 Mar	Taxi fare	49	9.12	1.52	7.60					
				73.57	4.56	24.26	16.65	9.60	5.00	13.50	
65.07	31 Mar	Bank									
	31 Mar	Balance c/d		100.00							
173.57				173.57							
100.00	1 Apr	Balance b/d									

(a)   You are to transfer the data from the petty cash book into the general ledger accounts (including cash book) as at 31 March 20-9. Note that a petty cash control is required.

(b)   Show the entry that will be recorded in the purchases ledger as at 31 March 20-9.

11.8   On returning from holiday, you are told to take charge of the petty cash book of Carr Trading. This is kept using the imprest system, the float being £150.00 at the beginning of each month. Analysis columns are used for VAT, travel, postages, stationery, meals, and miscellaneous.

There are a number of transactions for the month which have been authorised. All transactions, unless otherwise indicated, include VAT at 20%.

20-3

1 Aug	Balance of cash £150.00
4 Aug	Voucher no 39: taxi fare £9.60
6 Aug	Voucher no 40: postage £5.50 (no VAT)
9 Aug	Voucher no 41: marker pens £3.84
11 Aug	Voucher no 42: travel expenses £10.50 (no VAT)
12 Aug	Voucher no 43: window cleaner £14.40
16 Aug	Voucher no 44: large envelopes £4.80
18 Aug	Voucher no 45: donation to charity £10.00 (no VAT)
19 Aug	Voucher no 46: rail fare £10.60 (no VAT); meal allowance £6.00 (no VAT)
20 Aug	Voucher no 47: recorded delivery postage £2.30 (no VAT)
23 Aug	Voucher no 48: roll of packing tape £2.40
25 Aug	Voucher no 49: excess postage paid £1.50 (no VAT)
27 Aug	Voucher no 50: taxi fare £14.40

You are to:

•   Enter the transactions for the month in the petty cash book (PCB42).

•   Total the analysis columns.

•   Restore the imprest amount of petty cash book to £150.00 by transfer from the cash book.

•   Balance the petty cash book at 31 August 20-3 and bring down the balance on 1 September.

11.9 Towan Limited keeps an amount of petty cash in a locked box in the office. The imprest amount is £150 which is restored at the beginning of each month.

The following payments were made in June and have been recorded in the petty cash book:

3 June	Postage stamps	£5.85
7 June	Window cleaning	£12.50
10 June	Stationery	£7.25
15 June	Meal allowance	£8.00
18 June	Donation to charity	£10.00
20 June	Stationery	£9.47
24 June	Postage stamps	£3.65

At 30 June the petty cash remaining in the locked box comprised:

3 x £10 notes, 8 x £5 notes, 15 x £1 coins, 11 x 50p coins, 6 x 20p coins, 11 x 10p coins, 5 x 5p coins, 6 x 2p coins, 11 x 1p coins

You are to complete the following:

(a)

Total of petty cash payments for June		£
Cash remaining should be		£
Actual cash remaining is:		

	as at 30 June	
	number held	value (£)
£10 notes		
£5 notes		
£1 coins		
50p coins		
20p coins		
10p coins		
5p coins		
2p coins		
1p coins		
TOTAL		
Amount of discrepancy (if any)		£

(b) State what action should be taken when a petty cash book cannot be reconciled with cash in hand.

12 The initial trial balance

this chapter covers...

In Chapter 3 we saw how it is necessary to balance the traditional form of account (the 'T' account) from time-to-time, according to the needs of the business.

In this chapter we list in two columns the balance of each account from the ledger, distinguishing between those accounts which have debit balances and those which have credit balances.

These two columns of debit and credit balances form the initial trial balance.

The two columns are totalled and if the two totals are the same, it proves that the accounting records are arithmetically correct.

If the two totals are not the same, it shows that there is an error, either in the addition of the columns or in the double-entry bookkeeping. This error should be traced and corrected.

This chapter shows how to prepare a trial balance manually. Many accounting systems use computer accounting, where the computer prints out a trial balance, in which case the totals should agree.

Later in the chapter we look at the differences between:

■ capital expenditure and revenue expenditure

■ capital income and revenue income

We see why it is important to classify this income and expenditure correctly in the double-entry system – if this is not done, the accounts may show a false financial position for the business.

BALANCING THE ACCOUNTS

Before an initial trial balance can be extracted, it is necessary to balance each account in the general ledger. The balance brought down needs to be calculated correctly and shown on the correct side of the account. It is the balance brought down figure that is used in the initial trial balance.

Before moving on to the initial trial balance, do make sure that you are able to balance accounts accurately – please refer back to Chapter 3 if you wish to review this process.

PREPARING AN INITIAL TRIAL BALANCE

An initial trial balance is prepared – or extracted – from the accounting records in order to make an initial check of the arithmetical accuracy of the double-entry bookkeeping, ie that the debit entries equal the credit entries.

A trial balance is a list of the balances of every account from general ledger (including cash book and petty cash book), distinguishing between those accounts which have debit balances and those which have credit balances.

A trial balance is prepared at regular intervals – often at the end of each month – and the balances are set out in two totalled columns, a debit column and a credit column.

Read the notes set out below and refer at the same time to the example trial balance shown on the next page.

- The debit and credit columns are totalled and the totals should agree. In this way the trial balance proves that the accounting records are arithmetically correct.

- The balance for each account listed in the trial balance is the amount brought down after the accounts have been balanced.

- The order of accounts within the trial balance could be set out
    - in alphabetical order, or
    - in random order, or
    - in the order of final accounts, that is income and expenditure items from the income statement, followed by asset, liability and capital items from the statement of financial position

Trial balance of Ace Suppliers as at 31 January 20-4

Account name	Debit £	Credit £
Purchases	7,500	
Sales		16,000
Sales returns	250	
Purchases returns		500
Sales ledger control	1,550	
Purchases ledger control		900
Rent	1,000	
Wages	1,500	
Heating and lighting	1,250	
Office equipment	5,000	
Machinery	7,500	
Inventory at 1 Jan 20-4	2,500	
Petty cash	200	
Bank (cash at bank)	4,850	
Value Added Tax		1,200
J Williams: loan		7,000
Capital		10,000
Drawings	2,500	
	35,600	35,600

a note about the asset of inventory

We have seen in earlier chapters how businesses use separate purchases and sales accounts to record when the goods in which they trade are bought and sold. The reason for using separate accounts for purchases and sales is because there is usually a difference between the buying price and the selling price – the latter is higher and gives the business its profit. At least once a year, however, a business values the inventory it has on the shelves of the shop, for example, or in the warehouse. As inventory is an asset of a business, the valuation is recorded as a debit to inventory account. This means that there will – for most businesses – be a debit balance on inventory account representing the value of inventory held at the beginning of the financial year. This balance will continue until such time as the inventory is formally valued again – often at the end of the financial year.

The debit balance for inventory is shown in the trial balance, as seen above.

DEBIT AND CREDIT BALANCES – GUIDELINES

Certain accounts always have a debit balance, while others always have a credit balance. The lists set out below act as a guide, and will also help in your understanding of the initial trial balance.

debit balances

Debit balances are assets and expenses, and include:

- purchases account
- sales returns account
- non-current asset accounts, eg premises, motor vehicles, machinery, office equipment, etc
- inventory account – the inventory valuation, usually at the beginning of the year
- expenses accounts, eg wages, telephone, rent, discount allowed
- drawings account
- sales ledger control account (which records the total balances of trade receivables)
- petty cash control account

credit balances

Credit balances are liabilities, income and capital, and include:

- sales account
- purchases returns account
- income accounts, eg rent received, commission received, fees received, discount received
- capital account
- loan account
- purchases ledger control account (which records the total balances of trade payables)

Notes:

- **Bank control account** can be either debit or credit – it will be:
  - debit when the business has money in the bank
  - credit when it is overdrawn.
- **Value Added Tax account** can be either debit or credit – it will be:
  - debit when VAT is due to the business
  - credit when the business owes VAT to HM Revenue & Customs.

IF THE INITIAL TRIAL BALANCE DOESN'T BALANCE . . .

If the initial trial balance fails to balance, ie the two totals are different, there is an error (or errors):

■ either in the addition of the trial balance

■ and/or in the double-entry bookkeeping

how to find an error

The procedure for finding the error(s) is as follows:

■ check the addition of the trial balance

■ check that the balance of each account has been correctly entered in the trial balance, and under the correct heading, ie debit or credit

■ check that the balance of every account in general ledger has been included in the trial balance, together with the balance of cash book and petty cash book

■ check that analysis columns from the cash book (for settlement discount and VAT), and from the petty cash book (for VAT and expenses) have been entered to the general ledger accounts

■ check the calculation of the balance on each account

■ calculate the amount that the trial balance is wrong, and then look in the accounts for a transaction for this amount: if one is found, check that the double-entry bookkeeping has been carried out correctly

■ halve the amount by which the trial balance is wrong, and look for a transaction for this amount: if it is found, check the double-entry bookkeeping

■ if the amount by which the trial balance is wrong is divisible by nine, then the error may be a reversal of figures, eg £65 entered as £56, or £45 entered as £54

■ if the trial balance is wrong by a round amount, eg £10, £100, £1,000, the error is likely to be in the calculation of the account balances

■ if the error(s) is still not found, it is necessary to check the bookkeeping transactions since the date of the last trial balance, by going back to the financial documents and books of prime entry

The accounts supervisor needs to be informed if the trial balance still does not balance; he or she will give guidance as to what is to be done.

The Case Study that follows shows how an initial trial balance is constructed from a list of account balances.

INITIAL TRIAL BALANCE

situation

You work as an accounts assistant for Severn Valley Stationery. The company sells office products and equipment to businesses in its area.

Today the accounts supervisor has asked you to work on preparing an initial trial balance as at 30 April 20-4. The supervisor has given you the following list of balances to be transferred to the trial balance.

You are to place the figures in the debit or credit column, as appropriate, and to total the debit and credit columns.

Account name	Amount £	Debit £	Credit £
Vehicles	20,500		
Inventory	11,945		
Bank (overdraft)	8,297		
Petty cash control	110		
Sales ledger control	28,368		
Purchases ledger control	12,591		
VAT owing to HM Revenue & Customs	2,084		
Capital	23,237		
Loan from bank	20,500		
Sales	84,837		
Sales returns	1,089		
Purchases	51,054		
Purchases returns	2,210		
Discount allowed	105		
Discount received	215		
Vehicle expenses	3,175		
Wages	22,864		
Rent and rates	8,210		
Advertising	2,174		
Heating and lighting	968		
Travel costs	1,476		
Telephone	732		
Postages	591		
Miscellaneous expenses	610		
Totals	–		

solution

You take each balance in turn and enter it in either the debit balance column or the credit balance column.

You use the following guidelines:

DEBIT BALANCES (to go in the debit column)	**CREDIT BALANCES** (to go in the credit column)
• purchases	• sales
• sales returns	• purchases returns
• expenses (including discount allowed)	• income (including discount received)
• inventory	• capital
• sales ledger control	• purchases ledger control
• VAT (when refund is due from HM Revenue & Customs)	• VAT (when owed to HM Revenue & Customs)
• bank (cash at bank)	• bank (overdraft)
• petty cash control	• loan/bank loan
• non-current assets	
• drawings	

When you have entered the balances in the appropriate column, you then total the two columns of the trial balance – if the debit and credit totals are the same, this proves that the accounting records are arithmetically correct. If the trial balance doesn't balance, you follow the procedures for finding error(s) along the lines of those set out on page 246.

The initial trial balance of Severn Valley Stationery as at 30 April 20-4 then appears as shown on the next page.

Account name	Amount £	Debit £	Credit £
Vehicles	20,500	20,500	
Inventory	11,945	11,945	
Bank (overdraft)	8,297		8,297
Petty cash control	110	110	
Sales ledger control	28,368	28,368	
Purchases ledger control	12,591		12,591
VAT owing to HM Revenue & Customs	2,084		2,084
Capital	23,237		23,237
Loan from bank	20,500		20,500
Sales	84,837		84,837
Sales returns	1,089	1,089	
Purchases	51,054	51,054	
Purchases returns	2,210		2,210
Discount allowed	105	105	
Discount received	215		215
Vehicle expenses	3,175	3,175	
Wages	22,864	22,864	
Rent and rates	8,210	8,210	
Advertising	2,174	2,174	
Heating and lighting	968	968	
Travel costs	1,476	1,476	
Telephone	732	732	
Postages	591	591	
Miscellaneous expenses	610	610	
Totals	–	153,971	153,971

Note that the format of the initial trial balance shown above includes the original 'Amount' column to show you the process of transferring the account balances to the correct debit or credit column. In reality the initial trial balance is likely only to show the debit and credit money columns. It will also be headed up with the name of the business and the date of the trial balance.

The trial balance of Severn Valley Stationery is shown in its final form on the next page.

Severn Valley Stationery

Trial Balance as at 30 April 20-4

Account name	Debit £	Credit £
Vehicles	20,500	
Inventory	11,945	
Bank (overdraft)		8,297
Petty cash control	110	
Sales ledger control	28,368	
Purchases ledger control		12,591
VAT owing to HM Revenue & Customs		2,084
Capital		23,237
Loan from bank		20,500
Sales		84,837
Sales returns	1,089	
Purchases	51,054	
Purchases returns		2,210
Discount allowed	105	
Discount received		215
Vehicle expenses	3,175	
Wages	22,864	
Rent and rates	8,210	
Advertising	2,174	
Heating and lighting	968	
Travel costs	1,476	
Telephone	732	
Postages	591	
Miscellaneous expenses	610	
Totals	153,971	153,971

CAPITAL AND REVENUE EXPENDITURE AND INCOME

In the double-entry bookkeeping system, it is important to distinguish between:

■ **capital expenditure** and **revenue expenditure**

■ **capital income** and **revenue income**

The reason for making the distinction between these two types of classification is to ensure that the accounting system shows the true financial position for the business.

capital expenditure

Capital expenditure is expenditure incurred on the purchase, alteration or improvement of non-current assets. Non-current assets are items purchased by a business for use on a long-term basis.

Included in capital expenditure are such costs as:

■ delivery of non-current assets

■ installation of non-current assets

■ improvement (but not repair) of non-current assets

■ legal costs of buying property

An example of capital expenditure is the purchase of a car for use in the business.

Note that we use the word 'capitalised' to mean that an item has been treated as capital expenditure.

revenue expenditure

Revenue expenditure is expenditure incurred on purchases made by the business and on running expenses.

Included in revenue expenditure are the costs of:

■ purchases made by the business

■ maintenance and repair of non-current assets owned by the business

■ administration of the business

■ selling and distributing the goods or products in which the business trades

An example of revenue expenditure is the cost of petrol or diesel for the car used in the business.

capital expenditure and revenue expenditure – the differences

In the accounting system, it is important to classify correctly capital expenditure and revenue expenditure. An error in the double-entry accounting may show a false financial position for the business. For example, if the cost of the car was shown as an expense instead of as a non-current asset, the business will show a large motoring expense during the year but will not record that it owns the car as a non-current asset: in other words, the accounts will show an incorrect picture of the business.

Study the following examples: they show the differences between capital expenditure and revenue expenditure.

■ **£30,000 cost of building an extension to the factory, which includes £1,000 for repairs to the existing factory**

– capital expenditure £29,000

– revenue expenditure £1,000 (because it is for repairs to an existing non-current asset)

■ **a plot of land has been bought for £20,000, the legal costs are £750**

– capital expenditure £20,750 (the legal costs are included in the capital expenditure, because they are the cost of acquiring the non-current asset, ie the legal costs are 'capitalised')

■ **the business' own employees are used to install a new air conditioning system: wages £1,000, materials £1,500**

– capital expenditure £2,500 (an addition to the property); note that, in cases such as this, the amounts for revenue expenditure, ie wages and materials purchases, will need to be reduced to allow for the transfer to capital expenditure

■ **own employees used to repair and redecorate the premises: wages £500, materials £750**

– revenue expenditure £1,250 (repairs and redecoration are running expenses)

■ **purchase of a new machine £10,000, payment for installation and setting up £250**

– capital expenditure, £10,250 (costs of installation of a non-current asset are capitalised)

Only by recording capital expenditure and revenue expenditure correctly in the double-entry accounting system can the business know the correct expenses amount and the correct amount of non-current assets it owns.

capital income

Capital income is income received from non-regular ('one-off') transactions.

Included in capital income are receipts from:

- sales of non-current assets

- loans raised from banks and other lenders

- capital, or increases in capital, paid in by the owner of the business

revenue income

Revenue income is income received from sales made by the business and other regular amounts of income.

Included in revenue income are the receipts from:

- sales made by the business

- rent from business premises rented out

- commission for work done by the business on behalf of other businesses

- cash discount for prompt settlement of amounts due to suppliers

recording capital income and revenue income

As with capital and revenue expenditure it is important to record capital income and revenue income correctly in the double-entry accounting system so as not to show a false financial position. For example, if the money received from the sale of a non-current asset was shown as income from sales it would increase the sales figure and, at the same time, there would be no record against the non-current asset of the amount it was sold for.

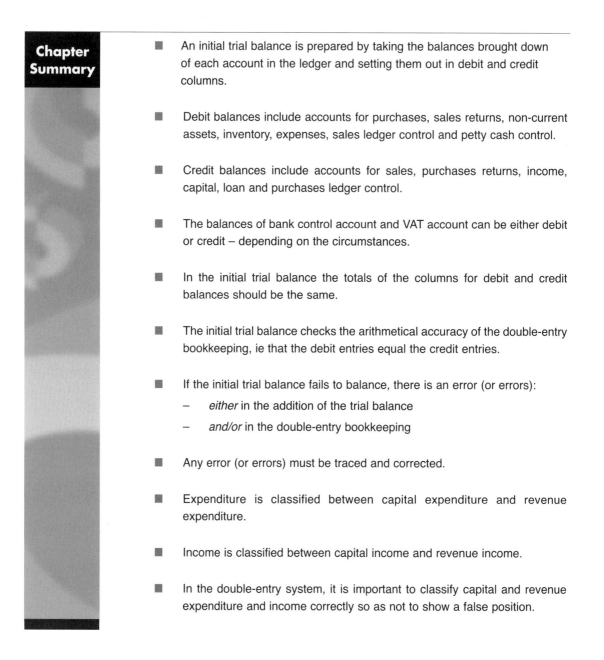

Chapter Summary

- An initial trial balance is prepared by taking the balances brought down of each account in the ledger and setting them out in debit and credit columns.

- Debit balances include accounts for purchases, sales returns, non-current assets, inventory, expenses, sales ledger control and petty cash control.

- Credit balances include accounts for sales, purchases returns, income, capital, loan and purchases ledger control.

- The balances of bank control account and VAT account can be either debit or credit – depending on the circumstances.

- In the initial trial balance the totals of the columns for debit and credit balances should be the same.

- The initial trial balance checks the arithmetical accuracy of the double-entry bookkeeping, ie that the debit entries equal the credit entries.

- If the initial trial balance fails to balance, there is an error (or errors):
  - *either* in the addition of the trial balance
  - *and/or* in the double-entry bookkeeping

- Any error (or errors) must be traced and corrected.

- Expenditure is classified between capital expenditure and revenue expenditure.

- Income is classified between capital income and revenue income.

- In the double-entry system, it is important to classify capital and revenue expenditure and income correctly so as not to show a false position.

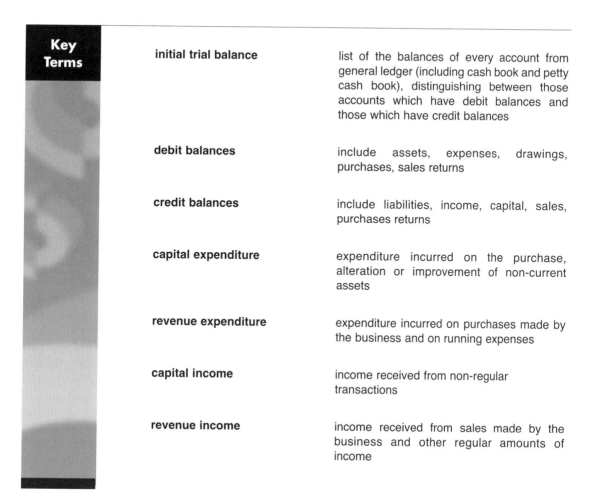

Key Terms		
	initial trial balance	list of the balances of every account from general ledger (including cash book and petty cash book), distinguishing between those accounts which have debit balances and those which have credit balances
	debit balances	include assets, expenses, drawings, purchases, sales returns
	credit balances	include liabilities, income, capital, sales, purchases returns
	capital expenditure	expenditure incurred on the purchase, alteration or improvement of non-current assets
	revenue expenditure	expenditure incurred on purchases made by the business and on running expenses
	capital income	income received from non-regular transactions
	revenue income	income received from sales made by the business and other regular amounts of income

Activities

12.1 Which one of the following accounts always has a debit balance?

(a) capital account

(b) purchases account

(c) sales account

(d) purchases returns account

Answer (a) or (b) or (c) or (d)

12.2 Which one of the following accounts always has a credit balance?

(a)   sales returns account

(b)   premises account

(c)   capital account

(d)   wages account

Answer (a) or (b) or (c) or (d)

12.3 Prepare the initial trial balance of Jane Greenwell as at 31 March 20-9, from the following list of balances:

	£
Bank (overdraft)	1,250
Purchases	850
Petty cash	48
Sales	1,940
Purchases returns	144
Trade payables	1,442
Equipment	2,704
Van	3,200
Inventory at 1 April 20-8	1,210
Sales returns	90
Trade receivables	1,174
Wages	1,500
Capital	6,000

12.4 You work as an accounts assistant for Pershore Products. The accounts supervisor has asked you to work on preparing an initial trial balance as at 30 June 20-2. The supervisor has given you the following list of balances to be transferred to the trial balance.

You are to place the figures in the debit or credit column, as appropriate, and total the debit and credit columns.

Account name	Amount £	Debit £	Credit £
Office equipment	12,246		
Bank (cash at bank)	3,091		
Petty cash control	84		
Inventory	11,310		
Capital	22,823		
Drawings	2,550		
VAT owing to HM Revenue & Customs	3,105		
Loan from bank	8,290		
Purchases ledger control	17,386		
Sales ledger control	30,274		
Sales	82,410		
Purchases	39,496		
Purchases returns	2,216		
Sales returns	3,471		
Discount received	298		
Discount allowed	517		
Wages	20,212		
Advertising	4,390		
Insurance	1,045		
Heating and lighting	1,237		
Rent and rates	4,076		
Travel costs	854		
Postages	721		
Telephone	954		
Totals	–		

12.5 You work as an accounts assistant for Arley Limited. The accounts supervisor has asked you to work on preparing an initial trial balance as at 31 December 20-6. The supervisor has given you the following list of balances to be transferred to the trial balance.

You are to place the figures in the debit or credit column, as appropriate, and total the debit and credit columns.

Account name	Amount £	Debit £	Credit £
Sales	101,269		
Sales returns	3,476		
Purchases	54,822		
Purchases returns	4,107		
Sales ledger control	25,624		
Purchases ledger control	18,792		
Discount received	399		
Discount allowed	210		
Rent and rates	3,985		
Advertising	4,867		
Insurance	1,733		
Wages	31,246		
Heating and lighting	3,085		
Postages	1,211		
Telephone	985		
Travel costs	2,311		
Miscellaneous expenses	107		
Capital	22,489		
Vehicles	22,400		
Inventory	12,454		
Petty cash control	85		
Bank (overdraft)	6,291		
VAT owing to HM Revenue & Customs	3,054		
Loan from bank	12,200		
Totals	–		

12.6 Classify the following as either *capital expenditure* or *revenue expenditure* by putting a tick in the relevant column of the table below.

		CAPITAL EXPENDITURE	REVENUE EXPENDITURE
(a)	purchase cost of vehicles		
(b)	rent paid on premises		
(c)	payments for purchases		
(d)	legal fees paid relating to the purchase of property		
(e)	cost of redecoration of the office		
(f)	cost of installation of air-conditioning in the office		
(g)	wages cost of own employees used to build extension to the stockroom		
(h)	cost of installation and setting up of a new machine		

12.7 Classify the following as either *capital income* or *revenue income* by putting a tick in the relevant column of the table below.

		CAPITAL INCOME	REVENUE INCOME
(a)	rent received		
(b)	commission received		
(c)	receipt from sale of old office equipment		
(d)	bank loan received		
(e)	receipts from sales		
(f)	cash discount received		
(g)	receipt from increase in owner's capital		
(h)	receipt from sale of property		

Answers to activities

CHAPTER 1: THE ACCOUNTING SYSTEM

1.1 (b)

1.2 True

1.3 (c)

1.4 (a)

1.5 (b)

1.6 (c)

1.7 (b)

1.8 (a)

1.9 (a) £10,500

(b) £6,720

(c) £3,000

(d) £155,000

(e) sales ledger and purchases ledger control accounts

CHAPTER 2: FINANCIAL DOCUMENTS FOR SALES

2.1 (a) delivery note (b) invoice
(c) statement (d) credit note (e) purchase order

2.2 (a) the percentage allowance given to customers who regularly deal with the seller.
(b) £159.50 - £47.85 discount = £111.65 plus VAT of £22.33 (rounded down) = £133.98

2.3

	total £	discount £	net total £	VAT £	invoice total £
(a)	160.00	32.00	128.00	25.60	153.60
(b)	400.00	80.00	320.00	64.00	384.00
(c)	40.00	none	40.00	8.00	48.00
(d)	8000.00	1600.00	6400.00	1280.00	7680.00

2.4

	net total	discount deducted	total after cash discount	VAT	invoice total*
(a)	128.00	3.20	124.80	24.96	152.96
(b)	320.00	8.00	312.00	62.40	382.40
(c)	40.00	1.00	39.00	7.80	47.80
(d)	6400.00	160.00	6240.00	1248.00	7648.00

*Remember that the VAT is normally added to the total before deduction of cash discount.

2.5   The problems are the urgency and the need for accuracy. If the wrong goods are sent the problems will be compounded.

Solutions: telephone or e-mail, and fax a copy of the order pointing out the error.

Best and quickest solution – telephone.

Important point – ask for a replacement corrected order to be sent (marked 'confirmation' to avoid duplication), so that a further check can be made. This is to make sure your position is strong, just in case the customer gets it wrong again! This type of problem can be sorted out at assistant level, but should be reported to the line manager when he/she returns.

2.6   Examples: Purchase order number, delivery note number, invoice number, inventory code, account number, credit note number.
The main importance of coding is for accurate cross referencing. It is also important for efficient filing.

2.7   (b)

2.8   (a)   Incorrect discount rate applied (10%), wrong addition for total. Goods total should be £76.00, VAT £15.20 and final total £91.20.

(b)   Total before discount should be £250.00. Corrected figures: goods total £225.00 (after deduction of 10% discount), VAT £45.00, final total £270.00.

2.9   Statement should be dated 31 July 20-3 and addressed to Mr Simpson.
The entries are:

20-3		debit £	credit £	balance £
1 July	Balance b/f	58.75		58.75
4 July	Cheque received		58.75	00.00
8 July	Invoice 10982	348.00		348.00
14 July	Credit note 2378		34.80	313.20
			TOTAL	313.20

CHAPTER 3: DOUBLE-ENTRY AND THE ACCOUNTING EQUATION

3.1   (c)

3.2   (b)

3.3   (a)

3.4

	debit	credit
Payment of wages		✔
Cash received from sales	✔	
Payment of an invoice by a credit customer	✔	
Payment of an insurance premium		✔
Loan received from a finance company	✔	
Loan repayment made		✔
Bank charges		✔

3.5

	debit	credit
Payment of wages	Wages	Bank
Payment of insurance	Insurance	Bank
Money received from sales	Bank	Sales
Purchases made	Purchases	Bank
Loan received from the bank	Bank	Loan
Loan repayment	Loan	Bank
Telephone bill paid	Telephone	Bank
Rates bill paid	Rates	Bank
Rent received from office let out	Bank	Rent received

3.6

Account	20-3	DR or CR	Details	Amount
Sales	1 May	Cr	Bank	975.00
	11 May	Cr	Bank	456.70
Telephone	6 May	Dr	Bank	265.00
Insurance	12 May	Dr	Bank	678.00
Bank Loan	14 May	Cr	Bank	5,000.00
Purchases	15 May	Dr	Bank	2,760.90

3.7

Debit balances: Purchases, Expenses, Customer Accounts, Assets

Credit balances: Capital, Liabilities, Supplier Accounts, Sales, Income

3.8

	debit	credit
Asset bought by the business	✔	
Liability (eg bank loan taken out)		✔
Capital introduced by the owner		✔
Sales made by the business		✔
Purchases made by the business	✔	
Expenses of the business	✔	
Customer who owes the business money	✔	
Supplier who is owed money by the business		✔

3.9 (b)

3.10

Assets	Liabilities	Capital
£	£	£
120,000	45,000	75,000
156,000	61,000	95,000
265,500	86,500	179,000
88,000	38,000	50,000
127,500	37,500	90,000
345,700	136,700	209,000

3.11

Transaction	Debit	Credit
Increase in capital account		✔
Increase in liability account		✔
Decrease in asset account		✔
Decrease in liability account	✔	
Increase in asset account	✔	

3.12

Debit			Bank Account			Credit
Date	Details	£	Date	Details		£
20-4			20-4			
3 Feb	Capital	10,000	10 Feb	Purchases		750
4 Feb	Bank Loan	25,000	14 Feb	Rates		450
6 Feb	Sales	1,340	15 Feb	Purchases		2,760
18 Feb	Sales	860	21 Feb	Advertising		138
25 Feb	Sales	2,640	28 Feb	Wages		3,560

Account	20-3	DR or CR	Details	Amount (£)
Capital	3 Feb	Cr	Bank	10,000
Bank loan	4 Feb	Cr	Bank	25,000
Sales	6 Feb	Cr	Bank	1,340
	18 Feb	Cr	Bank	860
	25 Feb	Cr	Bank	2,640
Purchases	10 Feb	Dr	Bank	750
	15 Feb	Dr	Bank	2,760
Rates	14 Feb	Dr	Bank	450
Advertising	21 Feb	Dr	Bank	138
Wages	28 Feb	Dr	Bank	3,560

3.13

(a)

Dr   Solo Supplies Account (Purchases Ledger)   **Cr**

20-3	Details	£	20-3	Details	£
31 Mar	Balance c/d	506.75	23 Mar	Purchases	248.00
			25 Mar	Purchases	78.75
			30 Mar	Purchases	180.00
		506.75			506.75
			1 Apr	Balance b/d	506.75

(b)

Dr   Atletico Supplies Account (Purchases Ledger)   **Cr**

20-3	Details	£	20-3	Details	£
23 Mar	Purchases returns	80.00	24 Mar	Purchases	120.00
26 Mar	Purchases returns	70.00	27 Mar	Purchases	360.00
31 Mar	Balance c/d	500.00	30 Mar	Purchases	170.00
		650.00			650.00
			1 Apr	Balance b/d	500.00

(c)

Dr			Trajan Sports Account (Sales Ledger)			Cr
20-3	**Details**	**£**	**20-3**	**Details**	**£**	
23 Mar	Sales	450.00	24 Mar	Sales returns	80.00	
26 Mar	Sales	70.00	30 Mar	Sales returns	70.00	
27 Mar	Sales	180.00	31 Mar	Balance c/d	550.00	
		700.00			700.00	
1 Apr	Balance b/d	550.00				

(d)

Dr			Office Expenses Account (General Ledger)			Cr
20-3	**Details**	**£**	**20-3**	**Details**	**£**	
4 Mar	Bank	75.20				
6 Mar	Bank	191.00				
8 Mar	Bank	34.65				
15 Mar	Bank	63.46	31 Mar	Balance c/d	364.31	
		364.31			364.31	
1 Apr	Balance b/d	364.31				

CHAPTER 4: ACCOUNTING FOR SALES AND SALES RETURNS

4.1 (a)

4.2 (a)

4.3 (a) • The financial documents for credit sales transactions are sales invoices that have been checked and authorised.

- The details and amounts of the invoices are entered into sales day book. In the money columns of sales day book is recorded:
  - total column, the final total of each invoice
  - VAT column, the VAT amount shown on each invoice
  - net column, the net ('goods or services total') amount of each invoice
- After sales day book has been written up for the week or month, it is totalled and the information from it is transferred into the double-entry system.
- The bookkeeping entries are:
  - the total of the total column is debited to sales ledger control account in general ledger
  - the total of the VAT column is credited to VAT account in general ledger
  - the total of the net column is credited to sales account in general ledger
  - the amounts from the total column for each separate transaction are debited to the subsidiary accounts of the customers in sales ledger

(b) • The financial documents for sales returns transactions are credit notes issued that have been checked and authorised.

- The details and amounts of the credit notes are entered into sales returns day book. In the money columns of the sales returns day book is recorded:
  - total column, the final total of each credit note
  - VAT column, the VAT amount shown on each credit note
  - net column, the net ('goods or services total') amount of each credit note
- After sales returns day book has been written up for the week or month, it is totalled and the information from it is transferred into the double-entry system.
- The bookkeeping entries are:
  - the total of the total column is credited to sales ledger control account in general ledger
  - the total of the VAT column is debited to VAT account in general ledger
  - the total of the net column is debited to sales returns account in general ledger
  - the amounts from the total column for each separate transaction are credited to the subsidiary accounts of the customers in sales ledger

4.4 (a)

Sales Day Book						SDB50
Date	Details	Invoice number	Account code	Total £	VAT £	Net £
20-5						
2 Apr	Malvern Stores	4578	SL110	66.00	11.00	55.00
5 Apr	Pershore Retailers	4579	SL145	78.00	13.00	65.00
7 Apr	E Grainger	4580	SL055	33.60	5.60	28.00
9 Apr	P Wilson	4581	SL172	69.60	11.60	58.00
12 Apr	M Kershaw	4582	SL090	91.20	15.20	76.00
14 Apr	D Lloyd	4583	SL095	79.20	13.20	66.00
19 Apr	A Cox	4584	SL032	39.60	6.60	33.00
22 Apr	Dines Stores	4585	SL048	122.40	20.40	102.00
23 Apr	Malvern Stores	4586	SL110	56.40	9.40	47.00
26 Apr	P Wilson	4587	SL172	42.00	7.00	35.00
29 Apr	A Cox	4588	SL032	98.40	16.40	82.00
30 Apr	Totals for month			776.40	129.40	647.00
				GL1200	GL2200	GL4100

(b)

GENERAL LEDGER

Dr		**Sales Ledger Control Account** (GL1200)			Cr
20-5		£ p	20-5		£ p
30 Apr	Sales Day Book SDB50	776.40			

Dr		**Value Added Tax Account** (GL2200)			Cr
20-5		£ p	20-5		£ p
			30 Apr	Sales Day Book SDB50	129.40

Dr		**Sales Account** (GL4100)			Cr
20-5		£ p	20-5		£ p
			30 Apr	Sales Day Book SDB50	647.00

SALES LEDGER

Dr		**Malvern Stores** (SL110)			Cr
20-5		£ p	20-5		£ p
2 Apr	Sales SDB50	66.00			
23 Apr	Sales SDB50	56.40			

Dr		**Pershore Retailers** (SL145)			Cr
20-5		£ p	20-5		£ p
5 Apr	Sales SDB50	78.00			

Dr		E Grainger (SL055)			Cr	
20-5			£ p	20-5		£ p
7 Apr	Sales	SDB50	33.60			

Dr		P Wilson (SL172)			Cr	
20-5			£ p	20-5		£ p
9 Apr	Sales	SDB50	69.60			
26 Apr	Sales	SDB50	42.00			

Dr		M Kershaw (SL090)			Cr	
20-5			£ p	20-5		£ p
12 Apr	Sales	SDB50	91.20			

Dr		D Lloyd (SL095)			Cr	
20-5			£ p	20-5		£ p
14 Apr	Sales	SDB 50	79.20			

Dr		A Cox (SL032)			Cr	
20-5			£ p	20-5		£ p
19 Apr	Sales	SDB 50	39.60			
29 Apr	Sales	SDB 50	98.40			

Dr		Dines Stores (SL048)			Cr	
20-5			£ p	20-5		£ p
22 Apr	Sales	SDB 50	122.40			

4.5 (a)

Sales Returns Day Book					SRDB18	
Date	Details	Credit note no	Account code	Total £	VAT £	Net £
20-5						
8 Apr	Pershore Retailers	572	SL145	24.00	4.00	20.00
12 Apr	E Grainger	573	SL055	33.60	5.60	28.00
16 Apr	D Lloyd	574	SL095	39.60	6.60	33.00
28 Apr	Malvern Stores	575	SL110	24.00	4.00	20.00
30 Apr	A Cox	576	SL032	48.00	8.00	40.00
30 Apr	Totals for month			169.20	28.20	141.00
				GL1200	GL2200	GL4110

(b)

GENERAL LEDGER

Dr	**Sales Ledger Control Account** (GL1200)		Cr	
20-5		£ p	20-5	£ p
30 Apr Sales Day Book	SDB50	776.40	30 Apr Sales Returns Day Book SRDB18	169.20

Dr	**Value Added Tax Account** (GL2200)		Cr	
20-5		£ p	20-5	£ p
30 Apr Sales Returns Day Book	SRDB18	28.20	30 Apr Sales Day Book SDB50	129.40

Dr	**Sales Returns Account** (GL4110)		Cr	
20-5		£ p	20-5	£ p
30 Apr Sales Returns Day Book	SRDB18	141.00		

Note: sales account not shown – see answer to Activity 4.4

SALES LEDGER

Dr	**Pershore Retailers** (SL145)		Cr	
20-5		£ p	20-5	£ p
5 Apr Sales	SDB50	78.00	8 Apr Sales Returns SRDB18	24.00

Dr	**E Grainger** (SL055)		Cr	
20-5		£ p	20-5	£ p
7 Apr Sales	SDB50	33.60	12 Apr Sales Returns SRDB18	33.60

Dr	**D Lloyd** (SL095)		Cr	
20-5		£ p	20-5	£ p
14 Apr Sales	SDB50	79.20	16 Apr Sales Returns SRDB18	39.60

Dr	**Malvern Stores** (SL110)		Cr	
20-5		£ p	20-5	£ p
2 Apr Sales	SDB50	66.00	28 Apr Sales Returns SRDB18	24.00
23 Apr Sales	SDB50	56.40		

Dr	**A Cox** (SL032)		Cr	
20-5		£ p	20-5	£ p
19 Apr Sales	SDB50	39.60	30 Apr Sales Returns SRDB18	48.00
29 Apr Sales	SDB50	98.40		

4.6 (a)

General ledger

Account name	Amount £	Debit ✓	Credit ✓
Sales	10,600		✓
Value Added Tax	2,120		✓
Sales ledger control	12,720	✓	

Sales ledger

Account name	Amount £	Debit ✓	Credit ✓
Bowne Ltd	960	✓	
Jamieson & Co	4,944	✓	
Pottertons	3,888	✓	
Wells plc	2,928	✓	

(b)

General ledger

Account name	Amount £	Debit ✓	Credit ✓
Sales returns	1,520	✓	
Value Added Tax	304	✓	
Sales ledger control	1,824		✓

Sales ledger

Account name	Amount £	Debit ✓	Credit ✓
Lloyd & Co	576		✓
Wyvern Stores	1,248		✓

4.7

Customer	Sales ledger account code
Dymock Trading Co	DYM003
Hedgehog Fashions	HED001
Jones & Co	JON002

Note: Dymock Trading Co is numbered '003' because an '002' account number has been allocated already for 'D'; similarly for Jones & Co where '001' has been allocated already for 'J'.

4.8   (a) & (b)

Sales day book

Date 20XX	Details	Invoice number	Total £	VAT £	Net £	Sales type 1 £	Sales type 2 £
30 June	Yanez & Co	1621	1,440	240	1,200		1,200
30 June	Napier Stores	1622	1,920	320	1,600	1,600	
30 June	Beale Ltd	1623	768	128	640		640
	Totals		4,128	688	3,440	1,600	1,840

CHAPTER 5: PROCESS PAYMENTS FROM CUSTOMERS

5.1   (d)

5.2   (b)

5.3   (a)   The remittance advice does not take account of the credit note issued on 10 November and so includes an overpayment of £49.00. Cool Socks should advise the customer, Trends, of this discrepancy and suggest that an adjustment could be made when the next month's payment is due, the credit remaining on the account for the time being.

   (b)   The remittance advice does not include payment of an invoice for £625.85 issued on 17 November and so the discrepancy is an underpayment. As the amount is large, Cool Socks should contact Vogue Limited and ask for payment. If the invoice is disputed, the problem should be looked into and resolved as soon as possible.

   (c)   RTC Fashions have underpaid their account because they have deducted 5% settlement discount when it was not offered (it is not included in the terms on the Chico Importers invoice). Additionally they have adjusted and underpaid the VAT by £5.60. Chico Importers should either ask RTC Fashions for payment of the shortfall of £33.60 immediately or advise them of the problem and suggest that an adjustment could be made when the next month's payment is due, the debit remaining on RTC Fashions' account for the time being. The decision depends on the relationship that exists between the supplier and customer.

CHAPTER 6: PROCESS DOCUMENTS FROM SUPPLIERS

6.1   (a)   purchase order

(b)   delivery note

(c)   goods received note

(d)   invoice

(e)   credit note

6.2   A delivery note is sent by the seller with the goods, a goods received note is an internal document used by the purchaser to record and action any discrepancies found when the goods arrive.

6.3   (a)

6.4   Credit note.

6.5   The errors are:

(a)   the goods were delivered to the wrong address

(b)   an incorrect customer discount has been applied (10% instead of 15%)

(c)   the wrong goods were sent (product code 4574 instead of 4573)

The total should have been £95 less 15% discount = £80.75 plus VAT of £16.15 = £96.90

The email should point out these errors and state that the disks are being returned for credit.

6.6   (a)   Errors on credit note:

– Wrong reference - should be 17643

– Product code incorrect – should be 919BK

– Should be gel pens, not rollerball pens

– credit should be for 2 boxes, not 3

– discount deducted at 20%, should be 10%

As the goods received are correct, the email should point out the errors on the credit note and ask for a revised document to be issued.

(b)

supplier a/c reference	general ledger a/c number
HE001	5010

CHAPTER 7: ACCOUNTING FOR PURCHASES AND PURCHASES RETURNS

7.1   (c)

7.2   (d)

7.3   (b)

7.4   (a)   • The financial documents for credit purchases transactions are purchases invoices, received from suppliers, that have been checked and authorised.

• The details and amounts of the invoices are entered into the purchases day book. In the money columns of purchases day book is recorded:

  – total column, the final total of each invoice

  – VAT column, the VAT amount shown on each invoice

  – net column, the net ('goods or services total') amount of each invoice

• After purchases day book has been written up for the week or month, it is totalled and the information from it is transferred into the double-entry system.

• The bookkeeping entries are:

  – the total of the total column is credited to purchases ledger control account in general ledger

  – the total of the VAT column is debited to VAT account in general ledger

  – the total of the net column is debited to purchases account in general ledger

  – the amounts from the total column for each separate transaction are credited to the subsidiary accounts of the suppliers in purchases ledger

   (b)   • The financial documents for purchases returns transactions are credit notes, received from suppliers, that have been checked and authorised.

• The details and amounts of the credit notes are entered into purchases returns day book. In the money columns of the purchases returns day book is recorded:

  – total column, the final total of each credit note

  – VAT column, the VAT amount shown on each credit note

  – net column, the net ('goods or services total') amount of each credit note

• After purchases returns day book has been written up for the week or month, it is totalled and the information from it is transferred into the double-entry system.

• The bookkeeping entries are:

  – the total of the total column is debited to purchases ledger control account in general ledger

  – the total of the VAT column is credited to VAT account in general ledger

  – the total of the net column is credited to purchases returns account in general ledger

  – the amounts from the total column for each separate transaction are debited to the subsidiary accounts of the suppliers in purchases ledger

7.5 (a)

Purchases Day Book						PDB36
Date	Details	Invoice number	Account code	Total	VAT	Net
20-5				£ p	£ p	£ p
2 Apr	Severn Supplies	6789	PL721	300.00	50.00	250.00
5 Apr	I Johnstone	A241	PL604	252.00	42.00	210.00
9 Apr	L Murphy	2456	PL659	222.00	37.00	185.00
15 Apr	Mercia Manufacturing	X457	PL627	216.00	36.00	180.00
19 Apr	AMC Enterprises	AMC 456	PL520	414.00	69.00	345.00
26 Apr	S Green	2846	PL574	474.00	79.00	395.00
30 Apr	Totals for month			1,878.00	313.00	1,565.00
				GL2350	GL2200	GL5100

(b)

GENERAL LEDGER

Dr	Value Added Tax Account (GL2200)		Cr
20-5	£ p	20-5	£ p
30 Apr Purchases Day Book PDB36	313.00		

Dr	Purchases Ledger Control Account (GL2350)		Cr
20-5	£ p	20-5	£ p
		30 Apr Purchases Day Book PDB36	1,878.00

Dr	Purchases Account (GL5100)		Cr
20-5	£ p	20-5	£ p
30 Apr Purchases Day Book PDB36	1,565.00		

PURCHASES LEDGER

Dr	Severn Supplies (PL721)		Cr
20-5	£ p	20-5	£ p
		2 Apr Purchases PDB36	300.00

Dr	I Johnstone (PL604)		Cr
20-5	£ p	20-5	£ p
		5 Apr Purchases PDB36	252.00

Dr			L Murphy (PL659)			Cr
20-5		£ p	20-5			£ p
			9 Apr	Purchases	PDB36	222.00

Dr			Mercia Manufacturing (PL627)			Cr
20-5		£ p	20-5			£ p
			15 Apr	Purchases	PDB36	216.00

Dr			AMC Enterprises (PL520)			Cr
20-5		£ p	20-5			£ p
			19 Apr	Purchases	PDB36	414.00

Dr			S Green (PL574)			Cr
20-5		£ p	20-5			£ p
			26 Apr	Purchases	PDB36	474.00

7.6 (a)

Purchases Returns Day Book						PRDB11
Date	Details	Credit note no	Account code	Total	VAT	Net
20-5				£ p	£ p	£ p
7 Apr	Severn Supplies	225	PL 721	60.00	10.00	50.00
14 Apr	L Murphy	X456	PL 659	96.00	16.00	80.00
21 Apr	AMC Enterprises	3921	PL 520	150.00	25.00	125.00
29 Apr	S Green	SG247	PL 574	81.60	13.60	68.00
30 Apr	Totals for month			387.60	64.60	323.00
				GL2350	GL2200	GL5110

(b)

GENERAL LEDGER

Dr		Value Added Tax Account (GL2200)			Cr
20-5		£ p	20-5		£ p
30 Apr	Purchases Day Book PDB36	313.00	30 Apr	Purchases Returns Day Book PRDB11	64.60

Dr		Purchases Ledger Control Account (GL2350)			Cr
20-5		£ p	20-5		£ p
30 Apr	Purchases Returns Day Book PRDB11	387.60	30 Apr	Purchases Day Book PDB36	1,878.00

Dr				Purchases Returns Account (GL5110)		Cr		
20-5			£ p	20-5			£	p
				30 Apr	Purchases Returns Day Book	PRDB11	323.00	

Note: purchases account not shown – see answer to Activity 7.5

PURCHASES LEDGER

Dr				Severn Supplies (PL721)		Cr		
20-5			£ p	20-5			£	p
7 Apr	Purchases Returns			2 Apr	Purchases	PDB36	300.00	
	PRDB11	60.00						

Dr				L Murphy (PL659)		Cr		
20-5			£ p	20-5			£	p
14 Apr	Purchases Returns			9 Apr	Purchases	PDB36	222.00	
	PRDB11	96.00						

Dr				AMC Enterprises (PL520)		Cr		
20-5			£ p	20-5			£	p
21 Apr	Purchases Returns			19 Apr	Purchases	PDB36	414.00	
	PRDB11	150.00						

Dr				S Green (PL574)		Cr		
20-5			£ p	20-5			£	p
29 Apr	Purchases Returns			26 Apr	Purchases	PDB36	474.00	
	PRDB11	81.60						

7.7 (a)

General ledger

Account name	Amount £	Debit ✓	Credit ✓
Purchases	8,040	✓	
Value Added Tax	1,608	✓	
Purchases ledger control	9,648		✓

Purchases ledger

Account name	Amount £	Debit ✓	Credit ✓
Seng Ltd	1,152		✓
Peall & Co	2,832		✓
Knightons	4,176		✓
Galeazzi plc	1,488		✓

(b)
General ledger

Account name	Amount £	Debit ✓	Credit ✓
Purchases returns	1,440		✓
Value Added Tax	288		✓
Purchases ledger control	1,728	✓	

Purchases ledger

Account name	Amount £	Debit ✓	Credit ✓
Martin & Co	1,056	✓	
Wentworth Stores	672	✓	

7.8

Supplier	Purchases ledger account code
Bridon Ltd	BRI003
Foster & Co	FOS001
Hirst & Co	HIR002

Note: Bridon Ltd is numbered '003' because an '002' account number has been allocated already for 'B'; similarly for Hirst & Co where '001' has been allocated already for 'H'.

7.9

Purchases day book

Date 20XX	Details	Invoice number	Total £	VAT £	Net £	Purchases type 1 £	Purchases type 2 £
30 June	Canoy Ltd	C350	1,608	268	1,340	1,340	
30 June	McVeigh & Co	5148	2,340	390	1,950		1,950
30 June	Robinsons	R/862	2,952	492	2,460	2,460	
	Totals		6,900	1,150	5,750	3,800	1,950

CHAPTER 8: PREPARE PAYMENTS TO SUPPLIERS

8.1 (c)

8.2 (a)

8.3 (b)

8.4 (c)

8.5 Invoice £150 on 8 March ref 76333 has been entered twice on the statement of account but only once in the purchases ledger. It is likely to be a duplication and should be queried with Luxon Traders. The likely outcome is a payment of £100 (invoice for £150 less credit note for £50).

8.6 Credit note £72.90 on 22 April appears in the purchases ledger but not on the supplier statement. Having checked that the credit note has been correctly posted to the purchases ledger account, you should query it with A Krauss Trading, as they may have posted it to the wrong account, or not posted it at all. The likely outcome is a payment of £269.85 (invoices for £233.25 and £109.50 less credit note for £72.90).

8.7

BACS REMITTANCE ADVICE

FROM:
Hetherington Limited
Unit 23 Wessex Estate
Langborne Road
Seatown SE8 5VZ

TO   Aldersgate Supplies
     10 Aldersgate Street, London EC1A 7GH

date: 3 October 20-5

date	your reference	our reference	payment amount £
08 09 20-5	Invoice 10945	PO85262	120.75
14 09 20-5	Invoice 10963	PO85271	380.25
20 09 20-5	Credit note 109	PO85248	(46.00)
		TOTAL	**455.00**

THIS AMOUNT HAS BEEN PAID BY BACS CREDIT TRANSFER DIRECTLY INTO YOUR BANK ACCOUNT AT ALBION BANK ACCOUNT NO 17643987 SORT CODE 99 43 83

8.8

REMITTANCE ADVICE

FROM:
Hetherington Limited
Unit 23 Wessex Estate
Langborne Road
Seatown SE8 5VZ

TO Sutherland & Co
67 Great March Street
Eastwick, EA3 9JN

date: 5 June 20-5

date	your reference	our reference	payment amount £
23 May 20-5	Invoice 7856	472984	345.90
29 May 20-5	Credit note 4562	472975	(87.50)
		CHEQUE TOTAL	**258.40**

Southern Bank PLC
Mereford Branch
16 Broad Street, Mereford MR1 7TR

date *5 June 20-5*

97-76-54

Pay *Sutherland & Co* ————————————————— only

Two hundred and fifty eight pounds 40p ————————

Account payee only

£ *258.40*

HETHERINGTON LTD

123456   97 76 54   68384939

Director

CHAPTER 9: THREE COLUMN CASH BOOK

9.1 (d)

9.2

GENERAL LEDGER

Dr				Capital Account			Cr
20-7			£	20-7			£
				30 Apr	Cash	CB70	2,000
				30 Apr	Bank	CB70	8,000

Dr				Bank Loan Account			Cr
20-7			£	20-7			£
				30 Apr	Bank	CB70	5,000

Dr				Rent Account			Cr
20-7			£	20-7			£
30 Apr	Bank	CB70	1,000				

Dr				Wages Account			Cr
20-7			£	20-7			£
30 Apr	Cash	CB70	800				

Dr				Drawings Account			Cr
20-7			£	20-7			£
30 Apr	Bank	CB70	500				

Dr				Vehicles Account			Cr
20-7			£	20-7			£
30 Apr	Bank	CB70	10,000				

9.3

(a) True

(b) False – the balance b/d of £918 on 1 May shows that, according to the cash book, there is a bank overdraft.

(c)

GENERAL LEDGER

Dr				Sales Account			Cr
20-5			£	20-5			£
				30 Apr	Cash	CB32	40

Dr		Commission Received Account			Cr
20-5			£	20-5			£
				30 Apr	Bank	CB32	48

Dr		Sales Ledger Control Account			Cr
20-5			£	20-5			£
				30 Apr	Bank	CB32	2,400
				30 Apr	Discount allowed	CB32	40

Dr		Bank Loan Account			Cr
20-5			£	20-5			£
				30 Apr	Bank	CB32	2,000

Dr		Purchases Ledger Control Account			Cr
20-5			£	20-5		£
30 Apr	Bank	CB32	3,200		
30 Apr	Discount received	CB32	50		

Dr		Purchases Account			Cr
20-5			£	20-5		£
30 Apr	Bank	CB32	96		

Dr		Office Equipment Account			Cr
20-5			£	20-5		£
30 Apr	Bank	CB32	2,600		

Dr		Wages Account			Cr
20-5			£	20-5		£
30 Apr	Bank	CB32	1,550		

Dr		General Expenses Account			Cr
20-5			£	20-5		£
30 Apr	Cash	CB32	80		

Dr		Discount Allowed Account			Cr
20-5			£	20-5		£
30 Apr	Sales ledger control	CB32	40		

Dr		Discount Received Account			Cr
20-5			£	20-5			£
				30 Apr	Purchases ledger control	CB32	50

(d)

SALES LEDGER

Dr					Lindum Limited				Cr
20-5				£	20-5				£
					30 Apr	Bank	CB32	2,400	
					30 Apr	Discount allowed	CB32	40	

PURCHASES LEDGER

Dr					Mereford Mills		Cr
20-5				£	20-5		£
30 Apr	Bank	CB32	3,200				
30 Apr	Discount received	CB32	50				

9.4 (a)

9.5 (a)

Dr					Cash Book					Cr
Date	Details	Acc code	Discount allowed	Cash	Bank	Date	Details	Acc code	Discount received	Cash	Bank
			£	£	£				£	£	£
20-2						20-2					
1 Jun	Balance b/d			280		1 Jun	Balance b/d				1,240
3 Jun	G Wheaton		5		195	10 Jun	Wages			165	
5 Jun	T Francis		2	92		12 Jun	A Morris		3	97	
18 Jun	H Watson		30		640	24 Jun	D Farr		2		65
30 Jun	Balance c/d				575	26 Jun	Telephone				105
						30 Jun	Balance c/d			110	
			37	372	1,410				5	372	1,410
1 Jul	Balance b/d			110		1 Jul	Balance b/d				575

(b)

Dr		Discount Allowed Account		Cr
20-2		£	20-2	£
30 Jun	Sales ledger control	37		

Dr		Discount Received Account		Cr
20-2		£	20-2	£
			30 Jun Purchases ledger control	5

CHAPTER 10: ANALYSED CASH BOOK

10.1 (c)

10.2 (a)

10.3

		True	False
(a)	Cash book is the book of prime entry for bank and cash receipts and payments	✔	
(b)	Cash book can be the double-entry account for bank and cash	✔	
(c)	The discount received column total from cash book is debited to discount received account in general ledger		✔
(d)	The VAT column total on the receipts side of an analysed cash book is debited to VAT account in general ledger		✔
(e)	The trade receivables column total from an analysed cash book is credited to sales ledger control account in general ledger	✔	

10.4

(a) - (b)

Dr (Receipts)

Date	Details	Acc code	Discount allowed	Cash	Bank	VAT	Cash sales	Trade receivables	Other income
20-7			£	£	£	£	£	£	£
12 May	Balances b/d			205	825				
12 May	Sales	GL			600	100	500		
13 May	Sales	GL		180		30	150		
13 May	T Jarvis	SL	3		155			155	
14 May	Sales	GL			720	120	600		
15 May	Cash	C			250				
15 May	Sales	GL		288		48	240		
16 May	Wyvern Council	SL	4		560			560	
			7	673	3,110	298	1,490	715	–
17 May	Balances b/d			387	1,816				

Cr (Payments)

Date	Details	Acc code	Discount received	Cash	Bank	VAT	Cash purchases	Trade payables	Other expenses
20-7			£	£	£	£	£	£	£
12 May	Rent	GL			255				255
13 May	Terry Carpets	PL	5		363			363	
14 May	Trade Supplies	PL	4		145			145	
14 May	Purchases	GL		36		6	30		
15 May	Bank	C		250					
15 May	Longlife Carpets	PL	4		291			291	
16 May	Purchases	GL			240	40	200		
16 May	Balances c/d			387	1,816				
			13	673	3,110	46	230	799	255

(c)   Transfers to general ledger:

- *discount allowed* column total of £7 is debited to discount allowed account and credited to sales ledger control account

- *discount received* column total of £13 is credited to discount received account and debited to purchases ledger control account

(d)

SALES LEDGER

Dr		T Jarvis			Cr
20-7		£	20-7		£
			13 May	Bank	155
			13 May	Discount allowed	3

Dr		Wyvern Council			Cr
20-7		£	20-7		£
			16 May	Bank	560
			16 May	Discount allowed	4

PURCHASES LEDGER

Dr		Terry Carpets		Cr
20-7		£	20-7	£
13 May	Bank	363		
13 May	Discount received	5		

Dr		Trade Supplies		Cr
20-7		£	20-7	£
14 May	Bank	145		
14 May	Discount received	4		

Dr		Longlife Carpets		Cr
20-7		£	20-7	£
15 May	Bank	291		
15 May	Discount received	4		

10.5 (a) **Cash book – credit side**

Details	Discount	Cash	Bank	VAT	Trade payables	Cash purchases	Vehicle expenses
Balance b/f							
Knowles & Co		30		5		25	
S Goulding		96		16		80	
Liyan Ltd	10		920		920		
Nelson Street Garage			132	22			110
Sandhu & Co			645		645		
Totals	10	126	1,697	43	1,565	105	110

(b) **Cash book – debit side**

Details	Discount	Cash	Bank	Trade receivables	Other income
Balance b/f		254	1,598		
Watkin Ltd			429	429	
P Pandya	12		1,522	1,522	
Matt Martin		235			235
Totals	12	489	3,549	1,951	235

(c) £363

(d) £1,852

(e)

Debit	✓
Credit	

CHAPTER 11: PETTY CASH BOOK

11.1   (c)
11.2   (a)
11.3   (d)

11.4   ✓

	✓
Debit	✓
Credit	

11.5   **General ledger**

Account name	Amount £	Debit ✓	Credit ✓
Petty cash book/Petty cash control account	75.00	✓	
Bank	75.00		✓

11.6

	Expense (excluding VAT) £	VAT £	Total £
(a)	8.00	1.60	9.60
(b)	4.00	0.80	4.80
(c)	2.00	0.40	2.40
(d)	2.05	0.41	2.46
(e)	4.67	0.93	5.60
(f)	2.90	0.58	3.48
(g)	7.30	1.46	8.76
(h)	0.80	0.16	0.96
(i)	0.83	0.16	0.99
(j)	7.86	1.57	9.43

11.7   (a)   **GENERAL LEDGER**

Dr   **Value Added Tax Account**   Cr

20-9			£	20-9			£
31 Mar	Petty cash book	PCB20	4.56				

Dr   **Travel Account**   Cr

20-9			£	20-9			£
31 Mar	Petty cash book	PCB20	24.26				

Dr   **Postages Account**   Cr

20-9			£	20-9			£
31 Mar	Petty cash book	PCB20	16.65	12 Mar	Petty cash book	PCB20	8.50

Dr   **Stationery Account**   Cr

20-9			£	20-9			£
31 Mar	Petty cash book	PCB20	9.60				

Dr   **Meals Account**   Cr

20-9			£	20-9			£
31 Mar	Petty cash book	PCB20	5.00				

Dr   **Purchases Ledger Control Account**   Cr

20-9			£	20-9			£
31 Mar	Petty cash book	PCB20	13.50				

Dr   **Petty Cash Control Account**   Cr

20-9			£	20-9			£
1 Mar	Balance b/d		100.00	31 Mar	Petty cash book	PCB20	73.57
31 Mar	Petty cash book	PCB20	8.50	31 Mar	Balance c/d		100.00
31 Mar	Bank	CB	65.07				
			173.57				173.57
1 Apr	Balance b/d		100.00				

Dr   **Cash Book**   Cr

20-9			Bank	20-9			Bank
				31 Mar	Petty cash	PCB20	65.07

(b)   **PURCHASES LEDGER**

Dr   **P Andrews**   Cr

20-9			£	20-9			£
18 Mar	Petty cash book	PCB20	13.50				

11.8

					Analysis columns					
Receipts	Date	Details	Voucher number	Total payment	VAT	Travel	Postages	Stationery	Meals	Misc
£	20-3			£	£	£	£	£	£	£
150.00	1 Aug	Balance b/d								
	4 Aug	Taxi fare	39	9.60	1.60	8.00				
	6 Aug	Postage	40	5.50			5.50			
	9 Aug	Marker pens	41	3.84	0.64			3.20		
	11 Aug	Travel expenses	42	10.50		10.50				
	12 Aug	Window cleaner	43	14.40	2.40					12.00
	16 Aug	Envelopes	44	4.80	0.80			4.00		
	18 Aug	Donation	45	10.00						10.00
	19 Aug	Rail fare/meal allow	46	16.60		10.60			6.00	
	20 Aug	Postage	47	2.30			2.30			
	23 Aug	Tape	48	2.40	0.40			2.00		
	25 Aug	Postage	49	1.50			1.50			
	27 Aug	Taxi fare	50	14.40	2.40	12.00				
				95.84	8.24	41.10	9.30	9.20	6.00	22.00
95.84	31 Aug	Bank								
	31 Aug	Balance c/d		150.00						
245.84				245.84						
150.00	1 Sep	Balance b/d								

Petty Cash Book   PCB42

11.9 (a)

Total of petty cash payments for June	£56.72
Cash remaining should be	£93.28

Actual cash remaining is:		
	as at 30 June	
	number held	value (£)
£10 notes	3	30.00
£5 notes	8	40.00
£1 coins	15	15.00
50p coins	11	5.50
20p coins	6	1.20
10p coins	11	1.10
5p coins	5	0.25
2p coins	6	0.12
1p coins	11	0.11
TOTAL		93.28
Amount of discrepancy (if any)		£ nil

(b) If there is a discrepancy – whether a shortfall or a surplus – it should be investigated promptly and, if it cannot be resolved, should be referred to the accounts supervisor.

CHAPTER 12: THE INITIAL TRIAL BALANCE

12.1 (b)

12.2 (c)

12.3

Trial balance of Jane Greenwell as at 31 March 20-9

Name of account	Dr £	Cr £
Bank (overdraft)		1,250
Purchases	850	
Petty cash	48	
Sales		1,940
Purchases returns		144
Trade payables		1,442
Equipment	2,704	
Van	3,200	
Inventory at 1 April 20-8	1,210	
Sales returns	90	
Trade receivables	1,174	
Wages	1,500	
Capital		6,000
	10,776	10,776

12.4

Account name	Amount £	Debit £	Credit £
Office equipment	12,246	12,246	
Bank (cash at bank)	3,091	3,091	
Petty cash control	84	84	
Inventory	11,310	11,310	
Capital	22,823		22,823
Drawings	2,550	2,550	
VAT owing to HM Revenue & Customs	3,105		3,105
Loan from bank	8,290		8,290
Purchases ledger control	17,386		17,386
Sales ledger control	30,274	30,274	
Sales	82,410		82,410
Purchases	39,496	39,496	
Purchases returns	2,216		2,216
Sales returns	3,471	3,471	
Discount received	298		298
Discount allowed	517	517	
Wages	20,212	20,212	
Advertising	4,390	4,390	
Insurance	1,045	1,045	
Heating and lighting	1,237	1,237	
Rent and rates	4,076	4,076	
Travel costs	854	854	
Postages	721	721	
Telephone	954	954	
Totals		136,528	136,528

12.5

Account name	Amount £	Debit £	Credit £
Sales	101,269		101,269
Sales returns	3,476	3,476	
Purchases	54,822	54,822	
Purchases returns	4,107		4,107
Sales ledger control	25,624	25,624	
Purchases ledger control	18,792		18,792
Discount received	399		399
Discount allowed	210	210	
Rent and rates	3,985	3,985	
Advertising	4,867	4,867	
Insurance	1,733	1,733	
Wages	31,246	31,246	
Heating and lighting	3,085	3,085	
Postages	1,211	1,211	
Telephone	985	985	
Travel costs	2,311	2,311	
Miscellaneous expenses	107	107	
Capital	22,489		22,489
Vehicles	22,400	22,400	
Inventory	12,454	12,454	
Petty cash control	85	85	
Bank (overdraft)	6,291		6,291
VAT owing to HM Revenue & Customs	3,054		3,054
Loan from bank	12,200		12,200
Totals		168,601	168,601

12.6

	CAPITAL EXPENDITURE	REVENUE EXPENDITURE
(a) purchase cost of vehicles	✓	
(b) rent paid on premises		✓
(c) payments for purchases		✓
(d) legal fees paid relating to the purchase of property	✓	
(e) cost of redecoration of the office		✓
(f) cost of installation of air-conditioning in the office	✓	
(g) wages cost of own employees used to build extension to the stockroom	✓	
(h) cost of installation and setting up of a new machine	✓	

12.7

	CAPITAL INCOME	REVENUE INCOME
(a) rent received		✓
(b) commission received		✓
(c) receipt from sale of old office equipment	✓	
(d) bank loan received	✓	
(e) receipts from sales		✓
(f) cash discount received		✓
(g) receipt from increase in owner's capital	✓	
(h) receipt from sale of property	✓	

Index

300

Trade discount, 28

Trial balance, 10-11

    initial trial balance, 242-250

Value Added Tax (VAT)

    cash book, 203

    definition, 32

    fraction, 32

    petty cash book, 224-225

Bookkeeping 1

Tutorial

11·00

6

David Cox
Michael Fardon

633006

AAT WISE GUIDES – for convenient exam revision

This handy pocket-sized guide provides the **perfect study and revision resource** for the AAT Level 2 Certificate in Accounting.

available for:

Bookkeeping 1
Bookkeeping 2
Working in Accounting and Finance
Introduction to Costing

Visit www.osbornebooks.co.uk for further information and to place your order.

Published by Osborne Books Limited
Unit 1B Everoak Estate
Bromyard Road, Worcester WR2 5HP
Tel 01905 748071
Email books@osbornebooks.co.uk
Website www.osbornebooks.co.uk

Design by Laura Ingham

Printed by CPI Group (UK) Limited, Croydon, CR0 4YY, on environmentally friendly, acid-free paper from managed forests.

MIX
Paper from
responsible sources
FSC® C013604

British Library Cataloguing in Publication Data
A catalogue record for this book is available from the British Library

ISBN 978 1909173 019